Peru
a journey in time

Peru
a journey in time

Edited by Cecilia Pardo
and Jago Cooper

The British
Museum

Published to accompany the exhibition *Peru: a journey in time*
at the British Museum from 11 November 2021 to 20 February 2022

Organised with the Museo de Arte de Lima, Peru

Supported by PROMPERÚ

Additional support by:

Mrs Ana Banon
Beatriz and Rupert Barclay
Carmen and Philip Byrne
Mrs Marcela Ganoza de Bombieri
Mr Philip Hirschler and Carina Alberti de Hirschler
Dr José-Carlos Mariátegui
Dr Luis Oganes
Mr Juan Carlos Verme

This exhibition has been made possible as a result of the Government
Indemnity Scheme. The British Museum would like to thank
HM Government for providing Government Indemnity and the
Department for Digital, Culture, Media and Sport and Arts Council
England for arranging the indemnity.

First published in the United Kingdom in 2021
by The British Museum Press
A division of The British Museum Company Ltd

The British Museum
Great Russell Street
London WC1B 3DG
britishmuseum.org/publishing

Reprinted 2022

Peru: a journey in time
© 2021 The Trustees of the British Museum

ISBN 978 07141 2491 9 (PB)
ISBN 978 07141 2492 6 (HB not for resale)

A catalogue record for this book is available from the British Library.

Further information about the British Museum and its collection
can be found at britishmuseum.org.

Images © 2021 The Trustees of the British Museum, courtesy
of the British Museum's Department of Photography and Imaging,
unless otherwise stated on page 237.

Designed by RITA PERES PEREIRA
Colour reproduction by ALTAIMAGE, LONDON
Printed in Belgium by GRAPHIUS

FRONTISPIECE
Earplug depicting a mythical figure. Lambayeque. AD 900–1300/50.
Wood, mother-of-pearl, shell. H. 10.5 cm, W. 8.8 cm.
British Museum, Am1960,06.1

FRONT COVER
Reduced-scale llama figure. Inca. AD 1400–1532. Gold. H. 6.5 cm,
L. 5.9 cm, D. 1.1 cm. British Museum, Am1921,0721.1

BACK COVER
The circular Inca terraces of Moray, Cusco region, AD 1400–1532.
© Douglas Peebles

Contents

Foreword by the President of the Republic of Peru

Today, we find ourselves in a unique and vibrant moment of history in the relationship between the United Kingdom and Peru. In a rapidly changing world, and with formidable challenges ahead, it is essential for nations to come together and cooperate to achieve greater goals. This process begins with understanding each other's cultures, traditions and history.

The British Museum's exhibition *Peru: a journey in time* is an unprecedented event that greatly strengthens the cultural, social and economic ties between both countries. And it does so by bringing our rich ancient history into the heart of London. The exhibition highlights the intriguing archaeological legacy of pre-Columbian societies, who inhabited the Andes hundreds and even thousands of years ago, in one of the most complex and challenging environments of the world.

The journey begins with an introduction to the geography and landscapes of the territories inhabited by ancient Peruvians. Understanding this context, its challenges and opportunities is key to conceptualising the development of the civilisations that arose. In chronological order, the exhibition showcases some of the most studied pre-Columbian cultures, starting with Chavín (1200–200 BC), located in the highlands; followed by the sacred desert, Paracas (900–200 BC) and Nasca (200 BC–AD 650); stories from the north: Moche (AD 100–800) and Chimú (AD 900–1400); and finally Wari (AD 600–900) and the rise of the Inca Empire (AD 1470–1532).

The timing of this exhibition could not be more fitting. Peru is celebrating 200 years of independence, and the United Kingdom was one of the first nations to officially recognise Peru's sovereignty. Now, two centuries later, we are thankful to have a partner of the calibre of the British Museum, one of the most visited and renowned museums in the world, and to share with you fascinating objects and ideas from ancient Peru. This exhibition will vividly illustrate how the people of the Andes and their culture flourished, becoming one of the six cradles of world civilisation.

Peru: a journey in time would not have been possible without the work of Peru's Export and Tourism Promotion Board, PROMPERÚ and its office in London. It is also the result of great efforts and cooperation between several institutions, both public and private, including our embassy in the United Kingdom. We hope that this exhibition and the invaluable information included in this catalogue contribute to a greater understanding of Peru, its history, heritage and culture.

Pedro Castillo Terrones, President of the Republic of Peru

Director's foreword

A single step through the front doors of the British Museum is always the first on a journey that can lead to a hundred untravelled worlds. The exhibition *Peru: a journey in time* provides the unique opportunity to explore the cultural origins of one of the most captivating regions in the world.

The fascinating range of material on display, which spans thousands of years and dozens of cultures, collectively challenges perceptions of how the world can be viewed and understood. From an intricately dyed Nasca textile, depicting hummingbirds bringing life to a desert landscape, to delicately modelled Moche portrait ceramics that introduce the visitor to a warrior who lived 1,000 years ago, every object reveals another clue as to how Andean peoples conceptually and constructively created their own path to societal success. From time moving backwards to mountains coming alive, life in the Andes reflects the independence of human ingenuity and their unique solutions to shared challenges. Among Andean societies without script-based writing systems, it is the symbology of the objects that must be relied upon to communicate cultural knowledge through time. This is nowhere clearer than in the use of the *khipu*, twisted, coloured and knotted strings used as mnemonic devices to hold information and convey stories. On display for the first time in their history are a series of wooden Moche figurines from the Macabi Islands. These dramatic figures, depicted as naked and bound in preparation for human sacrifice, are breathtaking – not only for their mystical beauty, but also for the revelatory way in which they present an alternative cultural understanding of death and ritual killing. Together, the objects in this exhibition exemplify an Andean understanding of time, in which the past is alive and entirely created in the present.

Peru: a journey in time emerges from more than a decade of discussions between colleagues in South America and the UK. Its Anglo-Peruvian co-curation embodies these dialogues and enduring relationships. My thanks to the Ministry of Culture, Peru and to the exhibition's lenders: the Amano Pre-Columbian Textile Museum, Lima; Complejo Arqueológico El Brujo | Fundación Augusto N. Wiese; Fundación Temple Radicati – UNMSM, Lima; the Gartner Collection, Lima; MALI – Museo de Arte de Lima; Museo Kuntur Wasi, Cajamarca; Museo Larco, Lima; Museo Nacional de Arqueología, Antropología e Historia del Perú, Lima; Museo 'Santiago Uceda Castillo' – Proyecto Arqueológico Huacas de Moche, Trujillo; Staatliche Museen zu Berlin, Ethnologisches Museum; and one private collection.

The vitality of Andean cultures and the knowledge they share allow us to travel through the living landscapes of Peru. I am deeply grateful to the Museo de Arte de Lima and for the unwavering support of the Peruvian government, which is testament to the power of international cultural collaboration. This exhibition would not have been possible without the support of PROMPERÚ; we thank them warmly for their generosity.

Hartwig Fischer, Director, British Museum

Timeline

14,000 BC	First evidence of people living in the Central Andean region
about 3500 BC	Domestication of camelids
about 3000 BC	People begin to cultivate maize
about 2500 BC	First evidence of textiles on the northern coast of Peru
about 2000–1800 BC	People begin to produce pottery
1200–200 BC	A system of beliefs develops from the Chavín pilgrimage centre of Chavín de Huántar in the northern Andean highlands and expands across the Central Andes
900–200 BC	The people of Paracas produce complex and beautiful textiles made of woven cotton and llama and alpaca fibres
200 BC–AD 650	The Nasca people from the southern coast create magnificent drawings in the desert
AD 100–800	The Moche civilisation rises in the north coast; its people are known for their narrative imagery depicted in pottery, metals and wall murals
about AD 300	The impressive ceremonial centre of Huaca de la Luna is built in the Moche valley
AD 600–900	The Wari people begin to rise from the highlands in Ayacucho and expand their influence to the coast. They introduce the *khipu*, later inherited by the Incas
AD 900–1470	Based on the northern coast of Peru, the Chimú culture establishes a large adobe city, known as Chan Chan
AD 1438	The Inca Empire is established and its influence spreads from the city of Cusco
about AD 1450	The citadel of Machu Picchu is built
AD 1532	Spanish conquistador Francisco Pizarro arrives in the port of Tumbes, and the last Inca, Atahualpa, is taken captive
AD 1533	Inca Atahualpa is executed, an event followed by the Spanish conquest of Cusco. The colonial period of Spanish rule begins
AD 1821	Peru claims independence from Spain

The main pre-Columbian cultures of the Central Andes

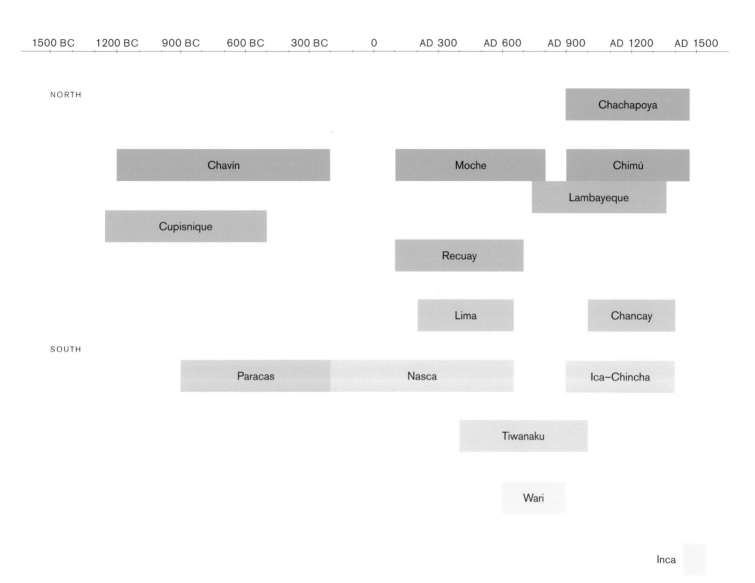

| 1500 BC | 1200 BC | 900 BC | 600 BC | 300 BC | 0 | AD 300 | AD 600 | AD 900 | AD 1200 | AD 1500 |

NORTH

Chachapoya

Chavín

Moche

Chimú

Lambayeque

Cupisnique

Recuay

Lima

Chancay

SOUTH

Paracas

Nasca

Ica–Chincha

Tiwanaku

Wari

Inca

PACIFIC

OCEAN

COLOMBIA

ECUADOR

Ingapirca

Amazon

BRAZIL

PERU

Kuélap

Sipán

Macabi Islands

Chan Chan

Huaca de la Luna

Huascarán ▲

Chavín de Huántar

Recuay

THE

Lima ■

Pachacamac

Wari

Vitcos

Choquequirao

Machu Picchu

Cusco

ANDES

Wari Kayan

Cahuachi

BOLIV

*Lake
Titicaca*

Isla del Sol y de la Luna

Tiwanaku

CHILE

■ • Modern cities

N
↑

Introduction

Cecilia Pardo and Jago Cooper

The past is often conceived as behind us, set in stone and the realm of the dead. In the Andes, nothing could be further from the truth. This book considers how the past is in fact very much alive in the present, continuing to influence our decisions and define our behaviours. The landscapes of the Andes are a living, breathing record of millennia of cultural practices and beliefs, not just metaphorically but actively. In learning about Andean narratives through objects, people and places, we can begin to change our perceptions and understandings of the past and present, and it is only by accepting the interrelationship between the past and present that we can prepare to plan for the future. For around 15,000 years, and continuing in the present day, the peoples of the Andes have created ways of life and understandings of the world that all cultures can consider and learn from. By reflecting on the cultural complexities of Andean societies, this publication seeks to challenge some of the cultural frameworks that have underpinned the historical interpretations made by Western societies. With the aid of cutting-edge archaeological research and expert scholarship from the region, it brings together the narratives of Andean peoples who have lived in one of the most geographically rich and climatically diverse regions in the world (fig. 0.1). It also gives space to contemporary voices from Peru in order to consider how the origins and legacies of pre-Columbian populations continue to influence the remarkable country today.

In the archaeological literature of the twentieth century, Andean societies from the Nasca to the Incas are often described pejoratively as not having developed writing, invented the wheel or used metal tools. This is not only factually incorrect, but also highlights how the criteria by which cultural successes or failures are decided are ethnocentrically framed by Western authors. This book tells a reframed narrative of Andean societies that enables readers to assess them through the powerful objects they created, such as a gold llama (fig. 0.2). This reduced-scale model, made as an offering to materialise the importance of the llama within Inca society, was shaped by hammering thirteen individual pieces of gold sheet into the final wrought figure. Andean peoples crafted objects like this from diverse materials such as ceramics, metals, wood and textiles, and used them to express their ideas and disseminate their beliefs.

The Andes are home to some of the highest inhabited areas in the world and the Pacific coast has hosted settlements that have thrived for millennia in some of the driest areas on the planet.[1] Andean peoples harnessed the power of their environment by developing large-scale irrigation systems, building filtration wells to obtain underground water and constructing more than two million acres of terraces for agriculture on the steep flanks of the Andes. Human ingenuity and technological innovation enabled populations to take advantage of the region's highly diverse ecological zones. These societies established the largest known pre-industrial road network (Qhapaq Ñan), which incorporated natural paths through the mountains to connect different regions and landscapes, from the Pacific coast to the Amazon tropical rainforest. Rather than rely solely on warfare in order to expand, states and empires created new territorial influences and loyalty by establishing strategic alliances and building on shared beliefs. The introduction from AD 600 onwards of the *khipu*, a system of knotted strings to hold and communicate information, served as a record of growing resources and expanding populations and even documented stories and poems.[2] It is these cultural achievements and choices, embodied in the objects they left behind, that tell the story of how there is more than one way of building a successful society.

HISTORY AND ARCHAEOLOGY

Between 15,000 and 12,000 years ago the descendants of the human populations who had once crossed the Bering Strait settled in the Central Andean region of South America. This Andean cultural zone centred on the territory now occupied by modern Peru, but at its peak it expanded to parts of Ecuador, western Bolivia, northern Argentina and Chile, and the extreme south-west of Colombia.[3] Over a long period of history, Andean peoples thrived by employing unique ways of living in one of the world's most geographically rich and diverse regions (fig. 0.3). Their particular vision of the world and their unique approaches to life, death, agriculture, power and economy were commonly misunderstood by the European, African and Asian migrants who arrived from the sixteenth century onwards.

FIG. 0.1 (PAGE 10) A map of Peru today

FIG. 0.2 Reduced-scale llama figure
Inca AD 1400–1532
Gold
H. 6.5 cm, L. 5.9 cm, D. 1.1 cm
British Museum, Am1921,0721.1

When in 1532, after two failed previous expeditions, Francisco Pizarro and his troops finally arrived in the port of Tumbes, on the north coast of Peru, they never imagined what they were about to encounter. While he was still in Panama, the messages that the Spanish conquistador had received from locals indicated that there was a rich territory in the south known as Virú, where gold was abundant – but this was not even close to what awaited their arrival.[4] The Inca Empire had been in existence for a little over a century, but its territories stretched more than 4,400 kilometres from north to south – four times the length of Britain. However, when the Europeans arrived the empire was in the midst of a civil war after Inca Atahualpa had beaten his brother Huáscar, following the death of their father, the former Sapa Inca Huayna Capac. The newcomers were to take advantage of this crisis, managing to capture and eventually execute Atahualpa before he could be crowned as the new ruler (fig. 0.4).

The *conquista* resulted in an incalculable loss of lives and the repression of Indigenous ways of life. Although Andean practices were subjugated under the imposition of new regimes, communities continued to thrive through endurance, adaptation and transformation. Cultural practices and beliefs were so deeply rooted that the construction of a new colonial society was possible only through the formation of alliances with Indigenous elites. For example, Inca iconography was maintained for many decades, in textiles as well as *keros* and *pacchas*, ritual drinking vessels that had been used for centuries and continued to endure. When the colonial regime ceased their attempts to change Inca accounting principles for the tax system, Indigenous communities and *curacazgos* (local rulers) continued to use *khipus* for accounting tasks.[5]

Scholars have been writing about Andean pre-Columbian societies for more than five hundred years in an attempt to 'decode' the long history and system of beliefs that guided these societies' own understanding of their existence. Beginning with the Spanish chroniclers, and followed by European explorers such as Alexander von Humboldt, Ephraim George Squier, Clements Markham, and Wilhelm Reiss and Alphons Stübel, as well as German archaeologist Max Uhle and the father of Peruvian archaeology, Julio C. Tello, by the twentieth century an early history of ancient Peru had been established.[6] In order to understand the complex narrative, archaeologists proposed that different Andean populations be labelled with names such as Chavín, Paracas, Nasca, Moche, Chimú and Wari, based either on local river valleys or contemporary names of the main archaeological sites associated with them. However, this long-standing empirical research often struggled to express a real understanding of the internal principles of these societies. Over time the academic disciplines of archaeology, anthropology, art history and ethnohistory have become closely linked to help us better understand enduring cultural practices.

THE STRUCTURE OF A JOURNEY IN TIME

The first section is a tripartite reflection on Peruvian culture: contemporary voices from Peru discuss connections between past and present, between societies that existed many thousands of years ago and those that exist today; a brief history outlines the curation of the British Museum's pre-Columbian acquisitions since the nineteenth century; and an essay on alternative Andean constructions of time explores how history is conceived and recorded, and the role of an institution such

FIG. 0.3 The mountains of Machu Picchu and Putucusi. The Inca site of Machu Picchu can be seen in the foreground.

FIG. 0.4 (BELOW) The meeting of the Incas and the Spanish conquistadors, from Francisco Xerez, *Uerdadera relacion de la conquista del Peru y prouincia del Cuzco llamada la nueua Castilla*, Seville: Bartholomé Perez, 1534. John Carter Brown Library

as the British Museum. Time is a crucial structural theme that runs across these texts. Andean societies thought of time as cyclical and interconnected, rather than linear and progressive. Within the Andean world, the past, present and future could happen at the same time, linked together in the same moment by objects, people or places. As time is not linear in this world, the past is not dead and finished, but rather it is alive and dynamic, continually playing an active role in the present. While this book follows a broadly chronological structure from 5,000 years ago until today, it is also a dialogue between a Western, linear construct of time and an alternative Andean reading of time, which is furthered by the inclusion of cross-temporal perspectives and cross-cultural thematic discussions that link together past, present and future.

The diverse landscapes, peoples and worldviews of Peru are the subject of the second section. Since humans settled in the Central Andes, cultures such as Chavín, Nasca, Moche, Chimú, Wari and Inca successfully adapted to arid desert coasts bordered by the Pacific Ocean, fertile river valleys coming down from the high Andean mountains and dense tropical rainforests stretching away into the Amazon basin. The use of marine resources and the cultivation of land depended on cultural knowledge and innovation, along with favourable weather conditions related to perceptions of divine forces. In the Andes nature itself was conceived as a living being, critical for survival, and was incorporated into shared belief systems, where the natural and supernatural worlds were intimately

The Paracas and Nasca peoples, who lived along the south coast of Peru, one of the most arid places on the planet, are discussed in section four. The Nasca transformed their rocky, infertile terrain into a sacred space by creating massive lines and drawings known as geoglyphs, which could only be seen in their entirety from the sky. Building on earlier traditions, they created the images by removing a top layer of earth and exposing the lighter sediment beneath. Ceramic depictions, offerings and remains of post holes (evidence for possible roofs or canopy structures) found here suggest that people walked along the lines and performed lively celebrations with music and dance. This use of music to bring life to the landscape shows the unifying force of Andean music and soundscapes.

In section five we encounter the Moche and Chimú cultures. While the Nasca developed in the south, the Moche established themselves in the northern coastal and inland valleys between AD 100 and 800 (fig. 0.5). Rather than a centralised state, it was formed of independent groups that lived in different valleys but shared common belief systems. The popularity of portrait ceramic vessels among the Moche helps to bring the individuals and roles within their society to life. They built large ceremonial centres with polychrome murals and increased cultivable land by developing large-scale irrigation systems, which sustained growing populations. The Moche created some of the most intriguing mythical narratives of the ancient world, visible in a limited number of scenes derived from rituals and myths. Archaeological finds have confirmed that some of the ceremonies depicted, aimed at guaranteeing the balance of nature and order in their world, actually took place in real life. The later kingdom of Chimú emerged on the north coast of Peru a few hundred years after the Moche had disappeared. Before they were integrated into the Inca Empire in the mid- to late fifteenth century, they conquered the northern territories of Lambayeque, a culture known for its skilful goldsmiths. Chimú's capital was based in Chan Chan, a 24-square-kilometre adobe-brick city with palaces, neighbourhoods and satellite towns, home to an estimated population of 70,000 inhabitants. Chan Chan was a cosmopolitan city where residents from all the Chimú territory would gather to participate in ceremonies, including child sacrifice, to honour the gods and their ancestors. Their reasons and justifications for killing, death and sacrifice help us to understand life in the central Andes.

connected. The development of these connections between settlements across the Andes resulted in the extraordinary 40,000-kilometre-long network of pre-Columbian Andean roads, many of which are still maintained and used today.

In the third section, we turn to early Andean cultures, travelling back to the second millennium BC, when permanent settlements were established alongside public buildings and sacred architecture. The development of agriculture and technology, including the introduction of ceramics, was key in this process, as it secured resources as well as the storage of water and food. Towards 1200 BC a new religion spread rapidly throughout the region from the ceremonial centre of Chavín de Huántar, located strategically in the highlands along roads that connected the coast and the Amazon. The new system of beliefs was focused on hybrid figures acquiring attributes from the feline, the bird and the snake. This imagery, carved in the stone walls of Chavín, was inspired by the principles of shamanistic rituals, where the consumption of hallucinogenic substances led to a trance-like state in which humans acquired divine attributes. Connections between Andean peoples and the environment are reflected in the history of Andean gastronomy and still alive today.

The sixth section discusses aspects of Wari and Inca culture. Towards AD 600 the southern highlands of Peru saw the rise of the Waris, thought to be the first empire in the Americas. They built urban-planned cities, professed an elite religion that was reflected in prescribed artistic canons and exercised influence from the southern highlands to the northern coast of Peru. It would take over five hundred years after the Waris had disappeared for the Inca Empire to emerge. The Inca Empire occupied a vast expanse, running 4,000 kilometres, from present-day southern Ecuador and Colombia down to northern Argentina and Bolivia, including all of present-day Peru. From their capital in Cusco, Incas incorporated multi-ethnic groups by establishing marital alliances, while imposing a distinctive architectural style with finely carved stonework and a formal language, Quechua, as well as an extensive network of roads. Their technological innovation and feats of engineering, which built on those of earlier cultures, enabled many areas of the Andes to have much higher population densities during Inca times than today.

The final section explores the endurance and resilience of Andean practices in spite of the trauma of the European conquest. Although traditions were suppressed, they managed to thrive through adapting and transforming: these practices were so integral to people's lives that the colonisers could only construct a new colonial society through forming alliances with the Indigenous elites. This endurance can be traced through objects such as *keros*, *pacchas* and textiles, as the case studies in this section reveal. An exploration of textile weaving reflects on one of the oldest Andean practices, dating back to at least 2500 BC. Even though traditional weaving has undergone important developments, the basic principles are still practised today. In different Andean communities, such as in Chinchero, in the Cusco region, traditional ways of weaving are continually present in the use of waist looms, raw materials (such as cotton and camelid fibres) and natural dyes, but most importantly in the symbolism still embedded as patterns in these fine garments. A special collaboration between the British Museum and Nilda Callañaupa Alvarez, founder of the Centro de Textiles Tradicionales del Cusco, has been key to incorporating an understanding of the views of local weavers and providing some context for the complex social change that has taken place during the twentieth and twenty-first centuries (fig. 0.6). This has resulted in a new commission produced by Nilda's collective of weavers, which has been acquired by the British Museum, thus marking the path for new ways of securing contemporary art for the Peruvian collection.

The Central Andes today is an integrated part of a globalising world reflecting a diversity of cultures, religions and ethnicities that have all undergone transformations during five centuries of population movement and economic and social change. Despite the dynamic and shifting landscapes, the enduring legacy of Andean peoples, places and practices continues. Quechua, the language that Incas disseminated through a vast empire, is still spoken by more than eight million people.[7] In similar ways, traditional pre-Columbian practices have remained in reinvented and adapted forms, responding to the needs and context of an evolving society.

FIG. 0.5 (OPPOSITE) Kneeling Moche warrior holding a club and a shield (vessel)
Moche AD 100–600
Pottery
H. 22 cm, W. 13.8 cm, D. 13.3 cm
British Museum, Am,P.1
Donated by Augustus Wollaston Franks

FIG. 0.6 Weavers of the Asociación de Tejedores Munay Ticlla de Pitumarca–Centro de Textiles Tradicionales del Cusco (CTTC) in the village of Pitumarca, Cusco, using traditional techniques to make textiles, 2021

1 Peru through time

Reflections on the Andean past

Nilda Callañaupa Alvarez, Manuel Choqque, Jago Cooper,
Victor Huamanchumo, Julio Ibarrola and Cecilia Pardo

Conceiving a project on the history of the Andes is about conversations and the sharing of knowledge just as much as it is about archaeology and research. In a global pandemic, these conversations with contributors in the Americas and Europe were based on long-standing relationships and new acquaintances, and often virtual by necessity. At the heart of these interactions are shared, and sometimes differing, views on how the legacy and meaning of an Andean past should be reflected on and disseminated to a wider audience. While the object-based study of pre-Columbian histories through archaeological investigation is the organisational focus for this publication, there is no substitute for the lived experiences and personal views on the extent to which a dynamic past continues to influence life and society in the Central Andes.

These wide-ranging discussions about the experience and continuities of Indigenous practice within the postcolonial context of a globalised world impact broader considerations about the role of archaeology in creating the framework for the past within a museum context.[1] While some contributors have expanded on their views in their own essays (see page 214), these are only excerpts from a much larger discussion. In the following paragraphs Peruvians Victor Huamanchumo, Nilda Callañaupa Alvarez, Julio Ibarrola and Manuel Choqque explain their own personal ideas about their relationship with their Andean legacies, and the potential connections between past and present.

Victor Huamanchumo is a third-generation fisherman from the town of Huanchaco in northern Peru (fig. 1.1). When he was a little boy, he watched his dad and grandfather make *totora* reed boats, which they used to go fishing, and when he turned fourteen it was his turn to build his own boat. People make boats from the reeds that grow by the coast and then paddle out to fish in the waters offshore. Fishermen in Huanchaco have two or three reed boats, so they can use one while the others dry. They inherited this technology from the Moche and Chimú people, who lived in this territory hundreds of years ago. During the time of the Chimú (AD 900–1470), reeds grew in a large area located in their capital city of Chan Chan, but they modified the coast and so now people can grow reeds in Huanchaco, his home town, which is very near the site of Chan Chan. Since you can see these *caballitos* (reed boats) in the pots the Chimú used to

make, they were used here then too. Huamanchumo explains that Gabriel Prieto has informed him that his same surname appears in texts written about the Chimú more than four hundred years ago (see page 140): 'I didn't know about that but my family has always lived in this area. I still teach people how to make these *totora* reed boats and hope that the younger generations don't just use the modern fibreglass boats, or that the problems with the fishing now mean that people don't use them or forget how to make them in the future. These ways of living with the local environment using knowledge passed down through generations are important to hold on to.'

Nilda Callañaupa Alvarez learned to weave when she was a girl in her hometown of Chinchero (fig. 1.2). She explains that when her people talk about ancestors, they do not think of it in years or as part of a long-forgotten past: 'We describe it as grandparents of grandparents … the connection is strong, they are in the weaving and also everywhere in the countryside around where people live. I don't know if people spend too much time thinking about cultures like the Wari or Chancay, to be honest, but people just continue to weave and live.' The knowledge of how to make the textiles and the different techniques that have been redeveloped in recent years comes from discussions between different generations and talking about what grandparents of grandparents used to do. In the last century, the introduction of new techniques from elsewhere is often what has encouraged people to make sure they hold on to the old knowledge, 'which is better – the textiles are stronger, the colours don't fade, just as we hope the memory of our ancestors doesn't fade either.'

Julio Ibarrola has always lived just a stone's throw from the archaeological site of San José de Moro on the northern coast of Peru (fig. 1.3). No one taught him how to make ceramics – he just learned by looking at archaeological examples he found and trying to copy some of the techniques. Nowadays he sources all his materials locally, using different rocks for the paints and tempers. Moulds, and once a kiln from the Moche period, have been found on archaeological sites, but they are very rare. There is no direct line of continuity of making these pots here where he lives. Now he makes dozens of elaborate ceramics and sells them to people who visit this incredible archaeological site. People around his area do not really have any connection to the site or the people who once lived here,

PAGE 16 A man walking down the Inca trail of Soledad de Tambo in the Andean highlands, in an image captured as part of the Qhapaq Ñan project 'Rutas Ancestrales' (Ancestral Routes)

FIG. 1.1 Victor Huamanchumo, a third-generation fisherman from Huanchaco, northern Peru, with some bundles of reeds, 2021

FIG. 1.2 Weaver and founder of the Centro de Textiles Tradicionales del Cusco, Nilda Callañaupa Alvarez, in Pitumarca, Cusco, 2021

FIG. 1.3 Potter Julio Ibarrola working on a large reproduction of a Moche vessel in San José de Moro, La Libertad, 2019

FIG. 1.4 Farmer and engineer Manuel Choqque in Piuray, Urubamba, 2021

which he says is a shame because it means that sometimes people do not treat the place as well as they should: 'There is a lot of building going on and sometimes the sites disappear and we lose all these objects from the past. The more work I have done making these ceramics, the more I am amazed at how good they were at making ceramics. Some of them are so complicated and well made, thin walls and well fired, and the painting is so delicate.'

Manuel Choqque runs a family project growing native potatoes at high altitudes in the Andes in his home village of Huatata, located near the Inca site of Chinchero, in Cusco (fig. 1.4). Members of his community have inherited the vast knowledge and experience the Incas had cultivating the land. The Inca Empire's capital was based in Cusco, and it expanded across a vast region in South America. Probably the most important thing he has learned from them is how they wisely benefited most from the land through crop rotation and other practical strategies. By sowing different crops, they let the soil recover from losing all its nutrients. For example, as the potatoes absorb nitrogen, phosphorous and potassium in great quantities, once they are harvested the ground is left poor in nutrients. So the following year, they must sow products such as tarwi (a high protein seed crop) or beans, which absorb nitrogen from the atmosphere and then give it back to the soil, thus helping its recovery. This knowledge was performed and tested in the circular terraces of Moray, an Inca agricultural research centre located near his village in the Sacred Valley of the Incas. Here Inca horticulturists experimented with different crops such as maize, potatoes and beans, to see what the best conditions were for them.

This project focuses on the ways in which differing understandings of Indigenous continuities and change through time have emerged from a postcolonial, globalising Peru; these conversations were inspired by some of the objects that have formed part of the exhibition *Peru: a journey in time*, which are also displayed in this publication. They include a North Coast vessel depicting a human figure in a *totora* reed boat not dissimilar from Victor Huamanchumo's (see fig. 5.30); several textiles with intricate designs and weaving techniques, methods currently being revived by Nilda Callañaupa Alvarez and the weavers in her community-based project (see page 221); a Moche fine-line vessel, a style which today inspires Julio Ibarrola (see fig. 5.21); and Inca vessels depicting agricultural tools that speak to the heritage of Manuel Choqque's community (see pages 188–9). When juxtaposed with the conversations above, some of these objects, dating up to 3,500 years old, help us to establish the links that prove the many ways the past is alive in the present, whether through ancient techniques that are still practised today or visual identities that continue in contemporary life. Each conversation inspires discussion about the customs and principles still alive and manifest in the present, even in the socio-political dynamics of a rapidly changing world. Together, they uphold a legacy of practice, of both cultural continuity and change.

The Peruvian pre-Columbian collections at the British Museum: a brief history

Cecilia Pardo

> *Chairman: You have, also, I imagine, Byzantine, Oriental, Mexican and Peruvian Antiquities stowed away in the basement?*
> *Franks: Yes, a few of them; and I may add, that I do not think it any great loss that they are not better placed than they are.*[1]
>
> Select Committee on the British Museum, 1860

The British Museum houses around 9,000 objects registered as 'Peruvian'. These include pre-Columbian ceramics, textiles, metals, wooden artefacts, silverwork and tapestries. It also holds a good selection of unregistered nineteenth- and twentieth-century photographs and a considerable number of slides taken during the course of field collecting in the 1980s, as well as objects acquired from local communities in Peru during the last fifty years, an ongoing task promoted by the Department of Africa, Oceania and the Americas and the Santo Domingo Centre of Excellence for Latin American Research.[2]

As an encyclopaedic museum, the British Museum's criteria for collecting objects from this region, as any other in the world, has changed significantly through time, a process influenced by the politics of the Museum, the norms of the curators, the early lack of interest in non-Western cultures and the international regulations for cultural property. An exhaustive, definitive account of the Peruvian history recorded in the collections is the subject of another study, but this brief overview of the pre-Columbian objects and how they arrived at the Museum is intended to shed light on how the cultures of Peru have been historically perceived and understood and how our curatorial approach has evolved and shifted over time.[3] Matters of further discussion are the magnificent pre-Columbian collections catalogued under other Andean countries such as Ecuador, Bolivia, Chile, Argentina and Colombia; during certain periods all of them, including Peru, formed part of the Central Andean region.

FIRST COLLECTIONS, FIRST EXPLORATIONS

Peru has been present at the British Museum since its inception. Sir Hans Sloane's founding bequest in 1753, which comprised around 2,000 objects, included three pre-Columbian pottery vessels belonging to the Moche (AD 100–800) and Chimú (AD 900–1400) cultures from northern Peru (fig. 1.5). Judging from how the collection was put together, and the objects' accession numbers (AmSLAntiq.726–728), they might have been acquired from one of Sloane's acquaintances in the early eighteenth century.[4] They formed part of the catalogue of 'Miscellanies' produced by the collector, although an annotation on the original record states that Sloane left a note referring to them as 'Antiquities' and not as 'Miscellanies', the first sign of a division that would come much later on in the history of the Museum.[5]

The journeys of exploration to South America by European naturalists and scientists from the late seventeenth to mid-eighteenth century – the time when the Sloane objects would have been taken from Peru – responded mainly to objectives such as charting the territory, spurred on by the ideals of Enlightenment, an intellectual and philosophical movement that aimed to further knowledge and focus on reason and science. Several well-known travel expeditions carried out by members of the Spanish viceroyalty during this period resulted in the formation of enormous collections at the bequest of a colonial order from the king of Spain.

FIG. 1.5 Fish-shaped stirrup vessel
Chimú AD 900–1470
Pottery
H. 14.4 cm, L. 21.3 cm, D. 7.6 cm
British Museum, Am,SLAntiq.726
Bequeathed by Sir Hans Sloane

Such is the case for Baltasar Jaime Martínez Compañón (1737–1797), who served as bishop of the northern coastal city of Trujillo. Between 1782 and 1785 he set up a team to explore his dioceses and commissioned an album of watercolour drawings entitled *Trujillo del Perú*, now in the Biblioteca Nacional de España in Madrid.[6] Produced by local artists, the drawings uniquely show the area's natural history, including its flora and fauna, as well as clothing, customs, maps and plans, and objects from the pre-Columbian cultures that developed in that region. The objects collected, as the result of those explorations, are currently housed in the Museo de América, Madrid. However, attempts to chronicle the history, geography and anthropology of Peru were only just beginning, not reaching their peak until the nineteenth century.

The Museo Nacional, the first institution devoted to preserving the country's national heritage, was founded in 1822, only one year after Peru had claimed independence from Spain. However, the weakness of most government-run institutions when it came to the unregulated export of Peruvian cultural heritage, combined with the growing number of narratives and memoirs on Peru that piqued the interest of foreign collectors and scholars, resulted in many collections being sent overseas. Travellers who wrote extensively about Peru's natural and cultural richness include German polymath Alexander von Humboldt (expedition 1801–3), English explorer and writer Clements Markham (1852–3, 1859–61), Swiss-American archaeologist Adolph Bandelier (from 1892), Austrian-French explorer Charles Wiener (from 1875) and Italian scientist Antonio Raimondi (from 1850).[7] Another explorer who spent some time in Peru during those years was American journalist Ephraim George Squier. After studying ancient North American publications and carrying out research on Central America, in 1863 he was appointed US Commissioner to Peru, where he undertook various studies. His *Peru: Incidents of Travel and Exploration in the Land of the Incas* (1877), an illustrated journal of his travels to different regions, remains one of the most important nineteenth-century accounts of Peru. The British Museum holds approximately thirty-three Moche and Chimú vessels collected by Squier on the northern coast. These objects arrived in 1931 with the purchase of the collection from the former Blackmore Museum in Salisbury, which contained Squier material from the Salisbury and South Wiltshire Museum.

Other collections gathered together from objects taken from Peru during those years were the ones formed by German archaeologist Max Uhle (1856–1944), which were sent to Berlin in 1895; the collections of Eduard Gaffron (1861–1931), sold to New York and Munich; and the important collection amassed by Peruvian collector José Mariano Macedo (1823–1894), sold to Berlin's Museum für Völkerkunde (now part of the Staatliche Museen), amid fear that its contents would be stolen by the Chileans, as war with the neighbouring country was imminent. In fact, three Recuay vessels now housed at the British Museum were acquired via Macedo in 1869.[8]

The practices and patterns of collecting manifested through these objects demonstrate an inherent bias when it comes to the representation of them in public and private spheres. Both museums and individuals contributed to a selective, Westernised interpretation of Peru's history and culture: they decided what was 'worth' preserving for future generations. This results in a narrower understanding of ancient Peru, in which objects that represent daily life are sidelined in favour of more decorative objects and textiles.

THE CONTRIBUTION OF FRANKS

One of the main figures who accounted for the early Peruvian collections at the British Museum was, without a doubt, Augustus Wollaston Franks (1826–1897). Franks was appointed as an assistant in the Department of Antiquities in 1851, and was later to become Keeper of the newly created Department of British, Medieval Antiquities and Ethnography, to which all material from non-Western worlds was assigned.[9] Around 900 Peruvian objects were collected between 1860 and 1900, decades that saw an unprecedented growth in the size and geographical span of the Museum's ethnographic collections, prompted by Franks and mainly through purchases and gifts rather than through excavations. By the end of his keepership the number of objects in the Ethnography Department had increased by about 8,000 and included objects from all around the world (fig. 1.6).[10] In 1877, Franks gave the museum objects from Ecuador, South Africa, New Guinea and Asia, including 'lip ornaments from Peru'.[11] Despite the fact that significant Peruvian objects were acquired during Franks's time at the Museum (see figs 0.5, 5.16 and 5.51), it is clear that the focus of the institution was to give priority to the study and display of the cultures that gave birth to Western civilisations. Franks's comment to the Chairman of the Select Committee, quoted at the beginning of this essay, makes it evident that he considered it no 'great loss' that these objects were hidden in the basement, out of sight and away from the public sphere; objects from cultures and places such as Mexico, Peru and parts of the Far East were not valued as highly as collections with a Eurocentric focus.

FIG. 1.6 Moche vessels on display at the British Museum, 1908

THE MACABI ISLANDS COLLECTION

Perhaps the most important set of objects donated by Franks was the group of Moche wooden sculpture figurines, textile and pottery fragments found in the guano layers of the Macabi Islands, located off the coast of La Libertad, in northern Peru. These objects represent a unique discovery as they contribute to confirming that ceremonial events during Moche times took place on the islands and that these probably involved human sacrifices to honour the gods, as portrayed in the iconography of the outstanding vessels (see fig. 5.28).[12] The wooden sculptures, some of them long staffs, depict officers in architectural structures and naked prisoners with ropes attached to their necks (fig. 1.7, and see figs 5.31–5.32, 5.34–5.37 and 5.58). The early records state that they were painted with red pigments, but as they were buried in several metres of guano for a long time, their appearance might have changed, darkening the wood, almost as if they had been polished.

Early accounts suggest that the sculptures were unearthed from the Peruvian guano islands before 1870, in the midst of guano mining. For more than forty years, Peruvian guano was exported mainly to the United Kingdom, through the firm Anthony Gibbs & Sons, which had opened offices in

Peru as early as 1822.[13] The firm had been granted the monopoly on trade by the Peruvian government and by 1856 they had managed to extract around 192,300 tonnes of guano. Between 1848 and 1875 about 20 million tonnes of guano were exported from Peru to North America and Europe, showing the level of reliance on this Peruvian natural resource.[14] During the first decades, the extractions were mostly focused on the Chincha Islands, on the southern coast of Peru. However, once these sources were depleted, other sites such as the Macabi Islands were exploited.

The Museum's early correspondence indicates that the Macabi collection arrived in two main lots, towards the end of 1871. The first one, composed of twenty-two objects, originally belonged to a certain Captain Newell but was transferred to his widow after his sudden death on his journey back home. The collection was sold to Franks, who subsequently left it as a gift to the Museum through J. W. Moore.[15] The second set of nine objects was collected by British scientist J. David Harris and donated by his father Josiah D. Harris to the Christy Collection.[16] Both sets might have arrived at the Museum at the same time, as they have correlative accession numbers (7416–7447). A later addition of five objects from the Macabi Islands was registered in 1986, acquired from Charles Thomas. Objects with the same provenance were to end up in other European institutions; such is the case of a textile from the Macabi Islands, which was acquired by the Ethnologisches Museum, Berlin in 1872, said to come from the Christy Collection too.[17]

It is interesting to note that, just after the end of the Second World War, the Macabi Island objects were to inspire studies carried out by Yale University. Correspondence from 1946 indicates that British-born ecology professor George Evelyn Hutchinson was collaborating with art historian George Kubler in order to set up a guano chronology[18] that would later result in an article published in the *Memoirs of the Society for American Archaeology* in 1948.[19] In his research, Kubler explains that the Macabi objects were discovered on North Macabi within an area of 67 square metres, at depths ranging from 4 to 20 metres.[20]

The colonial interests of Europeans working in Peru governed how pre-Columbian objects were sourced and disseminated worldwide. At that time the lack of access to certain regions probably had an impact on the selection of objects – notably, a disproportionate representation of coastal cultures and fewer examples of material culture from the highlands and the Amazon. A parallel can be found in the site of Machu Picchu, where evidence suggests that, although it was known locally, it remained largely untouched until the early twentieth century.

THE TWENTIETH CENTURY

The first half of the twentieth century saw a very important increase in Andean pre-Columbian artefacts added to the Museum's collection; this was at a time when Peru did not yet have official regulations on the protection of its cultural heritage property. During this period, Thomas Athol Joyce (1878–1942) and Hermann Justus Braunholtz (1888–1963) were two key figures responsible for the acquisition of Peruvian material. After being appointed in 1902, Joyce was responsible for the South American collections until his departure at the end of the 1930s, while Braunholtz served as a curator from 1913 and as Keeper of the newly created Ethnography Department from 1946 to 1953.

Joyce's interest in Peruvian material was underpinned by his *South American Archaeology: An Introduction to the Archaeology of the South American Continent with Special Reference to the Early History of Peru*, published in 1912.[21] During his time as an assistant curator, he received the important documentation Clements Markham had amassed during his visits to Peru, passed on to him with a note: 'To be given to Thomas A. Joyce after my death.'[22] The documents included Peruvian magazines;

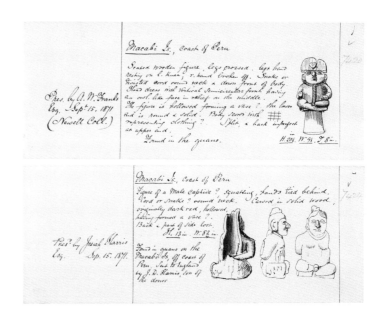

FIG. 1.7 Two handwritten acquisition slips recording wooden objects from the Macabi Islands, 1871

published catalogues of the archaeological collections of José Mariano Macedo (1881), Ana María Centeno (1876) and Enrique Mazzei (1891), which might have been on sale at the time; correspondence; and manuscripts of the transcriptions Markham had made of colonial documents. One example of this was the chronicle of Juan Diez de Betanzos, which was translated into English by Markham in 1909. Curiously, among the papers were also five different versions of the neo-Inca drama *Ollantay* and a volume of Justo Apu Sahuaraura Inca's *Memories of the Peruvian Monarchy, or Outline of the History of the Incas*, written in the 1830s and published in Paris in 1850.

In 1907 the Museum acquired a selection of 630 pre-Columbian objects from different cultures via Anna de Bolivar, from a collection formed by her relative Dr de Bolivar. As with most private collections at the time, it comprised a representative selection of vessels and textiles of different cultures, such as Moche, Lambayeque, Chimú, Nasca, Tiwanaku, Chancay and Ica, as well as colonial-era objects. Between 1909 and 1934 more than 280 pre-Columbian objects from Peru were donated by the London-based Dutch businessman Henry Van den Bergh. The objects, mostly from the north coast, stand out for their outstanding aesthetic quality (see figs 2.19 and 5.18). In addition, between 1914 and 1921 the Museum acquired more than 160 Peruvian objects from Scottish explorer and botanist Henry Ogg Forbes (1851–1932). Significantly, it comprised high-quality Nasca ceramic vessels as well as a great diversity of textiles.

FIG. 1.8 Textiles from Pachacamac presented to the British Museum for sale by Christian Theodor Wilhelm Gretzer around 1910

In 1910 Braunholtz was involved in a negotiation with Christian Theodor Wilhelm Gretzer (1847–1926) regarding the valuation for a possible acquisition of a group of pre-Columbian textiles from Pachacamac. Gretzer was a German textile collector and dealer who had lived in Lima during the last three decades of the nineteenth century. He formed two collections, both of which were subsequently sold to the Ethnologisches Museum.[23] The second one, formed some years later, contained around 10,000 textiles from Pachacamac and southern coastal sites. During these same years Max Uhle began his expeditions in Peru and was credited for making known the oracle and pilgrimage centre of Pachacamac (fig. 1.8). The negotiations that took place to acquire these Pachacamac textiles demonstrate the growing academic interest in the pre-Columbian cultures of Peru.

As well as Joyce and Braunholtz, who were actively acquiring new Peruvian artefacts from various collectors, the entomologist Mervyn G. Palmer (1879–1955) also

contributed to the Museum's archival history of Peru.[24] The Museum holds over fifty photographs of different sites taken by Palmer – Chan Chan, Pikillacta, Pachacamac, Tiwanaku, Cusco, Qenqo, Rumiqolca, Sacsayhuamán and Arequipa, as well as Tambo Colorado, one of the most important Inca coastal sites – and its archives house very detailed plans, drawings and a manuscript with a description of Tambo Colorado produced by Palmer in 1928. A group of eight Chancay textiles and a few Nasca pins, also collected by Palmer, were later donated to the British Museum through the Wellcome Institute for the History of Medicine.

In 1954 the Wellcome Institute, which housed material acquired by Sir Henry Wellcome in the first half of the twentieth century, donated more than 15,000 objects to the British Museum, of which 670 came from Peru. These included a rich variety of textiles from different periods, a good selection of Nasca and Moche pottery and some iconic Inca and early colonial objects (see figs 2.16, 3.22, 4.11–4.12, 4.31–4.34 and 6.24–6.25). Another significant Peruvian collection of around 324 items, which arrived at the Museum in three different batches, was donated by amateur archaeologist J. D. Spottiswoode. He had acquired his collection of pre-Columbian pottery in Pacasmayo, north of Trujillo, around 1907, and also obtained some stone objects from the caves near Moyobamba.[25]

As with the events of the late nineteenth century, the first decades of the twentieth century coincided with many collections leaving Peru to be housed in museums across the world. Importantly, this widespread collecting also occurred at a time when systematic archaeological initiatives were beginning in the country, which would end up being instrumental to a better understanding of its past.

THE MUSEUM OF MANKIND: EXHIBITIONS AND COLLECTIONS

The separation of the Department of Ethnography from the British Museum, which had been planned for decades, finally took place in 1970.[26] The new Museum of Mankind was housed in a building at 6 Burlington Gardens in Mayfair, originally built in 1869 as the headquarters of the University of London. It was conceived as a branch of the main Museum, intended to present exhibitions and public programmes that would allow the rotation of the permanent collections from non-Western cultures. In part, the Museum of Mankind's aim was to innovate and to change public perception with displays that promoted respect for the cultures that were represented, rather than merely presenting them as exotic or primitive.[27]

The exhibition on Moche vessels that took place between 1979 and 1982 was one of the more than 150 shows organised by the institution between 1970 and 1997 (fig. 1.9).[28] It is worth mentioning that the reorganisation of the Museum of Mankind into a separate building afforded it a certain freedom, which led to an exhibition trajectory quite different from that presented at the main site. It resulted in provocative, dynamic and innovative shows that sought to enable living cultures from the Americas, Oceania, Asia and Africa to represent their own views of how their histories should be interpreted and displayed. But thirty-four years after its creation, the Department of Ethnography at the Museum of Mankind was brought back into the main Museum premises in Bloomsbury, in the midst of an international postcolonial debate that questioned the Othering of non-Western cultures in museums. In 2004 this resulted in the renaming of the Department of Ethnography as the Department of Africa, Oceania and the Americas. A similar situation unfolded in North America. Many of the finest Peruvian objects now in The Metropolitan Museum of Art's collections, including feathered textiles, pottery vessels and masks, were originally acquired by the now-defunct Museum of Primitive Art. Its collections were intended to gather together early Indigenous art (then called 'Tribal' art). The word 'primitive', now heavily charged, contributed to the Othering of non-Western art forms and cultures.

Between 1970 and 1997 the Museum of Mankind commissioned mainly twentieth-century additions to its collections through curators or dealers, and by directly engaging with local, mostly rural communities. Several hundred Peruvian costume and textile objects from the central and southern highlands were acquired via Penny Bateman and Andrea Aranow, while collections from Amazonian groups, such as Shipibo, Campa and Machiguenga, were bought through Anna Lewington and Peter Gow. These fascinating objects and the growing contemporary collections of the Museum will no doubt be the focus of a different discussion. However, as witnesses to traditional Andean practices that have lasted for centuries, pre-Columbian objects make a substantial contribution to making a temporal link with the present and future of Andean societies in Peru. Since the collections have returned to the Museum's main site in Bloomsbury, the Peruvian presence has featured in installations within the Living and Dying Galleries and by the display of selected Nasca, Moche, Recuay and Chimú objects in the Enlightenment Gallery.

The pages that follow focus primarily on pre-Columbian collections from 1500 BC to AD 1500. But many objects produced in later periods – colonial, republican and even modern times – can still provide a glimpse of the vivid Andean cultures of the past, transporting us back through time. This is certainly the case with a number of contemporary objects that the Museum is currently acquiring, in which inspiration from the past seems to be the only viable way into the future.

FIG. 1.9 Poster for the exhibition *Moche Pottery from Peru* at the Museum of Mankind (1979–82)

An Andean journey through time

Jago Cooper

To a large extent, Western rational disbelief in the presence of ancestors and the efficacy of magic rest[s] on the rejection of ideas of temporal coexistence implied in these ideas and practices. So much is obvious.[1]

All existing facts and figures about human history can be learned given enough time but none of them can be truly understood until we change our perception of time itself. In the Andes the past is not behind us and the future is not ahead: both are in the present and connected by people. In order to understand any culture, it is essential to realise that the pillars of time and space can be conceived of in completely different ways. As anthropologist Johannes Fabian highlights in his observation quoted above, any cultural worldview or 'cosmovision' is built on a particular structure of time and space. Every aspect of a society's thought process and cultural values can be constructed differently, in a form that is no less valid or correct, just based on a completely different starting point. This chapter introduces alternative perspectives on time from the Andean world and critiques the common application of Eurocentric views of temporality. Acceptance that an alternative perspective is possible can not only help us to understand Andean cultures better, but also helps to dispel common pre-existing cultural assumptions and values.

For the Andean cultures represented within this book, time is not only linear and progressive (as in the Western tradition) but also parallel and interactive. The past, present and future are all happening at the same time and people's actions can directly change the reality of life in the other time dimension. This is not just a quirky point of cultural interest – it is a game-changing difference in our perception of the world, which alters everything about how people make decisions and how the societies discussed in this book were (are/will be) framed. 'The concept of linear time is one of the cornerstones of Judeo-Christian thought. Its importance lies beyond its continuity: the concept of linear time generates relationships that penetrate and mold all areas of thought and action.'[2] But what if everything someone in Europe thinks about time and space is wrong, or is at least different from the cultures in this book?

All European languages require distinct verbs for past, present and future and they deliberately separate them in a structurally linear way, a linguistic restriction brought into stark relief by the verb tenses used in this chapter. In fact, English does not really have the right vocabulary to describe some of the ideas presented here. In the Indigenous Quechua and Aymara languages, there is a word for the meeting of interconnected time and space: *pacha*. This embodies in material form the connections between past, present and future, bound together by physical space. *Pacha* can be seen operating in the Quechua language to describe places in the landscape, such as the pre-Columbian religious site of Pachacamac, on the coast 40 kilometres south of Lima; a material object named a *paccha*, such as a vessel used in ceremonies for containing or drinking a liquid (see fig. 7.29); or even a human being, such as the great Inca ruler Pachacuti.[3] Each of these words uses the root *pacha* because they refer to the ability to connect different timelines in space through materiality. In providing an alternative understanding of time from the outset, the objects discussed throughout this book take on a different role that reaches far beyond an increased historical knowledge of facts and figures. They become *pacha*, or temporal portals that connect the present, future and past together in a fixed point in space. They provide the reader with a glimpse between the interconnected realms of time and space in the Andean world. This viewpoint also reveals the unparalleled power and responsibility of a place like the British Museum, with its millions of objects acting as time portals. Museum objects become living microcosms of human experience and emotion that connect visitors with an explosion of life and enable them to journey through time and space.

THE ILLUSION OF CULTURE HISTORY

Archaeology, by definition, is the study of past peoples through the material remains they leave behind (fig. 1.10). Undergraduate students of archaeology are taught from the very first day to structure time and space in a highly ordered fashion. Calendar years and geographical boundaries that underpin the cultural historical frameworks are used by archaeologists to define artistic traditions, categorise cultural identities and interpret past societies. This is the simple universal system of time and space into which archaeologists order the cultural world. We take objects associated by

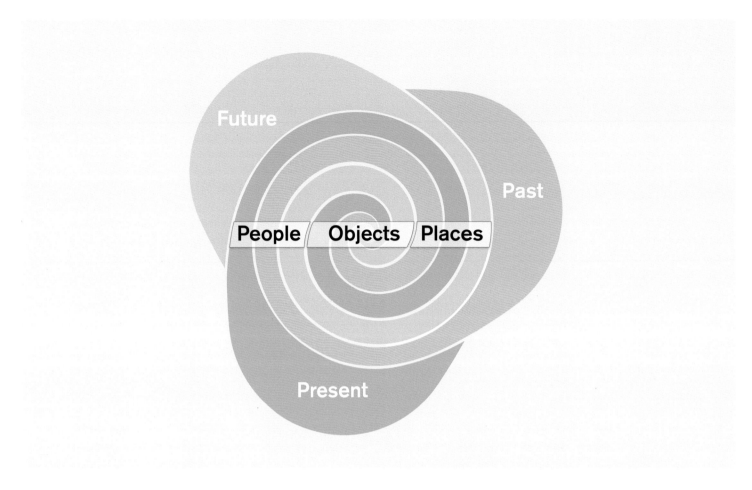

The diagram shows three overlapping shapes labelled **Future**, **Past**, and **Present**, with concentric rings at the centre containing the labels **People**, **Objects**, **Places**.

FIG. 1.10 (PAGE 28) The Intihuatana of Machu Picchu, a ritual stone possibly used in a similar way to a sundial, which formed part of the Inca calendar

FIG. 1.11 A visualisation of Andean time, showing how the past, present and future are interlinked and anchored by people, objects and places

similar styles, group sites with these similar objects and call them past 'cultures'. These cultures are often given arbitrary names based on the first excavation site where an object was found, or even an archaeologist's whim: the name often has absolutely no association with the actual peoples being named. Often archaeologists recreate these past cultures entirely in the present, using subjective cultural views and contemporary understandings of time and space. Archaeologists, and many scientists, study material remains and then write stories about the people who made them, framed within their own fundamental assumptions about how the world works. In a museum, these cultures and cultural stories are then displayed in isolated bubbles of time and space, which stretch along a single progressive linear timeline with retrospectively allocated facts and figures.

It is this comparatively recent and academically rigid conception of time and space that provides a conveniently neat way of understanding what is past, what is present and how we can interpret the world around us. However, if there is one thing I have learned during all my thirty years of studying and practising archaeology, it is that this cognitively reassuring but rigidly fixed system for ordering time and culture is a dangerous fiction. It is a self-interested and circular social construct built on the shaky foundations of hindsight, maladapted scholarship and post-rationalised authority. It encourages the creation of narratives that transpose cultural assumptions and normative values on to peoples who often have no voice to answer back and no ability to point out the cultural misappropriations. These misappropriations are currently being overturned by an ever-increasing clamour of voices speaking from around the world.[4]

Ironically, the European construction of how time works relies on understandings of the past being created in the present while pretending they are in the past. This overlooks all the implicit cultural assumptions and prejudices entailed by such an approach. The dangers of using this rigid and teleological framework for understanding world history are profound. It creates a narrow path for interpreting cultural values; it limits understanding of the process of social change; and it stops the possibility of a different future by relying on a restricted construction of the past. Therefore, if the material remains of the cultures represented in this book are to be understood in their own way, we need to understand the alternative construction of time and space within which they were created.

ANDEAN TIME

In the Andes, 'Western predilections about the structure of time need not apply', but how do we know what structures of time do apply?[5] There are three important caveats to this introduction to Andean time. The first is that this book covers more than two hundred generations of Andean cultures, so while this essay focuses on some of the key underlying principles of Andean time, it should not negate the diversity of the nuanced, varied and distinct temporal constructs that each Andean society created in their own way. The second is that Andean time is a highly active area of current research that pushes the boundaries of philosophical thought and this introduction is a subjective summary of this enormous corpus. The third is that the sources of knowledge of Andean time are multidisciplinary and not always aligned; therefore relevant in-depth studies from the disciplinary perspectives of archaeology, linguistics, cultural anthropology, architecture, art history or ethnohistory are cited, should you wish to delve deeper into the subject-specific sources.

The one thing that binds many Andean conceptualisations of time is the fact that the present, past and future are directly interconnected. Therefore the relationships between people (present), ancestors (past) and descendants (future) are/were/will be continually active and part of daily life. It also means that human actions in the present are directly linked to the past and future in an immediate sense, not separated by years or abstracted by time. A single action in the present could immediately impact the lives of ancestors and descendants. In many ways the idea of time in the Andean world is almost more like motion. Imagine that the past is not over and fixed in place, nor is the future unwritten and not yet started. Both past and future are alive and fully active in the present. People are alive, events are going on in all three timelines, and it is this dynamic interaction that creates life and the world people experience around them.

The aspects of Andean life that were able to connect these realms of time together and to provide some kind of temporal stability were vital to all Andean societies. The fundamental cultural anchors of time were places, people and objects. These anchors were brought together in Andean rituals which bound these concepts as one, creating the powerful cultural concept of time in the Andes (fig. 1.11). Reflected in that Quechua and Aymara word *pacha*, different times could be united in space. The physical reality of places, people and objects could bind time together and provide a human experience of temporal stability in which past and present could coexist in relative harmony.

In the Quechua language, spoken by more than seven million people throughout the Central Andes today, the relationship between past, present and future tenses is conditional on physical location. The language, and tens of millions who have spoken it for millennia, has a deep-rooted acceptance of the fluidity and interconnected nature of time.[6] A fluidity given solidity only by physical place or solid materiality. The Andean fluidity of time means that the future (*qhepa*) can literally be behind the present, and the past (*ñawpa*) ahead out in front. Conceptually this is still the way time is described in the Quechua language. The past is described linguistically as being ahead based on the logic that you can see some of what has already happened, while the future is behind you because you cannot see so clearly what is going on.[7] This concept of interconnected and parallel timelines underpins a different structure for thought and deed by the cultures discussed in this book. The consequence for how this impacts on all human decision-making and action is profound.

Instead of a single line of time between past, present and future, the Andean world can be conceived as multiple spiralling lines of time in which the fundamental principles of cause and effect are altered. In a linear conception of time each event has a meaning because it is permanent and unchangeable, whereas in a cyclical conception of time every event is reversible or transformable.[8] This lack of clear temporal order or structured rules for separating out the past, present and future in the Andean world creates (created/will create) a great sense of uncertainty. It also explains the importance to all Andean cultures trying to establish control of time, because the construction of places, the invested power of individuals, the creation of objects and the performance of ritual events helped to control time. In Andean society, 'to be bound up with time was to be linked to powerful forces'.[9] This complex understanding of cross-temporal time in the Andean world can be seen in the visual culture, values and actions of all the cultures in this book. For example, this is why the mummified remains of the dead would be carried around the streets, because they were

FIG. 1.12 The Thirteen Towers solar observatory, as seen from the ruins of Chankillo, c. 3rd century BC

still alive and an active part of daily life. The fluidity of time creates a rich opportunity for cultural freedom and creativity. Anthropologist Regina Harrison describes it as creating a world where the future that 'could come to be' is created in narrative form out of the symbolic material provided by 'a past that never was'.[10]

This Andean obsession with time also explains why cultures in the region always developed such intricate ways of mapping celestial movements, creating calendars and building observatories to record solar years and lunar months more than 1,800 years before Galileo made the same observations (fig. 1.12).[11] Calendars and observed astronomic cycles of the sun, moon, Venus, Pleiades and other stars were connected in the Andean world to the repetition of seasons and their vital role in agriculture. Due to the elusive nature of time, they devised calendars that were physically constructed in the landscape, where sacred places, special ceremonies and bespoke material offerings gave a physical permanence to time.[12] Through their observation of celestial orbits they understood the cyclical motion of time. Therefore their calendars and cultural framework for the human experience of time was circular rather than linear, with the past, present and future moving in the same direction while operating at the same time and remaining within a circular or spiralling loop. These cyclical periods of interconnected time could stop and start from scratch, with cataclysmic events often linked to natural or cultural upheavals. In the Inca world, this was a *pachacuti*, a cataclysm when the entire cycle of time would be re-set, the planetary hourglass turned over, and the past, present and future would all begin again.

In writing this chapter in a European language, I am inexorably bound by the structural language of linear time. This linguistic restriction is also why the visual language and meaning of the Andean objects in this book are so important. The objects, as physical embodiments of time, become a structural connection between past, present and future (fig. 1.13). By accepting the possibility of interconnected time, the objects can be freed from our linguistic and conceptual shackles and allowed to tell the powerful narratives of their creators.

MUSEUM TIME

An important consequence of this plural and parallel sense of time is that it fundamentally undermines the core Western idea of temporal progression and implicit cultural advancement that underpin so much of European identity. That idealised sense of social progress through time is the basis for understanding how Europeans got to where they are today, and by extension that past peoples are less developed and less sophisticated than people in the present or future.

An institution such as the British Museum, where the exhibition accompanying this book was created, is an interesting place to consider these issues and how conceptualisations of time influence wider reflections on global cultures. The Museum is an institution founded on the premise of cultural progress, a self-defined certainty proven by the people in charge of its creation wanting to understand and rationalise their intrinsic cultural success.[13] Such a position was built on the assumption that their cultural present is the definition of cultural progress/success/correctness. As anthropologist Paul Nadasdy points out,

> evolutionary assumptions and other 'time-distancing' devices … locate colonized 'others' in some other time – usually the static past. It is as though 'they' somehow got stuck in the past, while 'the West' continued its steady progress through history … it is the sacred duty of the colonizers, those magnanimous inhabitants of the present, to drag the 'primitive' and 'backwards' peoples they colonized – kicking and screaming if need be – into the temporal framework of the modern world.[14]

The idea that time is linear and progressive and that the past and future are not actively changed in the present seems a little ironic when you walk through the neoclassical architectural space and Enlightenment-era gallery designs of the British Museum. The entire Museum is a theatrical construct that makes assumptions about how a visitor in the present thinks about the past and reinforces them. Every decision made in the Museum is designed to influence perceptions of the past and present, whether explicitly so or not. Now imagine that the British Museum were founded within an Andean conceptualisation of time. The impact on the institution would be profound. The dead may understandably not be too happy and wish to more actively change the distanced and retrospective way in which they have been framed. An acceptance of a living past would directly challenge and help re-frame the metanarrative constructs of what constitutes human 'progress' and 'admired' cultural values. The active ability to connect the past, present and future would also highlight the vital role of a Museum for the past to change and in doing so alter the present and future. The point is that time and space underpin all cultural understandings and the lens through which other cultures are seen.

The rights and relevance of people in the past have little traction in a world where they are dead, gone and distanced from the present on a linear timeline. However, the morality and ethics of their treatment would completely change if they were present in the lives of the commentators. The impact of this worldview, with a direct relationship between a living present and a living past, would not only fundamentally alter the construct of the British Museum, it would also shatter cultural hubris. It would inject a sense of realism while opening the horizon for acceptance of a much more diverse set of cultural values, moralities and social ambitions. The fundamental basis upon which human progress was assessed would be up for much more healthy debate. This is exactly why an institution like the British Museum is so important, because it holds such extraordinary capacity to celebrate the cultural plurality of humanity, and this is exactly what this book aims to achieve. The brief Andean journey through time provided here is not merely conceptual curiosity – it is an attempt to bend and warp entrenched concepts of time because we know that in the ancient, contemporary and future Andes this is, was and will be the lived reality.

ANDEAN DECISION-MAKING

The preceding discussion has outlined how human decisions are framed by perceptions of time and space. These perceptions are the filing system for all knowledge we learn and therefore all cultural choices are framed by them. In changing the fundamental structure of how the mind conceives time and space, all human actions and decisions also change. The basis for establishing cultural values and deciding social responsibilities shifts. Andean peoples had (have/will have) a different understanding of time and space. Every human being places their understanding of their world within this different filing system – from their earliest learnings as a child to their amassed wisdom in old age. Every decision made then relies on this ordering of the world.

As an experiment, let us think about petrol. Today it is widely known that fossil fuel emissions are contributing to the destruction of the planet on which we live. However, hundreds of millions of people around the world still regularly burn fossil fuels every week. Now, just imagine for one moment that as you are filling up your car at a local petrol station, the cause of the problem of climate change, and the direct consequences of your actions are not in the distant past and future respectively, but immediate and experienced in the present connected to your physical location. Imagine your great-grandmother and great-grandchild physically standing with you in the same petrol station. Not as a hypothetical scenario, but as a lived experience in which you have the emotional relationship with your living family who are experiencing the consequences of your actions. Suddenly, your behaviour in the present is an active reality of the future,

FIG. 1.13 A large textile created using traditional techniques by weavers from the Centro de Textiles Tradicionales del Cusco (CTTC). Begun in 2018, this textile measures 120 × 110 m and took nearly a year to complete.

in which parallel times connect through place. A major problem with the use of a linear timeline is that the concepts of cause and effect are separated by time. This provides a mental distancing of responsibility and reduces people's sense of obligation to an unknown past and an unpredictable future. It gives us plenty of mental wiggle room to create well-reasoned arguments to justify the actions we choose to take in the present, 'knowing' the future is far away. However, this is not the case within Andean time, because the timeline is interconnected, and cause and effect are simultaneous, so all human actions have immediate impacts on the past and future. If this idea of interconnected time were the starting point and an active relationship between the present, past and future were accepted, then most people would immediately stop filling the car with petrol and pick up their great-grandchild. Decisions for human behaviours change when timelines are interconnected. Understanding this helps enormously to understand the choices of Andean peoples, particularly when related to important cultural choices such as sacrifice (see page 151).

This also helps to explain why certain psychoactive drugs played such an important role in Andean societies. In carefully prescribed ceremonies, trained individuals took powerful phenethylamines and tryptamines, which were absorbed into the bloodstream by ingesting drinks made from plants such as the San Pedro cactus (*Echinopsis pachanoi*) or Ayahuasca vine (*Banisteriopsis caapi*) found to the west and east of the Andes respectively. Intoxicants are often depicted in Andean iconography and have been found at pre-Columbian sites high up in the Andes, far from where they grow, alongside the carefully created equipment required to ingest them.[15] Their alkaloids energise $5HT_{-2A}$ brain receptors, disrupting the neuron transmission in the prefrontal cortex – or in other words, they fundamentally alter the way your mind receives, conceives and interprets thoughts. The temporary, and sometimes permanent, disruption of neurological function changes perceptions of time and space.

When taking these intoxicants, it is not uncommon to have physical face-to-face conversations with living ancestors (dead parents/grandparents) and living descendants (unborn children or children who have become adults). Ordinary experiences of time and space evaporate and are replaced with personalised journeys through the multiverse created by external stimuli, individual thought and psychoactive imagination. The ability to move through time and space augments established ways of conceptualising the world and so was a powerful tool in the Andean realm. It was (is/will be) a cultural mechanism for unlocking the restrictions of temporality and freeing the mind to wrestle with important decisions or life questions in a powerful way. Its relevance in the Andean worldview is clear as it reinforces the interconnected and parallel nature of time. The presence of mind-altering San Pedro cacti and the visual language of transformational beings, abstracted space and confluenced temporality is extremely common throughout Andean iconography. This symbolism across different Andean cultures reflects the similar cultural understanding of time and space shared by diverse societies.

While it is not necessary to take these psychoactive intoxicants in order to appreciate an alternative time, a willingness to accept the possibility is required to understand how interconnected time establishes the framework within which all Andean cultures can be better understood.

THE CULTURAL CONSTRUCTION OF TIME

This essay has attempted to disrupt established understandings of linear time and teleological cultural progress by providing a complementary Andean counterpoint in the form of cross-temporal understandings of accumulated cultural knowledge and cyclically shared understandings across time. This theme of time is continued throughout the book in order to frame the discussions and give context to the narratives of Andean peoples.

In reality, a wholesale shift in our temporal perceptions is a challenging task, because the reassuring handrail of history is often required to safely walk along the path of the Peruvian past. However, this essay encourages an openness to accept and celebrate the wonders of cultural plurality, temporal difference and cognitive dissonance: 'If we do not accept the plurality of the past, the plurality and possibility of the future is diminished.'[16] In the Andean world, the plurality of the past, present and future is clear. The future is not set in stone, nor is it the inevitable consequence of the past. It is dependent and contingent on the interconnected ways in which the past, present and future are conceived and acted on by people. The rigid linear progressive timeline of facts and figures denies people the ability to change a 'dead' past or to alter a prescribed future. By contrast, the plurality of the future is entirely possible when the plurality of the past is accepted – not as cultural exoticism and eccentricity from the norm, but as genuinely alternative constructions of the way in which people can conceive of the world around them and live with the planet they rely on.

Perhaps the greatest lesson of this journey through time in Peru is the realisation that often unquestioned assumptions about time can be built on fragile foundations. Dangerous ideas of cultural progress and absolved responsibility for past errors or future responsibilities unwittingly create a perilous position for a globalising world. It might be time to change perceptions of time and space a little in order to question the logic underpinning present human decision-making. The past and future may not be as far away as we think, and the objects and stories in this book hopefully bring this key Andean concept into existential reality.

2 Living landscapes: mountains, coast, rainforest

Time, space and living landscapes in the Andes[1]

Cecilia Pardo

Located on the western slopes of South America, the Central Andes is one of the few places in the world where complex societies developed independently from the rest of the world over a period of 14,000 years. Geographically, it comprises parts of modern sovereign countries such as southern Ecuador, western Bolivia, northern Argentina and Chile, and the main territory of Peru. The present volume is mainly focused on the area comprising the region within the boundaries of modern Peru. This country has one of the richest and most diverse and complex environments on the planet, with more than eighty life zones from the 116 existing worldwide.[2] It is formed of four main environmental habitats: a long strip of coastal deserts (fig. 2.1); a mountain cordillera with steep slopes and high altitudes reaching almost 7,000 metres above sea level; a tropical forest, which gives way to the Amazon (figs 2.2–2.4); and the Pacific Ocean, home to a rich variety of marine resources that societies have always depended on for survival.

In the coastal region the Pacific Ocean sees the meeting of two ocean currents. The cold Humboldt Current coming from the south and flowing in the direction of the equator creates a highly productive ecosystem with a great diversity of fish and molluscs. The El Niño, also known as ENSO (El Niño–Southern Oscillation), is a climatic event which occurs once every four years due to the heating of the Pacific Ocean. It brings hot weather from the north and has been the cause of environmental disruptions, such as heavy rains and floods, for thousands of years. Archaeological evidence suggests that ENSO events were already happening in Peru as early as the Moche period (AD 100–800). These climatic shifts have had a profound impact on Andean peoples over time, forcing them to constantly adapt to thrive in these challenging environments.

Forms of subsistence farming in the highlands have been very much based on access to different ecological zones through a system known as 'vertical control'.[3] These practices were introduced during pre-Columbian times as an efficient way to get the most out of a region where many different climate zones are contained within a small transect due to sudden changes in altitude. Vertical control of ecological zones allowed a great diversity of crops to be grown in different ecosystems and made them available to populations living at different altitudes, a system that went beyond community, ethnic, linguistic and even national boundaries.[4]

PAGE 36 View from the Choquequirao trail of the River Apurímac, Cusco region

FIG. 2.1 View of the archaeological site of Pachacamac, with the Pacific coast in the background

Thus, for example, a community living at 2,500 metres above sea level would have access to potatoes, which under normal conditions grow over 3,500 metres, or to coca leaves, which usually are cultivated in the Yunga region or in the eastern lowlands, at about 2,000 metres.

TIME IN THE ANDES

In the Central Andes, societies perceived time in a different way from how Western civilisations have understood time, and this was intrinsically linked to their culture and landscape – their dependence on agricultural cycles, rainy and dry seasons, where the sowing and harvest would determine survival, as well as their beliefs in the afterlife. In this belief system, where the deceased were transformed into ancestors who inhabited a parallel world of the divine, time was seen as circular and parallel rather than linear. Archaeologically, two major timelines dating from the 1960s have been used to understand the chronological history and cultural development of ancient Peru. The first one, proposed by anthropologist John Rowe and his colleagues from the University of Berkeley, defined periods based on the stylistic changes found in pottery, the principle material used to express ideas and shared beliefs.[5] According to this theory, the forms and decorations of the vessels mark temporal associations and changes. Thus, the epochs in which the influence of one region was imposed on another are known as 'horizons' – for example, Chavín, Wari and Inca – while those intervals dominated by local developments are known as 'intermediate' periods, a time where societies such as Nasca or Moche developed. The second timeline, proposed by Peruvian archaeologist Luis G. Lumbreras, organises periods based on the technological, social and political development of societies.[6]

CULTURES AND REGIONS

Societies in the Central Andean region became established in two main geographical areas, forming traditions with well-defined and common features. The northern tradition developed between the Piura and Huarmey valleys on the coast, and the Upper Marañón river basin in the highlands. Due to the arid deserts of the coast, societies that populated this region, such as Moche, Lambayeque and Chimú, had to modify the terrain, diverting river courses in order to undertake major irrigation works that helped to create arable land. They built large mudbrick ceremonial centres and created an ideological system in which humans interacted with animals and deified beings. The most common ceramic form

CHRONOLOGY BASED ON STYLISTIC CHANGES (1964)
JOHN H. ROWE

Preceramic	15,000–1700 BC
Initial Period	1700–1200 BC
Early Horizon	1200–200 BC (Chavín, Cupisnique)
Early Intermediate	200 BC–AD 550 (Mochica, Nasca, Recuay)
Middle Horizon	AD 550–800 (Wari)
Late Intermediate	AD 800–1400 (Chimú, Lambayeque, Chancay)
Late Horizon	AD 1400–1532 (Inca)

CHRONOLOGY BASED ON SOCIAL CHANGES (1969)
LUIS G. LUMBRERAS

Lithic	10,000–7600 BC
Archaic	7600–1700 BC
Formative	1700–200 BC
Regional Developments	200 BC–AD 600
Wari	AD 600–900
Regional States	AD 900–1400
Inca Empire	AD 1400–1532

was the stirrup-spout vessel. Generally, the motifs represented by the Moche were decorated in two tones: cream and reddish brown. In the highlands, the cloud forests proved ideal for the cultivation of tubers and maize, serving as the setting for early and ongoing developments from the Preceramic period right through to the arrival of the Spanish in the sixteenth century.

The southern tradition developed in the arid coastal valleys to the south of Lima, which connect to the inter-Andean valleys of Cusco and Apurímac and to the Lake Titicaca basin. On the coast, home to the Paracas and Nasca, the scarcity of water was a determining factor in their worldview. Rather than building large centres, their efforts were focused on underground canals and rituals associated with the earth, a sacred space inhabited by their ancestors. This is evidenced by the painted images on their ceramics, which are notable for the use of a diverse range of colours.

In the highlands, subsistence farming was determined by steep slopes and low temperatures, which were controlled through the construction of systems of agricultural terraces and pressurised irrigation. The farming of small grains and tubers, as well as the grazing of camelids, were decisive in their development. The Tiwanaku, Wari and Inca inhabited this region in different time periods.

Due to their location, the societies of central Peru shared features with both their northern and southern neighbours.

The Peruvian landscape is one of great diversity – from dry coastal deserts, to the high Andean mountains, and down to the tropical Amazon rainforest. These vastly different environments shaped and moulded the civilisations that inhabited them and their forms of production. The painted tunic opposite brings together all three (fig. 2.4): the painted feathers replicate the real Amazonian feathers on ceremonial tunics (fig. 2.2), the circular pattern might represent mountain lagoons, and the stylised wave pattern across the bottom edge shows the importance of marine life. This aspect is also demonstrated by the representation of fish in this ceremonial Nasca bowl (fig. 2.3).

FIG. 2.2 (LEFT) Feather ceremonial tunic
Inca AD 1400–1532
Cotton, feathers
H. 81.7 cm, W. 57 cm
British Museum, Am2006,Q.12

FIG. 2.3 (ABOVE) Bowl depicting two fish
Nasca 100 BC–AD 650
Pottery
H. 3.7 cm, Diam. 15.7 cm
British Museum, Am1939,24.3

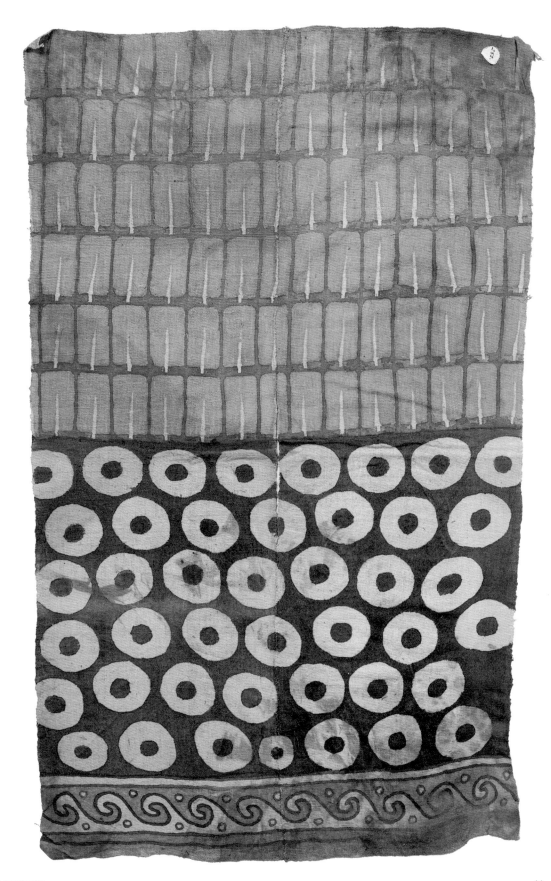

FIG. 2.4 Tunic
Chancay–Inca AD 1000–1470
Cotton, paint
H. 112 cm, W. 67.5 cm
British Museum, Am1907,0319.8

Thus, there is no single style unifying the different cultures of this area. In this in-between region, cultures such as Lima (AD 200–650) and Chancay (AD 1000–1400) arose. Although the appearance of the ceramics varies from one society to another, cultures like Lima and Chancay portrayed geometric motifs that were most likely inspired by textiles.

The tropical forest was populated by isolated communities until the Chachapoyas came into existence during the Late Intermediate period. Although little is known about this culture, they began to build Kuélap, a magnificent settlement located high up in the cloud forests, from around the seventh century AD. They also performed complex funerary practices, as is testified by sarcophagi located in very inaccessible locations, such as above river gorges.

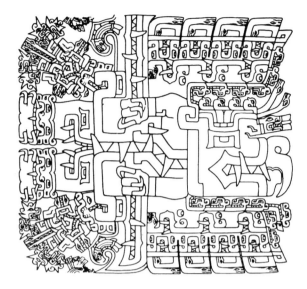

FIG. 2.5 A sculptural being with bird, feline and snake features from the Portal of the Falcons at Chavín de Huántar

SYMBOLIC ENVIRONMENTS

Landscape and environment played a fundamental role in the belief systems of Andean cultures. The use of marine resources and the cultivation of the land, both basic sources of food, depended to a large extent on favourable weather, which these cultures believed could only be controlled by divine forces. Basing their beliefs on their own surroundings, they attributed a sacred role to the elements of nature, conceiving them as living landscapes. They formed a repertoire of sacred animals and deified figures, represented in different mediums, whom they worshipped in ceremonies and rituals directed by the governing priests.

Three sacred animals were central to the pre-Columbian Andean worldview: the bird, the feline and the snake. This tripartite organisation of the cosmos, which may be observed from the Chavín onwards, is also associated with the world of the gods, the world of human beings and the world of the ancestors (fig. 2.5). The bird – usually depicted as an eagle or falcon – symbolises night-time, war and darkness, and is vested with anthropomorphic or supernatural features, depending on the activity being performed (fig. 2.6). For example, throughout Andean societies, shamans and warriors can be seen depicted with features of the owl and the raptor. The feline, often a jaguar or puma, symbolises might and power, with tails and fangs featuring heavily in the avatars of fierce warrior priests and of deities in the supernatural world (fig. 2.7). Lastly, the snake slithers across the earth and can travel underground to the site of the forbidden world in which the dead rest, allowing it to access the power and fertility of people's ancestors (fig. 2.8).[7]

Dualism was another important concept woven into the fabric of Andean society. It can be found as part of the *ayllu,*

FIG. 2.6 Vessel depicting a bird
Moche 200 BC–AD 500
Pottery
H. 18 cm, W. 11.8 cm, D. 12.8 cm
Museo de Arte de Lima, 2007.16.20
Donated by Petrus and Verónica Fernandini

The bird, the feline and the snake are central to the pre-Columbian Andean worldview and are therefore key to the world of the gods and ancestors. The bird is associated with the sky and is a symbol of the night-time and war. Shamans and warriors bearing features of the owl and the raptor can be seen throughout Andean societies. The feline figure displays might, its fangs, tail and other aspects often accompanying depictions of deities and fierce warrior priests. The snake can travel underground, where it has the supernatural ability to traverse the underworld, allowing individuals to access the powers of their dead ancestors.

FIG. 2.7 (ABOVE) Vessel depicting a feline
Moche 200 BC–AD 500
Pottery
H. 20 cm, W. 17 cm, D. 11 cm
Museo de Arte de Lima, 2007.16.25
Donated by Petrus and Verónica Fernandini

FIG. 2.8 (LEFT) Vessel depicting a snake
Moche 200 BC–AD 500
Pottery
H. 23.3 cm, L. 24.9 cm, D. 16.6 cm
Museo de Arte de Lima, IV-2.0-0037
Prado Family Bequest

Found in the deep seas of the Pacific Ocean, off the coast of Ecuador, *Spondylus* and *Strombus* shells have been imbued with high symbolic meaning for Andean societies for more than 4,000 years and have been interpreted as representing opposite forces of nature, such as feminine and masculine, moon and sun. They were used as funerary offerings, musical instruments and as raw material for producing fine adornments.

FIG. 2.9 (RIGHT) Stirrup vessel with representations of *Strombus* and *Spondylus* shells
Cupisnique 1250–500 BC
Pottery
H. 28 cm, W. 22.8 cm, D. 20 cm
Museo de Arte de Lima, 2007.16.2
Donated by Petrus and Verónica Fernandini

FIG. 2.10 (BELOW) A drawing of a stone carving from Chavín showing a fanged deity holding *Spondylus* and *Strombus* shells. Museo Nacional Chavín

a basic social unit rooted in pre-Columbian times. The division in moieties features in the organisation of agricultural work, festivities and community administration, and is a practice that endured the European conquest and remains even today. Other studies based on archaeological research suggest that dualism was and is also expressed in the way sacred animals were conceived. In Andean culture, the camelid belongs to the human realm (it signifies the day, domesticity and herding), while the deer belongs to the world of the ancestors (it represents the night, the wild and hunting).[8]

Moreover, the concept of dualism expressed in objects that imply this symbolism has existed since very early times, where the world was expressed and understood through universal diametric concepts such as feminine/masculine, sun/moon, up/down and so on. For example, *Spondylus* and *Strombus* shells, found in the deep warm waters of the Pacific Ocean, have been imbued with high symbolic meaning for Andean societies for more than 4,000 years (figs 2.9–2.10). They were considered important ritual objects and were used as sacred offerings to the gods, thought to symbolise the opposing and complementing forces of nature (fig. 2.9). While the *Strombus galeatus* is associated with the masculine, the *Spondylus princeps* is related to the feminine.[9] Other symbols of dualism are later expressed in objects such as a Moche stirrup vessel, which depicts two birds in carefully studied symmetry (fig. 2.11). It can also be seen in Inca and early colonial *keros*, wooden beverage containers used in pairs in ceremonies devoted to the Pachamama, or mother earth (see figs 7.18–7.20).[10]

The mountains, or *apus*, were key in the sacred Andean landscape. They had the power to watch over people and protect them, or to act as borders between different territories, a belief that still persists today. In some representations the mountains were depicted in sculptural models as the setting of supernatural events, ritual sites or as pure landscapes, in versions ranging from the highly naturalistic to more synthetic depictions. While some of these pieces feature mythological beings watching over ceremonies of ritual sacrifice, others show animals embodying sacred attributes as they emerge from the mountains, as if travelling between the world of the living and the world of the dead (see figs 2.21–2.22).

Another symbolic motif brought from nature is a stepped triangle that sometimes appears with a volute or spiral on top (figs 2.12 and 2.13). It is thought to have symbolised the wave, a representation of the forces at work in the ocean waters, and the throne on which rulers sat, investing them with great power and hegemonic might. Also interpreted as a synthesis of the constructions themselves – the *huaca* and the temple –

FIG.2.11 Stirrup vessel depicting the heads and necks of two identical birds
Moche AD 100–800
Pottery
H. 22.7 cm, W. 27.3 cm, D. 8.5 cm
British Museum, Am1909,1218.74
Donated by Henry Van den Bergh through the Art Fund

the triangle and the spiral were used as decorative elements on the ramps leading to principal enclosures, where the most important ceremonies were performed. An alternative explanation is that the union of the triangle and the spiral is a symbolic expression of the annual agricultural cycle, in which the mountain (the triangle) is responsible for bringing the water of the rivers (spiral) to the coast, fertilising the valleys and thus leading to nature's regeneration. According to interpretations of Moche iconography, it was thought that this occurred on the December solstice, coinciding with the start of the rainy season in the highlands.

Representations of architecture are another recurring theme in the broad repertoire of images inspired by the Andean landscape. Although some of these figures refer to sacred buildings that may have actually existed, the imprecise forms lacking in proportion raise questions regarding their function as mock-ups or models for construction. It is more likely that these objects were used to symbolise ritual spaces, in an attempt to perpetuate their likeness and meaning among different groups.[11] Some objects show buildings inhabited by divine beings celebrating special ceremonies, while others depict rituals directed by human beings in honour of their gods.

Recent studies connecting archaeology and iconography have proposed associations between such depictions and actual buildings, and existing archaeological findings have helped to demonstrate the relationship that may have existed between these objects and the most powerful figures of ancient societies.[12]

DISRUPTING THE ANDEAN BALANCE

The European conquest in the mid-sixteenth century had a major impact on different aspects of Andean society, disrupting its equilibrium – from introducing new diseases, to destroying local practices that had endured for thousands of years and breaking the harmony of the ecosystem. About sixty million lives were lost in the years that followed the arrival of the Spanish to the Americas. This was caused mainly by an onset of epidemics that local populations did not have antibodies to fight against,[13] but also by other factors such as warfare, slavery and seasonal food shortages. The depopulation in the Andes had a negative impact on the cultivable land; the decline in human labour resulted in a major decrease in levels of carbon dioxide in the atmosphere. Anthropologists have noted that globally the decline in CO_2 in this period lowered surface air temperatures by 0.15° C, speculating that one cause could have been the large-scale depopulation of the Americas after the arrival of Europeans.[14] In parallel, the new regime condemned local religious practices and aimed to eradicate all forms of Andean belief systems, in a mission known as the 'Extirpation of Idolatry'. The campaign took place during the seventeenth century and is recounted in an early colonial document by the Jesuit missionary Pablo José de Arriaga.[15]

However, in spite of this tremendous turmoil, Andean ways of life survived the colonial period and remained into the nineteenth and twentieth centuries, and through to the present. Their cultural practices were so deep-rooted that the construction of a new society could only be possible through alliances with the Indigenous elites. Various studies suggest that vertical control of altitudes for agriculture during pre-Columbian times is still reflected in current patterns in the highlands. Some communities still operate a shared network of administration and reciprocity, without depending on markets.[16] *Huacas* – sacred landscapes (including mountains, rivers and lakes), architecture and man-made objects – continued to be used as shrines and symbolic places of origin, where people could gather, devote offerings and pray for their wellbeing. As local populations grew again a new *mestizo* culture emerged, one that saw an increasing

FIG. 2.12 Vessel with painted stepped motifs
Moche AD 100–800
Pottery
H. 23 cm, W. 14 cm, D. 19.5 cm
British Museum, Am1858,0403.6

syncretism that would define Andean practices all the way to the twenty-first century. Hybrid traditions can be seen in rituals, community celebrations, religious processions and even in portable objects – these all managed to thrive through adaptation and transformation, incorporating elements and symbols of the Western world. For example, containers used in propitiatory ceremonies, such as *keros* and *pacchas*, and symbolic offerings, such as *conopas* (reduced-scale figurines in the form of camelids and crops, used to pray for good harvests), are still in use today, while many Indigenous communities continue to use coca leaves to thank the Pachamama, the magical mother earth. These surviving traditions demonstrate that Andean ways of living can thrive and endure.

The stepped triangle and spiral wave are two common aspects of
Andean iconography, often shown together. The steps represent
the mountains, and the spiral the water and waves that flow through
the valleys to the sea. Combining the two brings together a
representation of the agricultural cycle, the water coming down from
the mountains to the coast and thus fertilising the valleys on the way.

FIG. 2.13 Vessel in the form of a stepped
structure with volute
Moche 200 BC–AD 600
Pottery
H. 20.4 cm, L. 22.6 cm, D. 9.9 cm
Museo Larco, Lima, Peru, ML012932

White-tailed deer had a special significance among Andean societies and were a part of their mythology, as creatures able to transform into hybrid humans. In the upper coastal valleys, people carried out ritual deer hunts, in order to extract their blood as well as small bezoar stones (hard lumps built up around undigested material) from their stomachs. These were believed to have magical and healing properties and are still used in traditional medicine today.

Materials and materialities[1]

Cecilia Pardo

The beautiful and finely decorated objects left behind by pre-Columbian societies testify to the skill and mastery of trained artists, who were capable of transforming a wide variety of materials into fine objects with high symbolic value (fig. 2.16). Imbued with great artistic and aesthetic quality, they are true works of art. However, these items were not the result of free experimentation, but were guided by conventions within a broader system of production. Decorated objects were not used for activities in daily life, but were conceived as propitiatory items used in ritual ceremonies, funerary offerings (fig. 2.17) or as blank canvases for disseminating ideas. While clay, cotton, camelid fibres and metals were the most common materials for creating these objects, other mediums included stone, bone, feathers, wood and seashells (fig. 2.18).

Probably due to its plasticity and portability, clay was the primary material used in the creation of both domestic vessels and ritual vessels. The use of clays featuring different tonalities, the application of modelling and moulding techniques, and the finishes achieved through firing – the results of hundreds of years of experimentation – produced what is now recognised as one of the most important pottery traditions of the ancient world. Developing into a widespread tradition during the last millennia BC, at a time when fired pottery began to be circulated widely, master artisans demonstrated their great depth of knowledge in the creation of finely decorated vessels (fig. 2.19). From that point onwards, ceramics would become the main means for the dissemination of the belief systems that dominated during each period.

The most precious objects in ancient Peru were not necessarily made of gold and silver, but from woven threads of cotton and camelid fibres. Invested with a complex symbolism, textiles possessed a special value throughout the course of pre-Columbian history, and were used to transmit messages and establish social differences. Based on their manufacture and provenance, we know that some of these pieces were made to be worn by the elite during special ceremonies (fig. 2.20), while others were used as wall decorations. Textiles were made collectively and took months or even years to produce. The finest knits, however, mostly found in burial contexts, were made specifically to accompany the deceased on their journey to the afterlife. Archaeological records show that some of the textiles now on display in museums were in fact made especially for use as funeral offerings. Exhibiting a rich and complex iconography, they formed part of the grave goods, whether as wrappings for the cadaver, wall adornments in tombs or clothing.

The discovery and transformation of metals such as gold, silver and their alloys were the result of a long process of experimentation. Some of the most widely used techniques in the Andes included lamination, casting, rolling and hammering, methods that were complemented with embossing and fretwork, which were fundamental in the decoration of the pieces.

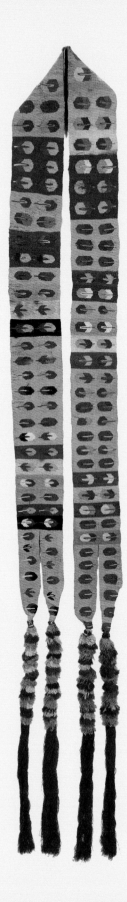

FIG. 2.16 (LEFT) Tasselled band painted with
feather motifs
Chimú AD 900–1470
Camelid fibres, cotton
L. 230 cm, W. 7 cm
British Museum, Am1954,05.486
Donated by the Wellcome Institute

FIG. 2.17 (BELOW) Funerary mask
Moche AD 100–800
Copper, shell
H. 20.8 cm, W. 29.5 cm, D. 8 cm
Museo de Arte de Lima, 1993.1.3
Donated by James Reid

Metal adornments shone or made noises, fulfilling important functions in rituals. Headdresses, breastplates, nosepieces and earpieces were probably worn for life by the governing class as symbols of prestige and status. Other objects were produced specifically for inclusion as part of burial offerings.

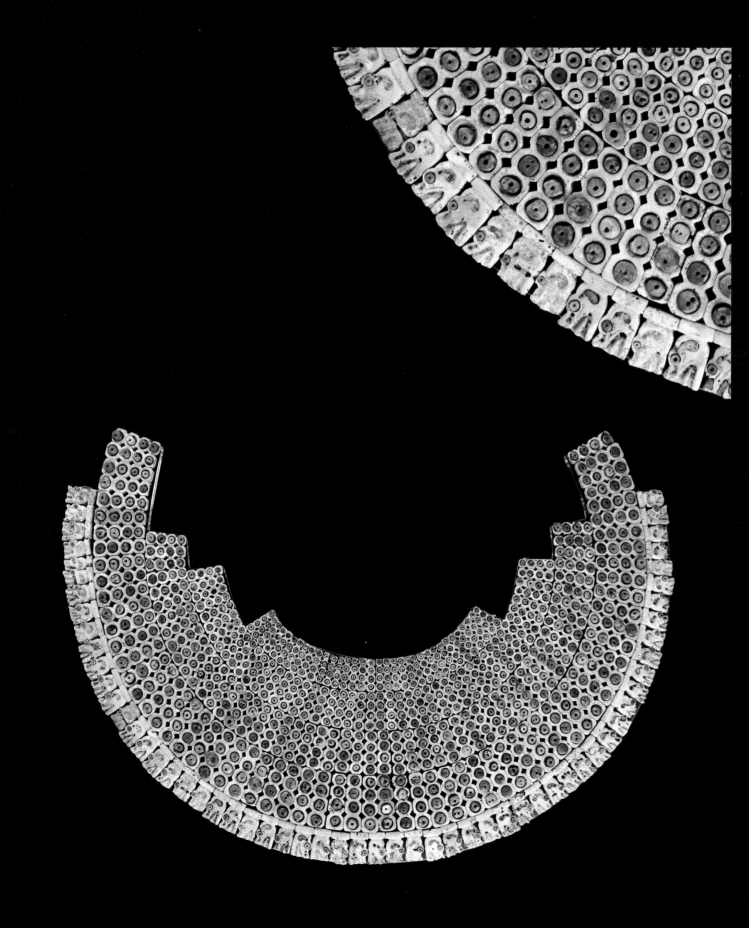

Materials exchanged with cultures from faraway places were used to produce sumptuous garments and accessories worn by high-ranking individuals, who would eventually be buried with them for the afterlife. While colourful feathers came from birds such as macaws from the Amazon tropical forest, semi-precious stones also were transported long distances, creating a network of luxury goods spanning areas such as modern-day Chile or Colombia.

FIG. 2.18 (OPPOSITE AND DETAIL)
Pectoral with feline heads represented around the edge
Cupisnique 1250 BC–AD 1
Shell, turquoise
H. 34 cm, W. 46 cm, D. 0.5 cm
Museo Larco, Lima, Peru, ML200007

FIG. 2.19 (LEFT) Vessel depicting a human figure playing a flute
Moche AD 100–800
Pottery
H. 30 cm, W. 24 cm, D. 14.7 cm
British Museum, Am1909,1218.11
Donated by Henry Van den Bergh through the Art Fund

FIG. 2.20 (ABOVE) Feathered tunic
Central Coast AD 1400–1532
Cotton, feathers
H. 141.5 cm, W. 81.5 cm
British Museum, Am1937,0213.12
Donated by John Goble

Sacred landscapes, time and livelihoods

George F. Lau

The Andes comprises three major natural regions: coast, mountains and tropical forest. Within each there is great environmental diversity, providing substantial resources for human use. In some regions, the ecological zones are found close together and can be crossed in quick succession, often in a day's journey. The land and sea can be bountiful, but also unpredictable, due to perils such as El Niño floods, earthquakes, drought and landslides, and long-term processes such as desertification and tectonic uplift. Economic and religious practices have sought to mitigate these risks. Villages based on traditional farming and herding practices became widespread during the first millennium BC. Highland peoples perceived their landscape as animate: mountains, lakes and the earth were considered sacred beings (figs 2.21 and 2.22). They were providers of scarce, unpredictable resources, such as water and fertility in relation to crops and animals. Their worship ensured the flow of food and resources in the Andes.

Andean populations organised their time and work by following the landscape's natural changes and rhythms. The sun's movement across the mountainous horizon marked the days, and the night's frosts returned when the sun disappeared in the west. The wet season (October to March) transformed these lands into mosaics of verdant agricultural fields. If the gods were pleased, harvests began in April and later sowing could repeat the process anew. Around AD 500, families began to keep their esteemed dead (in the form of ancestor mummies) in tomb repositories – small shrines, often located with or near standing monoliths (*huancas*) that watched over the fields. The stones and mummies were images of ancestors, guardians of the land and providers of rain; tilling the lands obliged mutual nourishment. Thus the agricultural cycle was also a ceremonial calendar, and the worship of mummies represented a sacred covenant with the divinities, safeguarding the land's renewal and reflecting the people's cultural understanding of time.

Farmers on the arid coast relied on rivers descending from the mountains to irrigate their floodplain fields (which included crops of maize, fruits, peanuts and squash). The harvesting of marine products (such as fish, shellfish, sea mammals and birds) was also seasonal. To help secure their livelihoods, people built monumental temples to mark and celebrate annual festivals and events. Offerings, including llama and human sacrifices, were made periodically to appease the gods, to ward off disasters and to guarantee the generosity of the sea and land.

FIG. 2.21 A view of livestock herders in the Andean highlands

The mountains, or *apus*, were of great importance to the Andean people and are often seen to have a sacred significance. Ceramic vessels such as this (fig. 2.22) can be seen throughout Andean art, depicting sacrifices, otherworldly events and ritual sites in the mountains. Some ceramics even show the mountains as anthropomorphic beings. The mountains were looked to for protection – watching over the people as well as acting as borders between groups.

FIG. 2.22 Sculptural bottle with mythological mountain scene
Moche AD 400–700
Pottery
H. 17.8 cm, W. 16.6 cm, D. 15.6 cm
Museo de Arte de Lima, 2007.16.30
Donated by Petrus and Verónica Fernandini

Qhapaq Ñan: the Andean road system

Jago Cooper and César Astuhuamán

The road system was not just a network that joined places and peoples, it was a framework for negotiating relationships between humans and a landscape with its own history and agency.[1]

The pre-Columbian road system of the Central Andes remains one of the most remarkable human achievements in successful environmental adaptation and collective cultural endeavour in the world (fig. 2.23). Studying how it was built, and its continued use today, reveals important insights into the relationship between Andean peoples and the mountains in whose awe-inspiring presence they live. Entirely constructed for humans to simply walk or run along, and to occasionally bring loads on the backs of llamas, these labyrinthine paths remain a captivating feature of the region today. Made up of stone-built paths clinging precipitously to the side of 1,000-metre vertical rock faces or intricately woven rope bridges traversing the melting glacial waters flowing down the mountains, today this road network[2] – or Qhapaq Ñan – is celebrated as the largest UNESCO world heritage site in the world.[3]

Just one 40-kilometre stretch of road, the Inca trail to Machu Picchu, attracts more than 150,000 people a year, but this is a tiny fraction of an enormous road system with so much more to walk along and explore. In fact, if the entire length of the road network were laid out straight it would be longer than the circumference of the earth itself.[4] The roads, found in the modern Andean nations of Peru, Ecuador, Bolivia, Chile, Colombia and Argentina, are built from stone, rope, earth and wood through dense cloud forest (fig. 2.24), over snow-capped mountains and across wide open desert sands. This network remains alive today, continually used to connect communities together. The roads are a living monument and physical manifestation of the cultural networks that unite peoples living throughout these beautiful and productive landscapes.

This Andean road network inspired awe in the first Europeans to arrive in Peru, their experience of road networks in medieval Europe paling into insignificance in comparison.[5] Pedro Cieza de León remarked in the 1550s:

In human memory, I believe that there is no account of roads as great as this, running through deep valleys, high mountains, banks of snow, torrents of water, living rock, and wild rivers … In all places it was clean and swept free of refuse, with lodgings, storehouses, sun temples, and posts along the route. Oh! Can anything similar be claimed for Alexander or any of the powerful kings who ruled the world?[6]

The road system in use when the first Europeans arrived included three major routes from north to south, stretching from northern Argentina to southern Colombia. One north–south route ran along the west coast, another crossed the top of the Andes and another, less studied and understood, ran along the eastern foothills of the Andes, connected through the river systems draining into the Amazon basin. There were then a whole series of interlacing east–west roads between these north–south routes, which created the network and facilitated the constant movement of Andean communities between different altitudes and environmental zones (fig. 2.25). This network of roads has organically grown throughout time, reflecting the waxing and waning of population sizes and concentrations throughout the region. For example, many of the routes in the eastern Andes, leading down the mountains into the Amazon, would have been far more busy and active than they are today, where many of these roads have remained untrodden for hundreds of years.[7]

The Andean road network is a living artefact of use, construction and modification, with some sections of road having been maintained for over 2,000 years. The different ways in which cultures, from the Nasca to the Incas, may have thought about planning and building the road system may have varied, but they all shared the experience of being part of this connected living network across the landscape. Like so many worldwide monuments honouring human achievement, the manual labour invested in constructing and maintaining this network over hundreds of years stretches into millions of hours of human effort.[8] In pre-Columbian times this work, done by hand, was not the product of enslaved peoples or soldiers driven by people in positions of power, aiming to physically dominate a landscape and maintain control. On the contrary, much of this road system was built by communities periodically coming together in shared endeavour, with the common purpose of building connections between themselves. Until this day, much

of the maintenance work on the sections still in use is done by local communities with *mink'a*, labour seasonally given up for projects of shared benefit and use (see page 219).

In many ways the Andean road network is timeless: re-walked and re-worked continuously by people with a shared desire for journeying. Conceptually, architecturally and materially, these networks are empathic with the environment. Every road carefully considers and adjusts to its distinctive local environment. The topography of the roads hugs the contours of the hills and they are commonly built from locally available and sustainable materials. For many stretches, Andean roads are the antithesis of the unyielding straight roads of the Roman Empire in Europe, built to a prescribed design by soldiers and enslaved peoples, smashing through nature and building over culture to create a centralised empire of control. These Andean roads were built in sympathy with local topography, environmental conditions, religious understandings and the specific needs of communities. The network symbolises the ability and understanding of Andean peoples to live with their environment and harness its potential without the need to destroy it in order to meet their needs. Roads would have seen trains of camelids laden with produce moving along the trade routes (fig. 2.26).

FIG. 2.23 (PAGE 56) A female weaver walking down a pathway in the village by Patacancha, Cusco region

FIG. 2.24 (ABOVE) An Inca road dug into the mountainside near Machu Picchu

FIG. 2.25 Map showing the extent
of the Inca road system known as
the Qhapaq Ñan

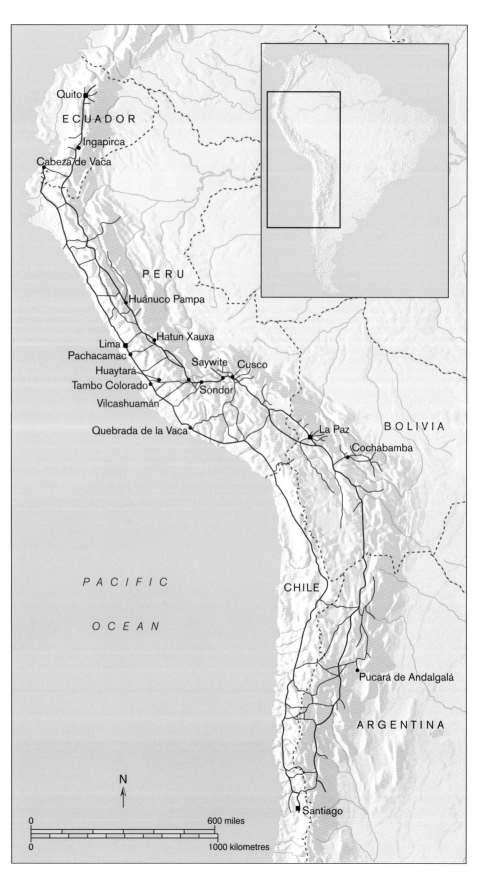

By walking along the more remote stretches of the pre-Columbian road network, it is possible to begin to understand aspects of Andean life through the archaeological buildings still standing: *tambos*, buildings used as way stations for *chasquis* (running messengers) carrying communications or important goods between handover points; *qolqas*, used to provision food and store trade goods; *huacas*, religious shrines to pay respect to the mountain deities (*apus*) and earth goddess Pachamama of the Andean pantheon; *pukaras*, forts for military garrisons and defensive protection; as well as every possible type of human settlement, from the smallest hamlet to the largest community.[9] This is the living cultural infrastructure built throughout a landscape, whose lifeblood was the road system itself. The often-used metaphor of roads as arteries for the world's body is particularly apt in the Andes, as the roads themselves have the potential to vitalise, or *camay*. The road is an integral part of the living landscape, the shared Andean worldview that connects the cultural, natural and supernatural realms.

The capacity of a road network to compress the time and space of lived human experience is important to acknowledge. It shows how collaborative human endeavour can change the time taken to move through a landscape or timescape dependent on the practical, architectural and ideological motivations of those involved.[10] A message would travel along a chain of *chasquis* from Cusco in the south of modern-day Peru to Quito in the north of modern-day Ecuador in just three days, a distance of 2,700 kilometres. This Inca vessel, which shows a muscled leg, allows us to imagine the fitness required of the *chasquis* (fig. 2.27). The road network literally changes the temporal relationship between people and their landscape because it reduces the time taken for people, goods and messages to travel between settlements.

This symbiotic connection between road and traveller, between practical and cultural, is why the Andean road system is so important. Over thousands of years it has created a map of the connections and diversity of the peoples living throughout the region.[11] 'Roads, in this respect, do more than connect places and traverse difference. As infrastructures, they bring people and things together in new configurations.'[12] By understanding the closely interconnected cultural and cosmological role of this road system within the lives of Andean peoples, we can see it as a cross-temporal map on which the different cultures and their material remains can be plotted.

The walk to the site of Chavín de Huántar over the Yanashallash pass traces one of the lowest altitude crossings over the eastern cordillera of the Andes at 4,700 metres above

FIG. 2.26 Vessel in the form of a camelid
Moche AD 100–800
H. 16.6 cm, W. 11.3 cm, L. 22.5 cm
Pottery
British Museum, Am1933,0713.58
Donated by Clarissa Reid

FIG. 2.27 Vessel in the form of a leg
and foot
Inca AD 1400–1532
Pottery
H. 22.8 cm, W. 6.6 cm, D. 11.8 cm
British Museum, Am1947,10.13
Donated by Mrs E. H. S. Spottiswoode

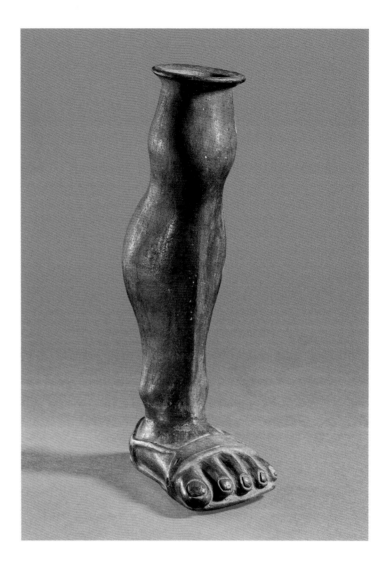

sea level. The site is at the heart of a transversal route through the Andes, connecting ancient settlements such as Sechín on the Pacific coast with the tributaries and peoples of the Amazon to the east. It is exactly the same journey traversed by hundreds of thousands of people living in the past, present and future. This shared experience of landscape connects everyone who has walked it and provides an important environmental and cultural context for the architecture, purpose and meaning of the Chavín site itself on arrival (see page 74).[13] The views of the surrounding mountains from the centre of the site, the sound of the water running through the carefully built underground channels, the structure of the Lanzón stone monument, enveloped within the underground shrine – all take on a different context if you have arrived there by walking over the top of the mountains, along the source of the river created by the melting ice, down into

the protected valley where the remarkable site of Chavín de Huántar has been for 3,000 years. The journey needs to be experienced as an environmental, cultural, climatic, historical and political landscape in order to understand Chavín's complexity, its sense of place and its relationship with other sites in the region.[14]

In many ways, the journeys these roads represent help to reflect that connection of shared experience between past, present and future; the setting, weather and environment frame the cultural landscape they connect. While the Andean road system is one of the greatest living artefacts of human achievement, it is also a physical journey that must be walked in order to truly appreciate and understand how these roads underpin the temporal and spatial connections between all the diverse peoples and cultures that make up the Andean world.

3 Chavín and early cultures

Early ceremonial centres in the Andes

Rafael Vega-Centeno Sara-Lafosse

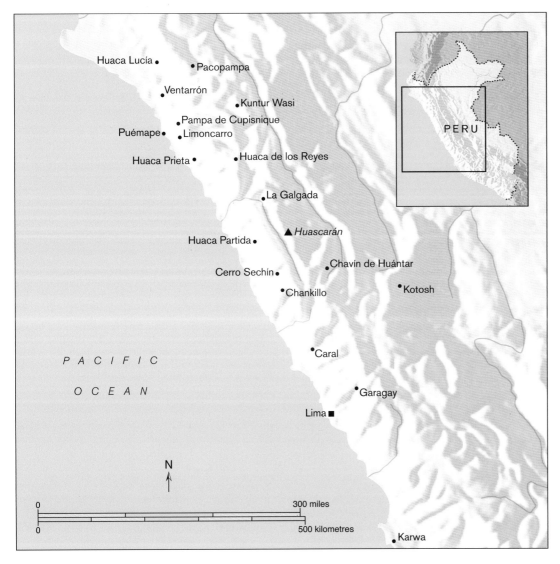

PAGE 62 The site of Chavín de Huántar

FIG. 3.1 (OPPOSITE) Vessel in the form
of a contortionist
Cupisnique 1250–500 BC
Pottery
H. 37 cm, W. 14.3 cm, D. 20.7 cm
Museo de Arte de Lima, 2007.16.10
Donated by Petrus and Verónica
Fernandini

FIG. 3.2 Map of the key early ceremonial
sites in the Central Andes

The emergence of different peoples in the Andes is linked to a series of social and political processes that started around 3000 BC. By then the inhabitants of the Central Andes had already lived in permanent settlements and had consolidated agricultural economies (in low and middle altitude zones) or livestock economies (in higher altitude zones). The variety of cultivated plants (tubers, fruits, grains and even corn) shows the dissemination of species across the Andes, revealing how people interacted across the regions. Moreover, in the coastal valleys, the farming of cotton facilitated the production of nets, which boosted fishing activity, thereby improving access to sources of protein.

It was in this environment that different manifestations of civilisation in the Central Andes developed. This complex process involved both social differentiation and centralisation, in response to the needs of growing populations. Productive diversification, ability and interdependency went beyond the domestic. Interdependency intensified the interaction between different regions, including the coastal plains, the inter-Andean basins and even the tropical forests of the

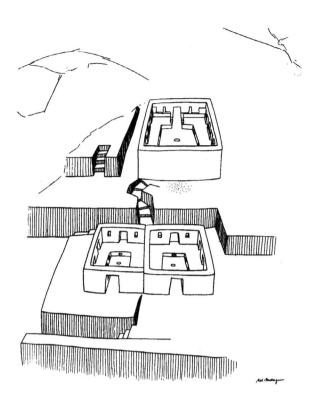

FIG 3.3 Reconstruction of the pre-Ceramic architecture in Kotosh, Huánuco

Amazon. These processes transformed the sociopolitical structures of smaller communities of farmers and shepherds into units of greater scale and complexity. Andean territory became fertile land ideal for the cultivation of beans, corn, potatoes and other crops, and the high plains became breeding grounds for llamas and alpacas. This was a transformative step towards the establishment of one of the six cradles of civilisation in the history of humanity – the other five are China, Egypt, Mesopotamia (present-day Iraq and Iran), the Indus valley (present-day Pakistan and Afghanistan) and Mexico.

The first evidence of these developments materialised in the construction of ritual buildings, as well as in the development of religious art.[1] Ritual buildings encouraged new forms of social organisation and political leadership, because their construction required strategies to recruit workers for non-domestic purposes. These buildings also became cosmological reference points for entire communities. Ritual is an evolved sociopolitical activity in which communities renew the relationships of their members and ancestors by coming together.[2] When populations settled permanently in different territories, they began to build a new identity where 'belonging' to the territory was key. In this context, claiming ownership to the land was legitimised by their ancestors' settlement in the past but also by their existence in the present. Therefore, promoting and controlling ritual activities by the use of a specially designed building or area to host them would become a key strategy of power. The ritual building thus became a space where, and through which, leaderships began to consolidate, which would eventually lead to the emergence of elites. In parallel, the rise of figurative art, made material at its outset in textile garments or clay figures (fig. 3.1), is evidence of the importance of expressing and communicating religious content to increasingly large audiences.[3] As part of this same tendency, objects of wood, shell and other materials were made more frequently, together with the use of minerals such as haematite, and contributed to the creation of religious images.

One important factor is that these changes occurred simultaneously across the Central Andean region, from the Lambayeque valley on the north coast to the Chillón valley on the central coast, including the high valleys to the Amazonian Andes (fig. 3.2). In this context, the significant development of the settlement of Caral in the Supe valley, as well as ceremonial centres such as Ventarrón in Lambayeque, El Paraíso in Lima and Kotosh in Huánuco (fig. 3.3) undoubtedly stand out.[4] The differences between regions in the ritual buildings' scale and design shows that although these were mostly autonomous processes, they were also the results of contact and interaction, thus forming the particular physiology of Andean civilisation as we know it.

Around 2000 BC new shifts took place in the region. The vast majority of existing ceremonial centres were abandoned, giving rise to new centres greater in scale and complexity. These changes coincided with the adoption of new technologies such as pottery, which had developed earlier in the northern Andes. The enormous ceremonial complexes built in the Casma valley, such as Sechín Alto or Moxeke, are significant examples from this period.[5] They were made up of flat-topped pyramids linked to patios and sunken circular plazas and incorporated iconographic narratives in the form of friezes and engraved stones, as well as stone objects for ceremonial use. One notable site is Cerro Sechín, which features a stone perimeter wall carved with complete and incomplete human figures, in an elaborate iconographic scheme whose subject is related to notions of order and chaos, represented allegorically in the articulation or disarticulation of the human body (fig. 3.4).[6]

Around 1100 BC further changes began to take place. Many of the temples that had flourished in Casma were abandoned and new ceremonial centres arose across the Central Andean territory. These centres were smaller than those from previous periods, but much more elaborate in

FIG. 3.4 Carved stones, *c*.2200–2000 BC, Cerro Sechín, Áncash

terms of spatial organisation and associated iconographic programmes. Moreover, during this epoch there were one or two ceremonial centres in each valley, evidence of a process of political and ritual centralisation, where the new centres had acquired hegemony over the surrounding regions. The following ceremonial centres deserve particular attention: Huaca Lucía and Huaca Collud in the Lambayeque valley, Huaca de los Reyes in the Moche valley, Cerro Blanco and Huaca Partida in the Nepeña valley, Garagay in the Rímac valley, Pacopampa in the Chotano valley, Kuntur Wasi in the Jequetepeque mountains, Campanayuq Rumi near Ayacucho and, especially, Chavín de Huántar in the Mosna valley, which is one of the most well-known sites today.[7]

The flourishing of regional ceremonial centres was related to the emergence of religious art, represented by the existence of fantastical characters of a hybrid nature, combining human figures with felines, birds of prey and reptile features. This created a pantheon of divinities that became characteristic of the Chavín and Cupisnique styles. Everything seems to indicate that this iconography was inspired by a shamanic cosmovision, where the trance process of the shaman enabled the acquisition of attributes and powers from natural beings. In this way, the shaman, filled with the powers of the fish eagle, the feline or the serpent, could travel to different realms of existence where he could interact with creatures from the present and the past (ancestors) and even project himself into the future. By these means, the shaman could also

obtain any necessary knowledge and information for his communities. According to this way of viewing the world, the representation of divinities resulted from contemplating the hybrid figure, which symbolised both anthropomorphic nature and the supernatural. This iconographic mechanism, with variations, would continue to be represented in the following periods (figs 3.6 and 3.11–3.12).

The objects that best reflect this system of artistic expression are those that come from the site of Chavín de Huántar. One of them, the stela known as the Lanzón, was found *in situ* inside the temple of Chavín, at the centre of the cross-shaped gallery (fig. 3.16). Evidence suggests that this is a representation of a main divinity of the earth's inner world (*ukhu pacha* in Quechua), a major divinity of this particular temple.[8] A study of Chavín's architectural stages has revealed that the Lanzón existed from the beginning and that the ceremonial building was developed around it, always preserving it as a referential axis.[9]

By 800 BC many ceremonial centres ceased to function, while a minority remained and grew in scale and power. There was a rise in pilgrimages from remote places to larger combined ceremonial centres such as Chavín de Huántar. Although this was the most prominent, it flourished alongside such centres as Kuntur Wasi, Pacopampa and Campanayuq Rumi. Archaeological evidence indicates that they were constantly interacting, creating a network of places of worship that facilitated the widespread circulation of exotic goods such as shells, obsidian and turquoise. Gold metallurgy in the Central Andes also became an established practice during this period. These metal pieces are fundamentally ornamental, including crowns, nose rings, pectorals or earrings (figs 3.10–3.12), and they commonly display an iconography that follows the stylistic patterns previously mentioned. The value of these metal pieces lay in their symbolic character and status rather than their exchange value, providing a good example of how new technologies were adopted because of social or political demands rather than economic ones.

Along with the growing influence of these centres came the first indisputable evidence of elites, who were given a special funerary treatment that started with the location in which they were buried. At this time, there were burials in the central platforms of the ceremonial buildings both in Kuntur Wasi and Pacopampa, representing a clear hierarchy between these special figures and the common people. In addition, the individuals buried at the temples had specific funerary offerings, among which were necklaces, pectorals, bracelets made of semi-precious stones such as turquoise, chrysocolla or lapis lazuli, and beads of *Spondylus crassiquama*. However, the most remarkable finds are gold crowns, nose rings and earrings decorated with religious themes, which were unquestionably signs of status, and ceramic vessels of sophisticated handwork. In the case of Kuntur Wasi, tombs from several platforms suggest different elite lineages had their own dedicated funerary spaces inside the ceremonial centre.[10]

Pacopampa provides evidence of exceptional circumstances: here a woman was buried on the main platform and the central axis of the temple. The site of her grave coincided with the burial of the whole platform and the construction of a new building above it, which could indicate that the death of this woman was linked to the end of a lineage and, as a consequence, a complete ceremonial structure was buried with her.[11] These indicate clearly the importance that the elite began to acquire in the life of Andean populations. More than representing the accumulation of consumable and exchangeable goods, the complexity of the funerary objects in Kuntur Wasi or Pacopampa emphasise goods that indicate the status of their bearer. This is related to a system of power where the main resource consisted of having people, rather than material goods, available to satisfy one's own desires. Following this principle, all means were used to provide legitimacy to those who sought control over people and their work.

Although burials with these characteristics have not been found at the site of Chavín de Huántar, it is evident that this

FIG. 3.5 The solar observatory and fortified temple at Chankillo, *c.* 3rd century BC

ceremonial centre was also governed by religious elites such as those found in Kuntur Wasi or Pacopampa. In addition, it is certain that Chavín became a hub for dynamic interaction, where traditions from the north, centre and south coincided, a fact that was reflected in the architectural design of the ceremonial centre and the iconographical programme of its stone art (see figs 2.5 and 2.10). The wall of the main building has carved stone heads belonging to human beings, anthropomorphous beings with feline traits and supernatural beings (fig. 3.13). These seem to represent the transformation of the human into feline (or another type of being), following the shamanistic cosmovision described above.[12] This was clearly an iconographic design intended to immerse the visitor in the religious aura of the ceremonial centre.

The gradual demise of the great ceremonial centres began around the year 500 BC. Chavín de Huántar was abandoned, while sites such as Kuntur Wasi continued to operate with increasingly less dominance. Moreover, new ceremonial centres arose in different regions, most of them smaller and simpler than their predecessors, and, in some cases, with defensive features such as perimeter walls. The site of Chankillo is a remarkable example of a ceremonial centre placed over a hilltop and protected by three concentric walls (fig. 3.5).[13] Evidence suggests that this was a time of increasing instability and conflict, and the era of the great ceremonial centres came to an end around 200 BC. This made way for new social structures in the history of Peru, characterised by strong regional identities such as those of Moche, Nasca, Lima, Recuay, Cajamarca, Xauxa and Huarpa.

The fine designs on this stone mortar and pestle from Pacopampa, Cajamarca, suggest that these objects were used in special ceremonies rather than in daily life. The motifs represent beings with feline, snake and bird features.

FIG. 3.6 Mortar and pestle with incised motifs
Pacopampa 800–200 BC
Stone
H. 7 cm, L. 10.8 cm, W. 8.1 cm (mortar);
L. 10 cm, D. 5 cm (pestle)
Museo Larco, Lima, Peru, ML300005, ML3500004

As early as 1250 BC, Andean societies began to represent figures worshipping the gods in symbolic ceremonies. These clay Cupisnique figurines have painted faces. One of them (below left) is holding a musical instrument, a trumpet made from *Strombus* shells. Such trumpets were produced by cutting off one of the shell's borders and replacing it with a copper nozzle.

FIG. 3.7 (BELOW LEFT) Human figurine holding a shell trumpet
Cupisnique 1250–500 BC
Pottery
H. 16.5 cm, W. 11 cm, D. 7 cm
Museo de Arte de Lima, 2007.16.16
Donated by Petrus and Verónica Fernandini

FIG. 3.8 (BELOW RIGHT) Human figurine
Cupisnique 1250–500 BC
Pottery
H. 19.5 cm, W. 10.5 cm, D. 8 cm
Museo de Arte de Lima, 2007.16.15
Donated by Petrus and Verónica Fernandini

FIG. 3.9 Line drawings of the human figurines.
Museo de Arte de Lima

This gold headdress and pair of ear plates were part of an elite burial found at the site of Kuntur Wasi, Cajamarca. They are decorated with embossed motifs of human faces with feline fangs and snakes' appendages, which marks a clear link with the belief system of Chavín de Huántar. The use of semi-precious stones and shells, in the detailed work of mother-of-pearl inlays, emphasises the long-distance exchange of goods that took place during this period.

FIG.3.11 Headdress depicting mythical feline heads
800–550 BC
Gold alloy
H. 19 cm, W. 47 cm
Museo Kuntur Wasi, Cajamarca, MKW-81304

FIG.3.12 Ear plates depicting feline features
800–550 BC
Gold alloy, shell
H. 23.6 cm, W. 11.3 cm (left); H. 23.9 cm, W. 11.3 cm (right)
Museo Kuntur Wasi, Cajamarca, MKW-81307 and MKW-81308

FIG.3.10 The tomb site at Kuntur Wasi, where the headdress and ear plates were found in 1997

The ceremonial centre of Chavín de Huántar

Cecilia Pardo and Peter Fux

Chavín de Huántar is without doubt one of the most impressive early monumental complexes of the Andes. For more than a century it was thought to be the site that gave birth to Andean civilisation.[1] However, today we know it is related to a broader religious phenomenon whose very nature transports us to the dawn of Peru's ancient history. The site is located in the Callejón de Conchucos in the northern highlands of Peru, at a central point between the coast and the Amazon lowlands. It lies in a steep mountain valley behind snow-capped mountains, a strategic location at an altitude of 3,200 metres, where the Wacheqsa river encounters the bigger Mosna river. It was built in different stages over a period of more than 800 years, between 1200 and 400 BC, and its monumental architecture and *in situ* sculptures have been crucial to our understanding of the renovations and additions to the site.[2] The heart of Chavín de Huántar was its ceremonial centre; its builders diverted streams to create underground waterways and built long underground passages to form an inner labyrinth. They sculpted and carved the most intriguing iconography in stone, featuring a repertoire of hybrid beings with feline, birdlike and serpentine attributes, which represent the power of animals and predators from the highlands and the tropical forests (fig. 3.13).

Chavín de Huántar served as a pilgrimage destination for local elites coming from distant regions, especially those living in the river valleys near the coast. Visitors would come to consult the oracle, pleading for favourable weather and fertility. Once they finally reached the temple, a unique experience awaited, one that would transport them into another world through the consumption of psychoactive substances. The roaring of the underground water flowing through the chambers, the enchanting sound of the conch shell trumpets (locally known as *pututos*), the mysterious stone-carved creatures and the sumptuously dressed priests acting as guides all added to the sense of spectacle.[3]

Above ground, Chavín's architecture, which includes big public plazas and secluded areas, shows that only select pilgrims participated in the intimate ceremonies. The chosen ones were allowed to proceed from the main plaza to the right-hand staircase and through a narrow gallery that led to the sunken circular plaza, where the preparation for the high point of the ceremony took place (fig. 3.14). The circular plaza displays *in situ* reliefs depicting the procession of humans and transformed beings carrying *Spondylus* shells and San Pedro cacti. Here, pilgrims would start going into trances by leaving their gifts to the gods and taking psychoactive substances. Their offerings were made in two underground galleries located near the plaza (fig. 3.15). In the first one, the Gallery of the Offerings, vessels of very different styles from various regions were found, which confirms that Chavín was in fact a pilgrimage centre.[4] The second one, known as the Gallery of the Strombus, contained twenty completely preserved *pututos*.

FIG. 3.13 A *cabeza clava* (a monolithic sculptural head) at Chavín de Huántar, Áncash

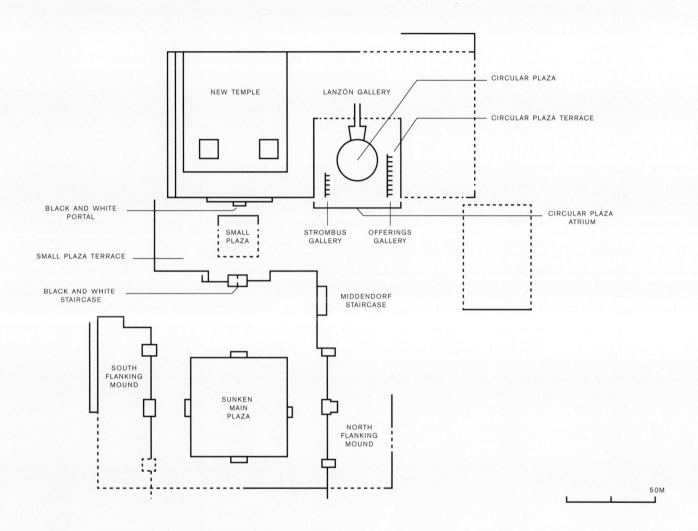

CIRCULAR PLAZA

CIRCULAR PLAZA TERRACE

NEW TEMPLE

LANZÓN GALLERY

CIRCULAR PLAZA ATRIUM

BLACK AND WHITE PORTAL

SMALL PLAZA

STROMBUS GALLERY

OFFERINGS GALLERY

SMALL PLAZA TERRACE

BLACK AND WHITE STAIRCASE

MIDDENDORF STAIRCASE

SOUTH FLANKING MOUND

SUNKEN MAIN PLAZA

NORTH FLANKING MOUND

50M

FIG. 3.14 A diagrammatic plan of the site of Chavín de Huántar

Strombus, a variety of conch shell from the deep seas in Ecuador, were turned into trumpets by cutting out one of the edges. They were used in temple rituals and played in chorus by specialist musicians. Their discovery in this context suggests that an established trade network of exotic goods took place in the Andean region from a very early date.[5]

From this space, pilgrims could finally access the gallery inside the temple's central chamber, where the Lanzón, a carved granite stela, could be seen (fig. 3.16). Those allowed to enter the inner labyrinth would encounter a deeply moving, solemn and unforgettable experience, which would strengthen their view of the world.[6] Once they had become accustomed to the dim light after the pitch-black and disorientating tunnels, they would recognise the intimidating face and form of the 4-metre-high, lance-shaped figure looming above them, with fangs, snake hair, claws and eccentric, upturned eyes – the oracle.

Apart from the Lanzón, there are two other well-known carved images associated with Chavín's architecture. The first one, the Tello Obelisk, named after archaeologist Julio C. Tello, shows two crocodile-like mythical creatures, perhaps one male and one female, from which other elements such as felines, shells, birds of prey, fanged profile heads, spider attributes and plants emerge (fig. 3.17). Although it is not known where the obelisk originally stood, it might have been in the middle of the circular plaza. The second, known as the Raimondi Stela after Italian explorer Antonio Raimondi, depicts a standing anthropomorphic deity holding staffs, with human, feline, avian and reptilian attributes and appendages emerging from the body. It was probably Chavín's main deity, which adopts features and power from predators. Where the stela stood within Chavín's buildings is still unknown.

Towards 300 BC the influence of Chavín de Huántar began to disintegrate. Many related sites were abandoned and pottery styles from the period changed rapidly, caused, according to some scholars, by a lack of a centralised state capable of maintaining long-term stability.[7] More recent studies suggest that a cataclysm which took place around 550 BC would have destroyed part of Chavín, debilitating its impact and prominence.[8] Whatever the reason, it is clear that a long-lasting system of beliefs that had reigned throughout the central Andean region during the first millennia BC had come to an end.

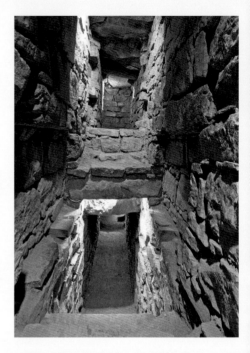

FIG. 3.15 Two of the underground tunnels at Chavín de Huántar

FIG. 3.17 Three views of the Tello Obelisk

The history of Andean food and gastronomy

Jago Cooper

Food practices are directly tied to Andean social organization, spirituality, and cultural perceptions regarding what is generally referred to as a sacred landscape.[1]

The eye-catching fact that there are more than 4,000 different types of potato in Peru provides just one colourful glimpse of the extraordinarily diverse and ancient roots of Andean gastronomy (fig. 3.18). Food represents the most basic and essential relationship created between people and their environment. The shared history of food knowledge, ingredients and culinary tradition connect all Andean cultures through time. Since the earliest settlers arrived in the Central Andes over 15,000 years ago, people have enjoyed the abundance of the region's food-rich terrestrial and marine habitats. A single 200-kilometre transect from west to east through the Central Andes includes nearly every habitat zone known to life. To the west, the Humboldt Current in the Pacific Ocean creates one of the most productive marine environments in the world, which currently provides coastal communities with over 3.8 million tonnes of fish every year. This abundance of marine food helped to underpin the success of all the coastal societies discussed in this book, from Paracas to Chimú. The vertiginous Central Andes are home to a series of niche microclimates as they climb up above 6,000 metres, which encourages species variability and unique plant and animal communities. To the east, the Amazon rainforest is the most biodiverse place on the planet. This dynamic regional abundance and diversity, combined with an exploratory human knowledge base grown over millennia, is why Peru has one of the most celebrated gastronomies in the world today.[2]

This diversity is important: an underlying principle of Andean food production is the curation of locally bespoke and environmentally appropriate foods. The diversity of climatic and environmental conditions means that people have always had to carefully cultivate plant variants suited to highly localised microclimate conditions. This explains why there are more than 4,000 varieties of potato, each originally specific to a local region. This sophisticated approach of growing the right crops for the environment – rather than trying to change the environment to suit the crop – is an important contrast with many other ancient cultures around the world. In many

ways, Andean agriculture is the antithesis of monoculture crop conditions, in which people rely heavily on a single crop grown in large uniform fields. In the Andes, the diversity of crops was key and carefully preserved.[3] A distinct advantage of this approach in the modern day is that diverse species can provide increased resistance to species-specific diseases, periods of drought and other locally impactful environmental hazards. In a way, understanding Andean relationships with food helps to reveal a cultural way of life far more powerful than the simple functional requirements of sustenance, as well

FIG. 3.18 Traditional products for sale at a market in Pisac, Sacred Valley region

as explaining the reasons for past human actions in their living landscapes. Put simply, plants and animals in the Central Andes shape the people and cultures who live there just as much as the other way around.[4]

It is not a coincidence that the earliest evidence for plant domestication is often found in the world's desert regions – they are one of the only environments where macro plant and animal remains can be preserved for millennia. The earliest preserved evidence for the domestication of plants in Peru, including peanuts and maize, is found from around 6,000 years ago in the Atacama desert. Along with the use of cotton and camelid fibres for weaving, together they demonstrate this very early domestic relationship with 'wild' life. However, it is important to note that an absence of evidence does not preclude even earlier plant and animal domestications, and origins of food cultures that sustained Andean peoples. Over the 5,000 years covered in this book, domesticated food species and cooking styles have been added to the Andean culinary repertoire using the wide range of ingredients available. Archaeological excavations have found plant foods including quinoa, potatoes, maize (fig. 3.19), peanuts, olluco, sweet potatoes, oca, beans, mashua, chilli, manioc, yacon, squash and seaweed; animal sources of food such as guinea pigs, llamas, vicuñas, alpacas, guanacos, deer, armadillos, sloths, monkeys, tapirs, peccaries, opossums and sea lions; and fish, turtles and shellfish; and all manner of birds.

The concept of plants and animals being part of a living landscape that is curated but not controlled or owned by people is important. None of the Andean cultures in this book represents a dichotomy between nature and culture; rather, each would perceive itself as part of an integrated ecology. This helps us to understand the prevalence of food in the iconography and objects of all Andean peoples. Food was heralded as the life source of culture and the manifestation of the cultural knowledge required for its care and production. This is why a ceramic vessel of a simple yucca root tuber is both a symbol of environmental knowledge and the embodiment of cultural pride. It illustrates that sustainable life is to be celebrated and respected (fig. 3.21). Food was considered sacred and commonly used in all offerings to ancestors and deities. Despite the distinctly different ceramic styles and vessel forms of the cultures from 1500 BC to AD 1500, food is commonly found at the heart of iconographic representation and narrative scenes, from the Nasca to the Moche. The continuity of this central role of food remains with us today. It is still common for Andean peoples to offer foods at places of worship and to spill liquids onto the floor for Pachamama, mother earth, before drinking themselves.

FIG.3.19 Vessel in the form of a maize plant
Nasca 100 BC–AD 650
Pottery
H. 24 cm, W. 7 cm
Museo Nacional de Arqueología, Antropología
e Historia del Perú, Lima, C-054994

This timeless practice is an action that reflects the need to responsibly nourish the life-giving environment. It is an obligation for all Andean peoples, who see themselves as being part of a mutually supporting and interdependent living world. Sustenance is reciprocal and integrated between people and their environment, not divided according to 'cultural' ability and 'natural' capital.

This ability to work with the natural environment in the process of food production is demonstrated through the making of chuño. This is the earliest example of intentional freeze-dried storage in the world. Small potatoes are left

outside in high altitudes overnight so that they freeze through completely; then during the day they are trodden on beneath the hot sun to squeeze out all of the moisture. This freeze, squeeze, thaw, dry process is repeated three or four times until the potatoes are fully dried out in the hot sun. By using this preservation method, *chuño* can be kept for up to a decade, and taken out at any time for eating, after having been reconstituted by being boiled up. *Chuño* has been found at Wari and Inca occupation sites, demonstrating the centuries-old history of this contemporary practice. This type of innovative food production, preservation and storage is reflected in different techniques across time and throughout the region (fig. 3.20). Such practices help explain the presence of so many *tambos* (storage buildings) found alongside the extensive Andean road network, allowing for the movement of these foods between the diverse environments from which they are harvested.

The role of food in bringing people together and strengthening cultural identities and beliefs is nowhere more apparent than in the making and consumption of *chicha*, an alcoholic drink made from fermented maize that has been a core part of Andean life for centuries.[5] Many scholars argue that maize beer is central to the development of all Andean societies, even proposing that the domestication of maize for beer pre-dates its use as a staple food (figs 3.19 and 3.22).[6] Every festival uses *chicha* to celebrate and in places where societies are underpinned by reciprocity and moral economies, rather than money and market economies, this role of beer as social contract is vital. The spoken salutations before drinking often herald the dead and record the obligations of the living, binding people together across time through their shared practice and location. *Chicha* is still often cooked, cooled and fermented in large earthenware vessels closely resembling ones made 3,500 years ago.[7] There is also evidence for continuities in the ways in which members of the community make *chicha* and the locally specific way it is prepared and drunk. This is also why the iconic *kero* drinking cup, intimately connected to this drinking culture, is such a powerful icon of continued practice and identity (see figs 7.18–7.20).[8]

More than 15,000 years of life in the Andes has seen named cultures such as the Nasca and the Moche come and go, and during the last 500 years the mountains have witnessed the concentrated effort to suppress and destroy Indigenous ways of life and living. However, the resilience of food heritage and culinary practice through time reflects the endurance of cultural continuity. The ability of food and Andean gastronomy to remain in place despite the coming and going of empire and dominion is testament to this quintessential aspect of Andean cultural resilience.[9] Equally unsung, and deserving of a book in itself, is the way in which Andean foods came to influence the world – from the potato-based diet of sixteenth-century Europe,[10] to the twenty-first-century explosion in the trend for quinoa as a superfood.[11] This unacknowledged influence of Andean societies on the wider world is perhaps symbolic. It demonstrates that a better understanding of the Andean ways of life represented in this book can create an alternative lens through which contemporary cultural choices and societal frameworks can be seen and understood.

Andean food knowledge is syncretic, accumulating through time and across cultures. Many of the core principles and practices of food were shared and endure to this day. This idea of food sustaining people and people sustaining food is both literal and symbolic in the Andean world. The careful preparation and circumscribed consumption practices pervade all Andean societies and connect cultures together across millennia. These shared Andean principles of food include reciprocal responsibility to the plants and animals from which food is made; embracing species diversity; celebrating the symbiotic sustenance of life through offerings and festivities; and reflecting the important role of food in the symbology and iconography of material culture. In exploring just a few elements of Andean food practices and knowledge, we can begin to understand the role of food in supporting the flourishing cultures of Peru and the rich gastronomy of the region.

FIG.3.21 Vessel in the form of a yucca
Moche AD 100–800
Pottery
H. 14.7 cm, W. 12.2 cm, D. 19.4 cm
Museo Larco, Lima, Peru, ML006641

FIG.3.22 Vessel of a mythical being holding a maize cob
Moche AD 100–800
Pottery
H. 19.5 cm, W. 11 cm, D. 10.5 cm
British Museum, Am1954,05.42
Donated by the Wellcome Institute

FIG.3.20 (OPPOSITE) A man farming potatoes in the fields near Queropuquio, Áncash

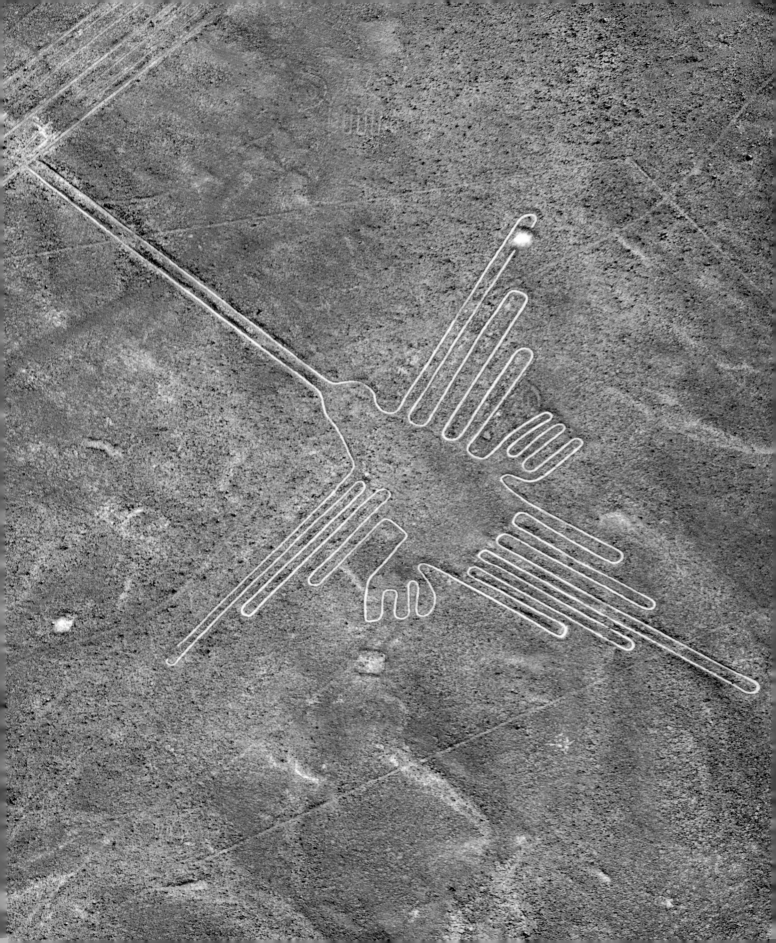

4 Paracas and Nasca: life and death in the desert

Paracas and Nasca:
life and death in the desert

Cecilia Pardo

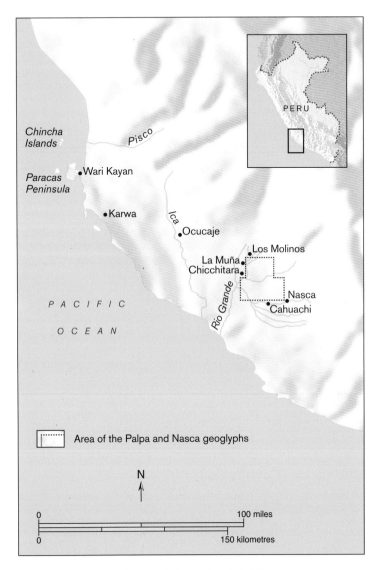

FIG. 4.1 Map of the main Paracas and Nasca archaeological sites

Considered one of the most outstanding and enigmatic pre-Columbian societies, the Nasca inhabited the southern desert coast and western slopes of the Andes between 200 BC and AD 650 (fig. 4.1).[1] This culture has been widely recognised for its famous geoglyphs: hundreds of huge lines, geometric figures and figurative images spread over more than 500 square kilometres. The Nasca Lines – this sacred space where the Nasca celebrated special events – were designated a UNESCO World Heritage Site in 1994. Glimpses of Nasca

culture can also be seen through surviving examples of colourful pottery and fine textiles. While the Nasca are most famous for these objects and the geoglyphs, today we know much more about the ways in which they lived and conceived their world.[2] By transforming their landscape with great creativity, the peoples of the Nasca managed to successfully adapt to, and thrive in, one of the most arid regions in the world.[3] They achieved this through technical innovations, but also by carrying out religious ceremonies to secure their ancestors' safe journey to the afterlife and at the same time to appeal to the benevolence of their gods (fig. 4.2).

Recent studies carried out by multidisciplinary projects suggest that although living conditions in the region were less extreme than today, they grew increasingly more difficult over time. Towards 100 BC, climatic changes resulted in a long process of desertification that eventually forced populations to abandon the lower lands and settle in higher altitudes, a process that might have led to the collapse of this culture.[4] However, human activity could also have contributed to altering the ecological balance, mainly caused by the deforestation of *huarango* (*Acacia* and *Prosopis*), the local tree (fig. 4.3).[5] Even though the Nasca valleys carried water seasonally, in the middle valleys, where the cultivated fields were located, water ran several metres below the surface. In response to this, the people organised a system of water extraction through underground galleries known as *puquios* (see page 102).

THE BEGINNINGS: PARACAS

The Nasca arose from the Paracas, a culture that developed around 700 years before in the valleys of Pisco and Ica, 200 kilometres to the north of Nasca. Genetic studies of DNA samples have proved that the Paracas and Nasca were the same people, who shared similar beliefs – for example, both cultures were conscious of the need to ensure the supply of water for agriculture and believed it was provided by their ancestors as givers of life.[6] Peruvian archaeologist Julio C. Tello gave this culture its name after he had discovered over 429 burials at the site of Wari Kayan in the Paracas peninsula between 1925 and 1930. Each funeral bundle contained up to fifty objects, including burial mantles, turbans, tunics and other accessories (fig. 4.4). Thanks to the arid climate of the

coastal desert, they were found to be strikingly well preserved. Since this amazing discovery, however, the debate about the boundaries between Paracas and Nasca has remained unresolved.[7] It stems from the similarity between the images embroidered on the mantles used to wrap the funerary bundles found here and those that were depicted in Nasca iconography. Strangely, however, the ceramics found with the bundles were not typical of Nasca, but instead featured a different style, lacking any sort of decorative elements. Therefore, Paracas and Nasca seemed to represent different phases in the development of a single population, which succeeded in progressively adapting to its environment and shared a similar ideological base, although their religious practices and beliefs appear to have become increasingly complex.[8]

Towards the end of the Paracas culture, groups migrated from the north and the highlands and settled in the southern valleys of Nasca, where new cultural traditions were developed around the ceremonial centre of Cahuachi. Situated on the left bank of the Nasca river, this site covers an area of 24 square kilometres. Cahuachi controlled the distribution of water obtained from the infiltration galleries and it served as the starting point of the paths that led to the

PAGE 82 The Nasca hummingbird geoglyph, created between 200 BC–AD 500

FIG 4.2 (ABOVE) The valleys and pampas of the Nasca region, with the killer whale geoglyph in the foreground

FIG 4.3 (BELOW) A *huarango* tree in Nasca

ceremonial area where the geoglyphs feature. Its location between the Andes and the Pacific Ocean also enabled it to play a strategic role in relations between the highland and coastal communities. While there are different hypotheses regarding its function, all specialists agree that Cahuachi was the most important centre of Nasca society in its early phase (AD 50–300). Cahuachi's apogee is thought to have ended around AD 400, possibly as a result of two floods and a major earthquake – drastic upheavals that led to its sudden abandonment and the reorganisation of Nasca society.[9]

THE NASCA GEOGLYPHS

The landscape of Nasca has a particular feature that differentiates it from other coastal regions. This is an area of the Andes where a coastal cordillera runs across the region, from north to south. Thousands of years ago, the depression between the cordillera and the Andes became filled with rounded boulders and finer sediments, creating a vast plain commonly known as 'pampas'. These pampas were crossed by rivers fed by seasonal rainfall coming from the Andes, forming coastal valleys that could be used for agriculture through the implementation of irrigation systems.[10] The peoples of Nasca conceived the pampas as a ritual space, a massive blank canvas on which hundreds of enormous figurative linear drawings could be created between the 60 kilometres of Pacific Ocean coastline and the foothills of the Andean mountains. Evidence of human activity has been found here, including ceramics, offerings and the possible remains of roofs and other elements that reveal living spaces where the inhabitants of Nasca came to worship their gods as part of their permanent search for water and fertility.[11] Lines converging on special mounds indicate spaces where the population would gather to carry out key ceremonies. Some Nasca art gives us a sense of how these celebrations might have taken place. One ceramic model discovered by Tello during the 1920s depicts a procession scene comprised of five dressed human figures who hold offerings and musical instruments, accompanied by five dogs (fig. 4.5). Birds from the rainforest are also depicted, hinting at an advanced trade network spanning to the Amazon. Tello associated this image with the pilgrimages that might have taken place in the Palpa and Nasca pampas.

SOUNDS AND MUSIC RITUALS

No other pre-Columbian culture has left us such a diverse corpus of musical instruments as the Nasca – not only

FIG. 4.4 Julio C. Tello opening a Paracas funeral bundle wrapped in textiles, 1938

through images that provide context for its ritual use, but also through the evidence of the objects themselves. The sheer number of instruments such as panpipes, whistles, drums and trumpets in museum collections and found via archaeological discoveries reveals the importance of music for these societies.[12] One of the main discoveries corresponds to a 1995 excavation by Italian archaeologist Giuseppe Orefici in Sector Y13 in Cahuachi, which comprises twenty-seven damaged ceramic panpipes. The theory is that the objects would have been broken intentionally as part of an offering – described by Orefici as a 'sacrifice' – and would have been used in propitiatory ceremonies.[13]

These panpipes might have given great sounds to the celebrations conducted by priests or shamans, who would be dressed up in colourful clothing and masks. In these ceremonies, the consumption of psychoactive substances was paramount. Through special rituals, the shaman acquired supernatural powers that allowed him to call on the gods and make the people's entreaties a reality. One such ceremony depicted on a Nasca pottery vase shows a musician playing one *antara* flute while holding another in his hands (fig. 4.38). He wears face paint and a headdress in the form of a snake, an allusion to the supernatural world. Beside him is a San Pedro cactus, surrounded by a group of vessels used for the consumption of this hallucinogenic plant. The main figure,

FIG.4.5 Model of a ceremonial
procession in the desert
Nasca 100 BC–AD 650
Pottery
H. 10.8 cm, L. 14.3 cm
Museo Nacional de Arqueología,
Antropología e Historia del Perú,
Lima, C-055308

who is shown in mid-transformation, is flanked by two
groups of musicians.

As well as wind instruments, a variety of drums played a
crucial role in the ritual – especially the so-called drum-vessels,
which were created in ceramic and reached 1.5 metres in
height. Some of these were decorated with the most complex
scenes in Nasca art, which have helped us to understand the
role that ancestors, deities and human sacrifices played in
these societies.[14]

A HISTORY OF RESEARCH

The surviving chronicles and documents from the sixteenth
to the mid-seventeenth centuries, when Peru was a Spanish
colony, offer little information on the Nasca region. The
earliest known historical reference is that made by Pedro Cieza
de León around 1553, in which the chronicler mentions that

> in the main valley of this Nasca region, there were
> great edifices with many deposits, which the Ingas
> [sic] had made. Throughout all of these valleys, and
> all of those through which they passed thereafter,
> runs the beautiful and great road of the Ingas, and
> in some parts of the sand dunes there are signs so

that they could keep to the path that they were
to follow.[15]

Over the following centuries, study of the region was overlooked,
and the full extent of the geoglyphs was unknown until well
into the twentieth century, when aerial photography arrived
in Peru in the 1930s. The German archaeologist Max Uhle
began the first scientific investigations on the southern coast in
the early twentieth century. Despite this being the official start
of archaeological studies of this region – Uhle was responsible
for introducing new scientific practices such as stratigraphy to
the Andean region – the reconstruction of Nasca history had
already begun decades earlier, with the formation of the first
private collections. By the time Tello began his explorations
on the southern coast around 1915, Uhle had already left the
country. On his first expedition to the area, Tello found that the
looting of archaeological sites and the sale of collections outside
Peru had increased considerably.[16] This plundering, which had
begun towards the end of the nineteenth century, intensified
following Uhle's discoveries. Indeed, his scientific achievements
resulted in unintended negative consequences, drawing
unwanted attention and sparking the interest of collectors and
museums around the world, as well as local antiquarians such as
Alexander, Jancke, Ringold, Welsche and Brignardello.[17]

This unique object shows a scene of eight women seated around three large vessels. They wear headdresses and are taking part in a ceremony to prepare and consume *chicha*, an alcoholic drink made from fermented purple maize. Scenes like this remain a common sight throughout the Andes today. Here, one woman plays a drum to accompany the ritual. Two pyramid-like structures around the edge suggest that the ritual is taking place within a built, architectural space.

FIG. 4.6 Celebration scene with music and beverages
Nasca 100 BC–AD 650
Pottery
H. 24 cm, W. 20.3 cm
Museo Nacional de Arqueología, Antropología e Historia del Perú, Lima, C-055264

Severed heads are commonly depicted in Andean art in both stylised and realistic depictions. Such heads are thought to have been taken from vanquished foes and were used in fertility ceremonies and rituals. In art, they are featured painted onto bowls, sometimes held by mythical beings and sometimes with fruit or plants sprouting from the heads to emphasise the duality of life and death. The heads even appear as small ceramic replicas with closed eyes and pinned mouths.

FIG. 4.7 Vessel in the shape of a severed human head
Nasca 100 BC–AD 650
Pottery
H. 14.5 cm, W. 12.2 cm, D. 12.5 cm
British Museum, Am1954,05.50
Donated by the Wellcome Institute

FIG. 4.8 Bowl with painted human heads
Nasca 100 BC–AD 650
Pottery
H. 8.6 cm, Diam. 17.3 cm
British Museum, Am1941,04.39
Donated by Lady Dow Steel-Maitland

Archaeological records indicate that textiles now part of museum collections were once specially produced as funerary offerings. They formed part of the paraphernalia that accompanied the deceased on the trip to the afterlife, as part of the mummy bundle or as garments decorated with fantastic drawings. In the Paracas and Nasca textiles, the embroidered images on the plain weaves depict mythical figures, which represent the transformation of the deceased into ancestors. They are identified by the diadems and nose masks they wear, as well as by the severed heads they carry with them.

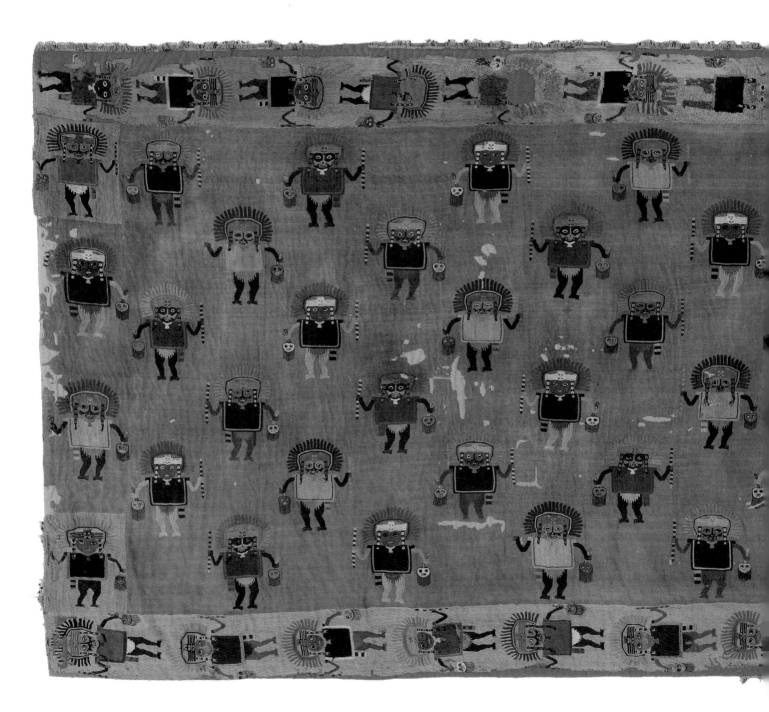

FIG. 4.9 (LEFT) Mantle depicting human figures
with feline mouth masks holding severed heads
Early Nasca 100 BC–AD 100
Cotton and camelid fibres
H. 142 cm, W. 286 cm
Museo de Arte de Lima, IV-2.1-0002
Prado Family Bequest. Restored with
a grant from the Bank of America Art
Conservation Project

FIG. 4.10 (BELOW) A figure holding a severed
head depicted on the textile, line drawing by
Rember Martínez

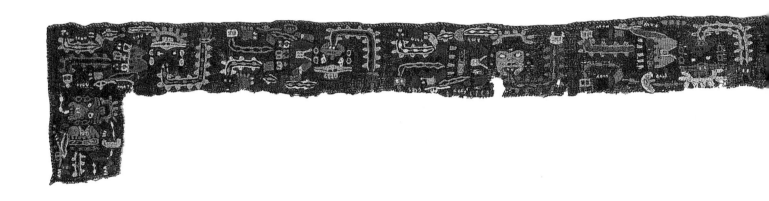

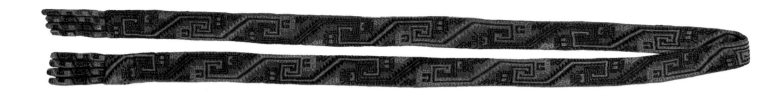

FIG. 4.11 (ABOVE TOP)
Mantle border fragment depicting mythical beings
Nasca 100 BC–AD 200
Camelid fibres, cotton
H. 10 cm, W. 172 cm
British Museum, Am1954,05.562
Donated by the Wellcome Institute

FIG. 4.12 (ABOVE MIDDLE, AND DETAIL RIGHT)
Headband with motifs of feline-like beings
Paracas 500 BC–AD 1
Camelid fibres, cotton
H. 4.5 cm, W. 218 cm
British Museum, Am1954,05.590
Donated by the Wellcome Institute

FIG. 4.13 (ABOVE, AND DETAIL RIGHT)
Fragment of a mantle border with three-dimensional
representations of birds and flowers
Nasca AD 100–400
Camelid fibres, cotton
H. 3 cm, W. 39.5 cm
British Museum, Am1931,1123.21.a

The depiction of women in Nasca pottery dramatically increases around AD 400. This coincided with the collapse of the ceremonial centre of Cahuachi and possibly signifies a restructuring of society. Women are often depicted naked and voluptuous, seated and with their genitals exposed – all symbols of fertility, which was of particular importance to a desert society.

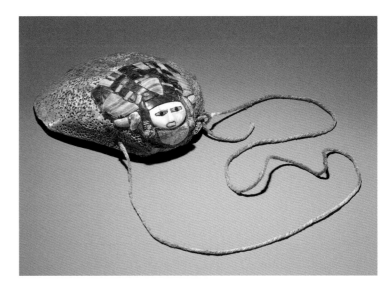

FIG. 4.14 (ABOVE) *Spondylus* shell depicting a female face
Nasca 100 BC–AD 650
Shell, mother-of-pearl, resin, string
H. 13.4 cm, W. 12.5 cm, D. 4.4 cm
British Museum, Am1913,1020.1
Donated by Louis Colville Gray Clarke

FIG. 4.15 (LEFT) Vessel of a man and woman copulating
Nasca 100 BC–AD 650
Pottery
H. 13.4 cm, W. 15 cm, D. 3.7 cm
British Museum, Am1954,05.806
Donated by the Wellcome Institute

FIG.4.16 Vessel of a woman with long hair,
wearing a cape decorated with mythical beings
Nasca 100 BC–AD 650
Pottery
H. 15.9 cm, W. 14.8 cm, D. 14.6 cm
British Museum, Am1939,-.8

When scientific investigations finally began in 1925 there were already more than one hundred examples of Late Paracas textiles – a tradition closely related to the origins of Nasca – held in public and private collections, both in Peru and abroad.

For a long time, research dedicated to clarifying the nature of the lines and geoglyphs of Nasca and Palpa was separated from investigations into Nasca culture. American professor Paul Kosok (1896–1959), however, was responsible for the first scientific research into the geoglyphs, also known as the 'Nasca Lines'. Initially he believed that the lines may have been used as irrigation canals, but he later confirmed that they were not deep enough to have fulfilled such a function. After mapping the lines and discovering the existence of figures, Kosok became the first to suggest that they may have formed part of an ancient astronomical calendar.[18] With the help of his interpreter, a young German mathematician named María Reiche, he continued with the painstaking task of measuring the lines and figures. For over half a century, until her death in 1998, Reiche carried out the arduous labour of protecting the lines from her modest home located in San Pablo, in the Ingenio valley (fig. 4.17).[19] Kosok's hypothesis of the astronomical calendar remained popular for several decades, until the emergence of studies that argued for a different interpretation, centred on the idea that the geoglyphs had a ritual function.

Starting in the 1980s, archaeologists began to consider the cultural context in their efforts to grasp the nature of the geoglyphs. They observed, for example, the relationships between the settlements, the landscape and the geoglyphs, including evidence of discoveries that revealed the performance of different activities on top of the drawings themselves. Johan Reinhard, for example, associated them with sites used for the cult of fertility, while others, such as Anthony Aveni, based their theories on ethnographic and ethnohistorical evidence, proposing an interpretation of the lines as a centre with 'rays' tied to strategic points for water sources.[20] In recent decades, the application of innovative technologies in archaeology has allowed for new perspectives on the nature and construction of the geoglyphs. The use of satellite images and geodesic tools, for example, has helped to establish a preliminary chronology of the pampas at different moments in time.[21]

The excavations undertaken by Helaine Silverman between 1984 and 1985 were specifically aimed at situating Cahuachi – the most important archaeological site associated with the culture – within the broader context of pre-Columbian cultures and the development of Nasca society.[22] Starting in 1982, the Centro Italiano Studi e Ricerche Archeologiche Precolombiane, led by Giuseppe Orefici, undertook the Nasca Project, which continues to this day. The project's initial objective was to analyse the early Nasca ceramic style (c. AD 50–300) in relation to the Nasca geoglyphs, in order to later carry out work at sites such as Pueblo Viejo, Huayurí and Cahuachi. The archaeologists Markus Reindel and Johny Isla, co-directors of the Nasca-Palpa Project, have played a crucial role in recent Nasca archaeology. However, in spite of major recent contributions and evolving approaches, there are still aspects about which we know very little.[23]

Environmental causes hastened the end of the Nasca civilisation around AD 650. Paleoecological records have demonstrated that the process of desertification reached an extent where survival in the lower valleys was no longer possible. As rivers coming from the highlands did not carry enough water down into the deserts, populations were forced to move and resettle in new sites located in higher regions where agriculture could still be practised.[24] Other cultural factors might also have influenced the collapse of Nasca. The number of images of warriors depicted in art increases significantly, starting around AD 350–400, due to social changes that occurred at this time, when pressure on Nasca society forced populations to relocate to other areas of the Rio Grande river basin. The role of the warrior–shaman from early phases of the civilisation – when Cahuachi served as the primary ceremonial centre – is thought to have been replaced later on by the presence of military leaders in charge of secular tasks. Towards AD 600 the Wari culture arose in the southern highlands near Ayacucho. The Wari had very successful adaptive agricultural techniques and complex irrigation technologies, alongside a strong militaristic outlook and an alternative religious approach. The archaeological evidence seems to suggest that they were not aiming to conquer the old Nasca territory, but instead to make use of the area's natural resources, such as gold and copper deposits and semi-precious stones.[25] Objects dating to this period include ceramics and textiles decorated with stylised motifs, which originated in the southern highlands, in a style known as 'Nasca–Wari' (see page 175).

In spite of the demise of the Nasca, their legacy lives on in the amazing geoglyphs that remain etched into the landscape. Conserving and protecting around 500 square kilometres of lines and drawings in the desert is certainly no easy task. María Reiche devoted her entire life to studying and protecting the geoglyphs; today she is considered an icon in Peru. Sadly, by the time Reiche arrived, the lizard geoglyph had already been cut into two in the 1920s in order to build the Pan-American Highway (see fig. 4.23). In the past decades, important initiatives such as the Nasca-Palpa Project have been focused on highlighting and providing resources to access valuable archaeological sites that remain unknown

to visitors and even to the local populations.[26] Research was focused on the settlements and geoglyphs of the Palpa region, which resulted in an updated chronology, establishing that the precedents of the Nasca geoglyphs were to be found in Paracas.

These contemporary investigations have also helped to document sites that had never before been studied in depth. For example, in the cemetery at La Muña, located near Palpa, the largest burials of Nasca elites currently known to exist have been discovered. At least twelve tombs were registered on terraces with large adobe walls. Although the tombs were sacked during the 1930s, it has still been possible to recover relevant information on Nasca funerary architecture, along with a group of objects that formed part of the funeral bundles. In Chichitara, another site located in the lower Palpa valley, the project registered over 150 anthropomorphic and zoomorphic images carved in stone. A careful analysis of the images, facilitated by the creation of three-dimensional photogrammetric models, was able to date them to the Initial (1700–800 BC) and Paracas (900–200 BC) periods. Furthermore, the valley's incorporation into a Geographic Information System (GIS) made it possible to study its spatial relationship with its surroundings, with paths that connected the valley to locations in the highlands. Based on their very nature, the petroglyphs – man-made interventions in the natural terrain – may have been forerunners to the geoglyphs, which, although they began with the Paracas, would ultimately reach their peak in Nasca.

Today, historians and archaeologists are still working to identify and document the geoglyphs and other elements of Nasca and Palpa heritage. During 2017 and 2018, Johny Isla and Luis Jaime Castillo collaborated to record unidentified geoglyphs.[27] They carried out aerial surveys of the mountain slopes around the city of Palpa, using drones and photogrammetry techniques in order to identify archaeological features that had not yet been discovered – which had helped to preserve them.[28] More recently, Peruvian artist Rita Ponce de León and Argentine-born performance artist Tania Solomonoff have undertaken an art project aimed at understanding the relationship between Nasca communities and their heritage.[29] These cross-cultural endeavours, which aim to document, preserve and promote the hidden histories of these peoples, will be a valuable resource for future generations.

FIG. 4.17 (OPPOSITE) German scholar
María Reiche sitting in front of one of
the geoglyphs, 1993

Ancestors played a key role in Nasca society, in an environment where gathering resources was key to survival. The ancestors were seen as intermediaries between the two worlds and a way of guaranteeing that these resources would be abundant. They are often depicted wearing nose rings with feline whiskers or with other animal attributes such as those of the bird and whale.

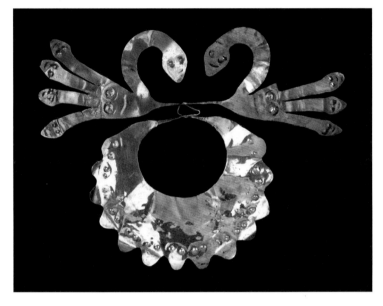

FIG. 4.18 (LEFT) Armlet
Nasca 100 BC–AD 650
Gold
H. 8.8 cm, W. 5.9 cm
British Museum, Am1921,0321.1

FIG. 4.19 (TOP) Diadem
Paracas 900 BC–AD 200
Gold
H. 8.1 cm, W. 24 cm
Museo Nacional de Arqueología, Antropologia
e Historia del Perú, Lima, M-2841

FIG. 4.20 (ABOVE) Nose ring in the shape
of feline whiskers and snakes
Nasca 100 BC–AD 650
Gold
H. 10.2 cm, W. 13.5 cm, D. 0.5 cm
British Museum, Am1952,10.1

The Nasca's principal deity is known as 'the mythical' or 'masked being'. This human-like being adopts the traits of different animals, and can be recognised by its nose piece with feline whiskers, diadem and necklace with trapezoidal beads. Thought to have originated from the earlier Paracas culture's Oculate Being, the form of the deity became increasingly stylised over time, before disappearing as the Nasca culture faded with the dawn of the Wari Empire.

FIG.4.21 Bowl depicting the Nasca mythical
being
Nasca 100 BC–AD 650
Pottery
H. 13 cm, W. 27.5 cm
British Museum, Am1914,0731.1

FIG.4.22 Drawing of the mythical being
depicted on the bowl. British Museum

Walking the lines: exploring the meaning of the Nasca geoglyphs

Peter Fux

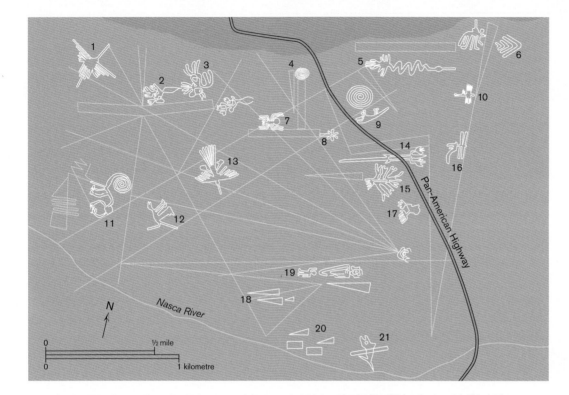

Pre-Columbian petroglyphs and geoglyphs have always fascinated archaeologists as well as antiquarians, cultural tourists, people interested in history and even fantasy authors. In the field of archaeology, some researchers have insisted on exploring and interpreting such geoglyphs as a separate genre of finds and as something distinct from archaeological context. This approach is particularly evident in the archaeological research history of the Nasca region. Twentieth-century Peruvian archaeologist Toribio Mejía Xesspe interpreted the now world-famous geoglyphs in the desert of Nasca in their extensive context, in relation to the culture that produced them, and he was followed by researchers who focused their attention on only the geoglyphs themselves. The most prominent of these scholars was German-born mathematician María Reiche, who devoted her life to studying and protecting the lines, providing a framework for later studies.

In recent decades the Nasca-Palpa Archaeological Project, led by the Peruvian archaeologist Johny Isla and his German colleague Markus Reindel, is the best example within the framework of interdisciplinary research. Since 1995 they have not only documented and studied in detail the geoglyphs and rock art sites of the region, but also undertaken thorough investigations encompassing settlement and grave archaeology, climate and landscape history and anthropological studies.[1] This broad approach has allowed

FIG. 4.24 Aerial view of the whale geoglyph
(number 21 on the map opposite)

for the interpretation of the geoglyphs and rock art sites in their natural and cultural context. Considering that the landscape was integrated into the cultural space through its imagery, and that images are symbolic expressions whose meaning can be understood only in their cultural context, this holistic approach seems imperative.

The resulting interpretation can be summarised as follows: the function and meaning of the petroglyphs and geoglyphs of the Nasca region changed throughout history. In the earlier Paracas period (900–200 BC), people placed the figurative geoglyphs on the valley slopes so that they could be seen easily from the river valley. Compared to the huge drawings of the later Nasca period, they are of modest dimensions. Numerous rock art sites are also known from the Paracas period. Their study has revealed that they are lined up along former long-distance trade routes connecting the oasis valleys of the coastal region with the highlands, within a day's walk of one another. It might be the case that the ground drawings served as a form of orientation by giving character and place names to the landscape through their images, while the rock art sites could have served as campsites for the long-distance trade caravans. Were they protective images intended to ward off raiders?[2]

The geoglyphs of the Nasca period (200 BC–AD 650) are much larger and are located on the high plain plateaus (or pampas) between the river valleys (fig. 4.23). They were clearly not created with the intention to be seen and read: if their makers had wanted this they would not have placed the giant drawings in the plain, but would have designed them on the slope, like the Paracas had done hundreds of years earlier. It is noticeable that the figurative representations in particular – which preceded the huge geometric forms and represented pelicans, birds or whales (fig. 4.24; see page 82 and fig. 4.2) – are each designed as a single continuous line, with an entrance into the figure and an exit parallel to it, as if they were devised to be walked through. The later spirals, lines, zigzag shapes and trapezoids could reach lengths of more than a kilometre. A number of found altar buildings, post settings and offerings, which are clearly associated with the geoglyphs, suggest that ritual actions were performed in these spaces. Geomagnetic measurements of the strongly compacted soil prove that the images were intensively walked through, perhaps as part of important fertility ceremonies, in order to appeal to the will of the gods.[3]

The pampas still form an impressive intermediate zone between the fertile river valleys below and the water-giving mountains above. Climatic-historical research points to a dramatic drying of the region during the Nasca period. It is likely that the people ritually walked the figures in large groups, accompanied by rhythmic music and under the influence of psychoactive substances. The shapes of the geoglyphs were revealed during this process but soon disappeared again. Could these rhythmic walks have been part of a ritual to encourage water and fertility? This is one explanation that an archaeological approach could reveal, but the mysteries of the geoglyphs may never be fully uncovered.[4] Today they represent one of the most captivating and elusive archaeological discoveries in the world, challenging us to think about these ancient peoples in a very different way.

FIG. 4.25 Vessel in the form of a mythical whale
Nasca 100 BC–AD 650
Pottery
H. 29.4 cm, W. 25.4 cm, D. 7.3 cm
Museo Larco, Lima, Peru, ML013684

Searching for water in the desert

Cecilia Pardo

The Nasca managed to survive in one of the most arid deserts in the world. How were they able to supply their people with rich diets based on crops such as maize, beans, potatoes and squash? Agriculture was of great importance to Andean societies and their economy, and as with any desert society the key to this was maintaining a relatively good supply of water. They also required land that was fertile in order to grow cotton, the main raw material used for the production of fine textiles. Although the lower and upper valleys in the Rio Grande drainage basin received seasonal water supplies, in the middle valleys – precisely where the farming areas were located, and thus where abundant water supplies were required – the water flowed up to 10 metres below the earth's surface.

In response to this challenge, the Nasca found a creative solution: they developed a complex and innovative hydraulic system of subterranean aqueducts, known as *puquios*. This entailed using gravity to take water from the subsoil to the surface through a series of channels and open ditches. The water was stored in ponds and reservoirs, from which it was distributed to the crop fields. The *puquios* enabled the Nasca to have a dependable supply of water throughout the year. This system, which continues to be used today, ensured the success of their agricultural practice (fig. 4.26).

FIG. 4.26 The Nasca channels and ditches, redrawn from a diagram by Katharina Schreiber

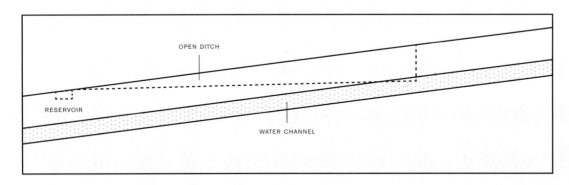

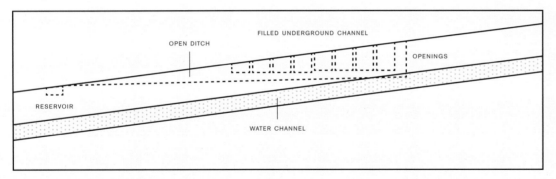

According to modern studies, today there are about thirty-five *puquios* in use out of the fifty which would have worked in the past. These have been transformed and adapted by adding concrete and wood to reinforce the ancient structures.[1] In Cantalloc, Nasca, spiral ladders leading into the underground channels have been made out of stones in order to encourage tourism and visits to the site (fig. 4.27). Although there are no written records of the Nasca, the existence of these sophisticated systems reveals that they used a social and collaborative approach to generate resources and survive in the desert.

FIG. 4.27 The Cantalloc aqueducts, near Nasca

Colours of life in the Andes: a scientific perspective

Joanne Dyer

Historically, the origin and date of textiles were largely determined by style and iconography. Increasingly, the application of scientific techniques is slowly overturning long-held assumptions concerning chronology, the sources of materials and availability of dyestuffs, and providing new insights into textile production, dyeing practices, trade and the economy in ancient cultures.

Two textiles from the south coast of Peru were investigated scientifically as part of a project on Andean textiles carried out at the British Museum between 2011 and 2014.[1] The two textiles are chronologically separated by some 1,000 years and dye analysis has determined that the choice of colourants in each case, particularly the red and green colourants, showed a shift in dyeing practice that occurred around the Wari period. Thus, whereas indigo, likely from *Indigofera* sp., continued to be used as a source of blue, plant sources of red (probably *Relbunium* sp.) used in more ancient textiles, such as in the early Nasca textile with the hummingbirds (fig. 4.28), were replaced by insect-based red dyes in later textiles.

These later dyes were based on species of cochineal, either domesticated or wild, which are native to higher elevations, indicating that they were probably acquired by the south-coast dyers and weavers through trade with these regions.[2] Cochineal is still used today and is a very versatile dye that can produce different shades of red and purple, particularly in mixtures with indigo, as can be seen from the colourful coca bag (see fig. 6.24). It has been suggested that environmental changes may have been responsible for the change in dyeing practice.[3] It is unknown whether this change also affected the use of green colourants, but analyses have shown that green baccharis, a form of the yellow colourant source *Baccharis* spp. which had undergone fungal attack and produced a green dye, was used specifically in Paracas-period textiles but not in later periods. Green baccharis (in combination with indigo) was found in the bright green shades seen in the hummingbird textile.

The above analyses required samples to be taken from the textiles, but modern scientific imaging advances mean that a good preliminary indication of the dyes present, and their distribution, can now be determined non-invasively. We can create a series of images known as 'multispectral images', which are acquired using different wavelengths of light from the ultraviolet to the infrared, with certain wavelengths of light being more effective at detecting particular dyes. Thus, UV light can be used to excite the pink luminescence typical of certain red plant dyes (fig. 4.29, top part), whereas false colour images, obtained from a combination of reflected visible and infrared light, can determine the distribution of indigo in the textile, which appears in shades of red (fig. 4.29, bottom part). The use of this technology to identify the particular kinds of dyes used on these textiles can reveal important insights into when and how different cultures in Peru gained access to them, their horticultural practices and how techniques were adapted over the course of centuries.

FIG. 4.28 Tasselled textile fragment with embroidered hummingbirds
Early Nasca 100 BC–AD 200
Camelid fibres, cotton
H. 25 cm, L. 229 cm
British Museum, Am1933,1216.2
Donated by Henry Van den Bergh through the Art Fund

FIG. 4.29 Two multispectral images of the hummingbird textile, with UV-induced luminescence (top) and in infrared-reflected false colour (bottom). The latter shows the presence of indigo dye in red.

The sound of time passing:
Andean music and soundscapes

Jago Cooper and Dianne Scullin

The sound an ocarina makes when blown today is the same as when it was played 1,500 years ago. Paradoxically, sounds are both timeless and exist in only one moment. Music in the ancient Andes was much more than a recreational enjoyment – it was living history. It helped to provide a connection between Andean people, ancestors, time and place. The first Europeans to arrive in the Andes in the sixteenth century referred to Andean peoples using music to record time. The chronicler Juan Diez de Betanzos describes the moment he arrived in the Inca capital, Cusco: '*mamaconas* [Inca female state officials] and servants were singing about each ruler as they had succeeded one another up to that time. And that was the order that was followed from then on. Thus they preserved the memory of them and their times.'[1] Music and songs played an important role in recording oral histories and reinforcing cultural identities. Prior to the invention of recorded sound, any musical event existed in only one time or place. Yet the reproduction of events and rituals involving sound, using the same instrumentation and music, connects a present performance to all performances that have occurred previously, especially in the memories of those participating (fig. 4.30).

Evidence of musical instruments in the Andes exists from the earliest cultures such as Chavín, through to the Incas and up to today. The types of musical instruments recovered from archaeological contexts are primarily aerophones, objects that require human breath to produce sound. These include trumpets, ocarinas, whistles, flutes, panpipes and whistling vessels (figs 4.31–4.32). Additionally, rattles, bells and drums provided accompanying rhythm. The instruments were often elaborately decorated and made from diverse materials including reeds, ceramics, bones, shells and animal hides.[2] While some instrument types, such as whistling vessels, ceased to be used after the colonial period, others such as flutes, ocarinas, panpipes and shell trumpets continue to be played today as part of many current Andean musical traditions.[3]

The use of wind or breath as the primary basis for Andean music reflects the importance of naturally created sounds in the landscape. Sound was used to communicate between humans and the spirits residing in their surroundings. In fact, water, wind and acoustical properties were important aspects for Andean peoples to consider when planning architecture and patterns of settlement. The ritual offerings

FIG. 4.30 A member of a local youth association playing music during the Virgen de la Candelaria festival in Puno

excavated within the underground water channels at the site of Chavín de Huántar included six shell trumpets, which were recently played again for the first time in 3,000 years.[4] These recent experiments revealed that the acoustic result is a roaring sound like that made by a caiman: this echoes through the chamber that contains the Lanzón Stela (see fig. 3.16), which bears carved crocodilian creatures and sits within the tunnels surrounded by water beneath the site. The engraved stone walls of the courtyard above depict a procession of people carrying symbolic objects of *Spondylus* and San Pedro

FIGS 4.31–4.32 Whistles in the form
of a mythical being and a bird
Nasca 100 BC–AD 650
Pottery
H. 7.3 cm, W. 4 cm, D. 2 cm (top);
H. 6.9 cm, W. 2.8 cm, D. 2.5 cm (bottom)
British Museum, Am1954,05.194,
Am1954,05.195
Donated by the Wellcome Institute

cacti and playing the shell trumpets as they walk. Therefore, the architecture of the entire site was constructed with music and sound at its heart – because these provided a way to enact spiritual beliefs physically and to communicate with otherworldly beings. Musical instruments acted as devices that helped people to experience time and connect with the other temporal realms of Andean beliefs.

While it remains tempting to equate modern Indigenous Andean musical practices with those of the past, many if not most ancient Andean musical traditions would sound nearly incomprehensible as music to modern audiences familiar with Western musical aesthetics.[5] A large proportion of Andean musical instruments intentionally sound dissonant or 'out of tune'. Instruments achieved this either through combining tones that were very close together, a soundscape echo of Andean dualism, or through producing pitches that intentionally deviate from an in-tune note. These types of sounds are not a result of lacking the necessary technology to produce tuned instruments, but because the makers actively chose to create instruments to play out-of-tune sounds. For example, studies of the Nasca panpipes found at Cahuachi show that they were created with a precise tuning pitch

Panpipes, or *antaras*, were very popular among the Nasca. Many depictions of ceremonies and rituals feature players and numerous clay examples have been found at archaeological sites. One particularly striking find was the discovery of twenty-seven broken panpipes by Giuseppe Orefici at Cahuachi in 1995. These instruments were thought to be deliberately broken as a form of sacrifice, possibly in a ceremony to promote agricultural fertility.

FIG. 4.33 Panpipes
Nasca 100 BC–AD 650
Pottery
H. 49.5 cm, W. 22.7 cm, D. 2.5 cm
British Museum, Am1954,05.207
Donated by the Wellcome Institute

FIG. 4.34 Panpipes with painted designs
Nasca 100 BC–AD 650
Pottery
H. 18.9 cm, W. 9.7 cm, D. 1.4 cm
British Museum, Am1954,05.848
Donated by the Wellcome Institute

FIG. 4.35 An offering of broken panpipes
excavated by Giuseppe Orefici at the site
of Cahuachi, 1995

carefully in mind (figs 4.33–4.34).[6] Many Moche whistles
and ocarinas made and played at the site of Huacas de
Moche sounded two adjacent pitches simultaneously, creating
dissonance and pulsating beats.[7] The pitch and resonance of
music were key in Andean culture. The music helped to bring
together ancestors and the landscape they share with their
descendants. Thinking about sound helps us to imagine now-
silent archaeological sites as busy, noisy places full of music and
life. Scholars such as José Pérez de Arce propose that a concept
of music existed in the past in the Andes that was different
from the present Western sense. He writes, 'The artisans who
made these artefacts were influenced by a concept of sound
very typical of the Andes and very strange to the European
concept, which is to play in the pure timbral dimension of
the flute, without melody or with a minimum of it.'[8]

Andean knowledge was mnemonic in how it was recorded
and communicated. People used repeatable patterns to help
remember and share information. This is embodied in the
use of *khipus* (knotted strings used as recording devices) and
also the scenes on certain ceramics, which used symbols and
recognisable visual identifiers to help record and tell narrative
stories. The mnemonic structure of music and the use of
sound as a tool for sharing stories underpinned important
ceremonies. This is why musical instruments are frequently
found within religious contexts. For example, in 1994 a temple
complex was excavated in the heart of Cahuachi and dozens
of deliberately broken and carefully placed ceramic panpipes
were found (fig. 4.35).[9] This breaking of the panpipes is often
interpreted as a form of ritual sacrifice of their life force.

Ordered by colour and sound type, they were found next
to other carefully placed religious offerings, including sixty-
four sacrificed camelids, two human heads and a young
man with his head removed and placed between his legs.
The panpipes averaged 40 to 60 centimetres long, but also
included enormous ones up to 86 centimetres in length.
Their placement within the temple was interpreted by the
excavators as evidence of a connection between music and
cycles of time, because 'within that spiral of cyclic births
and deaths, the *antaras* [panpipes] would be related with
the stages of death, fertilisation, and penetration into the
earth'.[10] In a similar vein, situating music within the Nasca
belief system of life and death reveals a different dimension
to the depictions of people playing these instruments while
walking along the Nasca Lines. It helps us to understand the
Nasca Lines not as inanimate works of abstract art but as
loud musical spaces for human ceremonies and processions.
The interconnected nature of sound and movement is also
evident in the Quechua word for song, *taki*, which means
rhythm and movement at the same time.[11] Such an indication
of animation and action is useful when considering musical
objects or episodes represented in Andean narrative scenes
(figs 4.36–4.39).[12] The whistling vessel, a uniquely Andean
instrument, requires the combination of the movements of
air and water to produce sound.[13] Sound is energy; it is always
inherently and undeniably the result of action and movement.
This fundamental nature of sound animates the seemingly
inanimate, whether it be musical instruments, landscapes or
ritual sites.

This striking drum relates the Nasca worldview, including the capture in ritual combat of the defeated enemies, who are firmly grasped by the hair by ancestral beings identified by their feline mouth masks. One of the most intriguing features are the five ancestral deities, showing different family lineages. Towards the top, hanging from a branch, we can see a human being with a corpse-like appearance, a trophy head on a rope and a being transformed into an ancestor. These three images depict the primary theme of this myth: the capture of the defeated party in ritual combat, the use of his head as a trophy and offering, and his transformation into an ancestor.

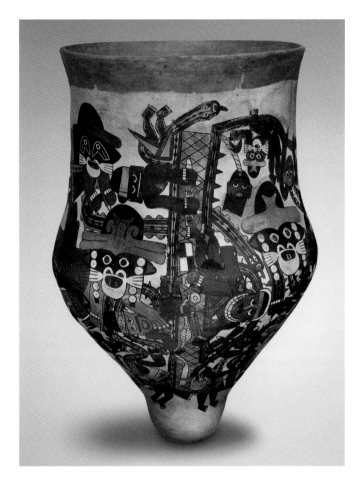

FIG.4.36 Ceremonial drum depicting a mythical scene
Nasca 100 BC–AD 650
Pottery
H. 115 cm, W. 78 cm, D. 78 cm
Private collection on loan to the Museo de Arte de Lima

FIG.4.37 The mythical scene on the ceremonial drum,
line drawing by Daniel Morales Chocano. Museo de Arte
de Lima

Nasca rituals are depicted on objects like this vessel. Through the use of music and the wearing of headdresses, such as this one in the form of a snake, the shaman calls upon the powers of the animal world to aid him in his travels. The San Pedro cactus depicted in the drawing below was a strong hallucinogenic, which would transform and transport the shaman into the world of the gods and ancestors.

FIG. 4.38 Vessel depicting a ritual, including music and hallucinogenic substances
Nasca 100 BC–AD 650
Pottery
H. 18.9 cm, W. 16 cm
Museo Nacional de Arqueología, Antropología e Historia del Perú, Lima, C-065296

FIG. 4.39 The design on the other side of the vessel, line drawing by Carla Vanesa Rodríguez Rodriguez-Prieto. Museo de Arte de Lima

5 Unwritten histories: Moche and Chimú

Stories from the north

Julio Rucabado

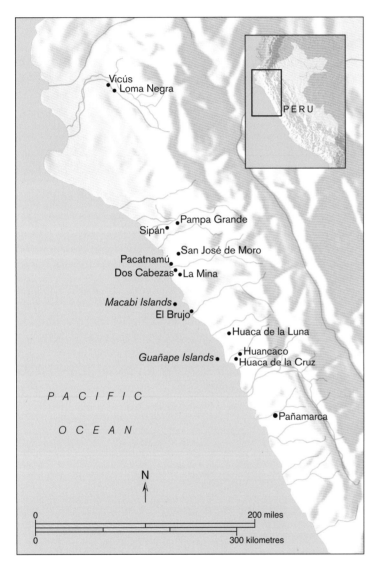

PAGE 112 Mural walls at Huaca de la Luna, AD 100–800
FIG. 5.1 Map showing the major Moche archaeological sites

Following the abandonment of early ceremonial centres, new forms of cultural, economic and political development began to emerge in the Central Andes. It was during this shifting period (c. 400 BC–AD 100) that several of the northern coastal valleys – Moche, Virú, Santa, Nepeña, Casma and Huarmey – began to receive migrant groups from the surrounding mountains. The presence of these foreigners created tensions and provoked disputes about territories and resources, especially among those communities whose development depended on the productive capacity of crop fields and an efficient system of irrigation.[1] Although there is little surviving evidence of violence, the figure of the armed warrior, fighting in duels or placed atop structures or buildings, became a common topic of representation in the art of coastal societies in this period, suggesting the formation of an elite class of warrior–leaders.[2]

THE MOCHE: FACES OF POWER

From around AD 300 to 800, a new political order developed in several northern coastal valleys (fig. 5.1), which were independent territories linked by common belief systems and a distinctive visual culture. Recognised as Moche (also Mochica or Muchik), this culture stands out for its ceramic vessels, now housed in different museums around the world.[3]

When looking at scenes depicted in Moche narrative art, one recognisable figure is the mythical hero or ancestor, a character whose presence and action in the imaginary assured the order and wellbeing of the world: the idea of him became concrete through those who led public and ritual life.[4] The Moche leaders, chief warriors and priests assumed political, military and religious roles informed by mythical stories. The legitimacy and prestige of these leaders were determined by a number of attributes: the ability to perform theatrical rituals; the understanding of natural and cosmological mysteries; the capacity to control artisanal production and the acquisition of exotic goods; the management of irrigation canals; and the ability to maintain the validity of a system of battles and ritual sacrifices. Thus, narrative art helped to reinforce and communicate the symbolic power and authority of the new elites during Moche's rise.

These characters were represented on fine sculptural vessels (figs 5.2–5.5), where we can identify various decorative elements such as helmets, caps and headdresses, handkerchiefs and headbands, animal-shaped diadems, prominent ear flaps, nose rings and necklaces, as well as different types of hairstyle, face paint, tattoo and scarring.[5] The range of forms and decorative motifs, as well as their different combinations, seem to suggest a division between the roles or social types. In some cases, the headdresses and ornaments are similar to those

The human portrait vessels of the Moche provide a rare glimpse of actual people of pre-Columbian Andean societies. These vessels feature specific traits of real individuals, including missing eyes and cleft palates. It is clear from their clothing and accessories, such as earpieces and headdresses, and the use of face paint that these figures held high-ranking political, religious or military roles.

Of all these societies, only the Moche produced portraits in the strictest sense of the word. Although there is no concrete information on the function of this genre, recent studies have noted recurring features in several of these pieces, making it possible to identify particular people depicted at different stages of their lives. The purpose of these portraits thus seems to have been to memorialise specific individuals who held important positions.

FIG. 5.2 (ABOVE) Stirrup vessel in the form of a human portrait
Moche AD 100–800
Pottery
H. 24.6 cm, W. 13.7 cm, D. 17.8 cm
British Museum, Am1947,16.13

FIG 5.3 (LEFT) Stirrup vessel in the form of a human portrait
Moche AD 100–800
Pottery
H. 32.6 cm, W. 19 cm, D. 22.2 cm
British Museum, Am1947,16.12

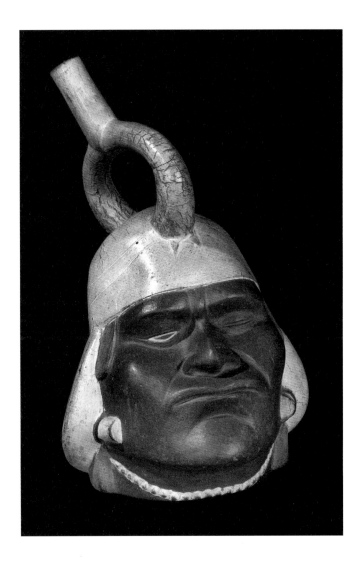

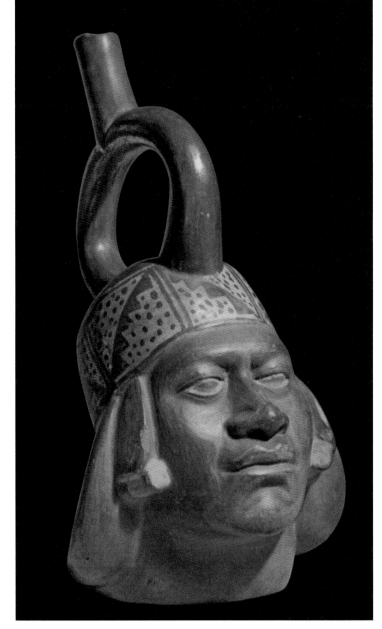

FIG 5.4 (ABOVE) Stirrup vessel in the form
of a human portrait
Moche AD 100–800
Pottery
H. 18.9 cm, W. 16 cm
British Museum, Am1880,0405.1
Donated by Edward Frederick North
and D. Pedro Galvez

FIG.5.5 (RIGHT) Stirrup vessel in the form
of a human portrait
Moche AD 100–800
Pottery
H. 27.1 cm, W. 15 cm, D. 14.5 cm
British Museum, Am,+.1308
Donated by Augustus Wollaston Franks

worn by mythical characters, which is the case for the diadem with a feline form, usually associated with the figure of the Moche hero. The distribution of these objects, technologies and iconographic themes along the entire northern coast provides evidence of both a vast network for the exchange of goods and the power of the Moche's elite to control their production and circulation.

Some face portraits present particular attributes such as scars or wounds, probably suffered during ritual battles. One vessel shows the head of a man who has lost his left eye (fig. 5.4), an injury that could have frequently occurred in conflict, especially when trying to knock off headdresses using club heads. Although the Moche face portraits represent only male figures, archaeological research has revealed the existence of elite Moche female leaders, who fulfilled the role of priestess and guided the rituals dedicated to the moon goddess, a central figure in the Moche pantheon.[6]

RITUAL PARAPHERNALIA

Specialised craftspeople in workshops supervised by the local governments were responsible for the process of producing textile garments, ornaments and objects for ceremonial use.[7] There, they would work with various raw materials, from gold and silver alloys, to seashells such as *Spondylus* and nacre, to stones such as turquoise, chrysocolla and lapis lazuli, to cotton and camelid wool fibres. The combination of these materials enabled the creation of the set of clothes and adornments that embellished and distinguished Moche leaders at public events. The production of objects such as a breastplate (see fig. 2.18), composed of hundreds of beads made from shells and chrysocolla, was the result of a long series of operations that involved procuring and processing raw materials from

different and remote regions. Special care was given to the metallurgical and goldsmithing work, which sought to harness the physical attributes of metals such as gold, silver and copper. The radiance of the metal plates reflecting in the light and the particular sound of them clashing against one another must have generated unique effects and left spectators in awe.[8] Some objects, such as a set of bimetallic nose rings, feature creatures that are characteristic of Moche art, such as serpents, felines, birds and crustaceans (figs 5.7–5.12). The particular style of these objects must have also been used to distinguish the Moche elite from other neighbouring societies, such as the Recuay, Cajamarca and Vicús.

When leaders died, their bodies were buried with this paraphernalia in order that they were prepared to continue their duties in the afterlife, in some cases assuming the identity of their mythical ancestor. This was the case for those individuals buried in graves or platforms in the various valleys where the Moche elites were able to consolidate their political and ideological system. The burials of warrior priests have been found in sites such as Sipán, Úcupe and Dos Cabezas.[9] One notable feature of grave goods at sites such as these is the use of metallic masks: together with headdresses and other special objects, they played a transcendental role in the process of transformation and ancestralisation of the dead person (see fig. 2.17).[10]

The burial of a female leader known as 'Señora de Cao' (Lady of Cao) is a special case. She was found in the grounds of the Huaca Cao Viejo, the main ceremonial centre in the Chicama valley.[11] Her tattooed body was covered with layers of cloth and embellishments and she was surrounded by objects representing weapons (clubs and spear-throwers), which were usually associated with male roles. Furthermore, her main headdress, which displays a feline portrait, appears

FIG. 5.6 Presentation of the cup, ritual battle and sacrifice of prisoners, line drawing from a ceramic vessel held by the Museo Nacional de Arqueología Antropología e Historia del Perú, Lima. Moche Archive, Dumbarton Oaks, Trustees for Harvard University, Washington, DC, PH.PC.001_0110

This set of nose rings, part of a larger group, was found inside a tomb belonging to a very important female leader who lived on the north coast of Peru around AD 200–400. Besides their high aesthetic quality, they convey aspects of dualism, which is expressed in pairs of identical motifs depicted in gold and silver, two opposed but complementary metals associated with the sun and moon.

FIGS 5.7–5.12 Six nose rings depicting human beings, animals and geometric patterns
Moche AD 100–400
Gold, silver, semi-precious stones
H. 6 cm, W. 5 cm, D. 0.5 cm (largest piece)
Complejo Arqueológico El Brujo | Fundación Augusto N. Wiese, PACEB-F4-00003, 00002, 00014, 00015, 00027 and 00030

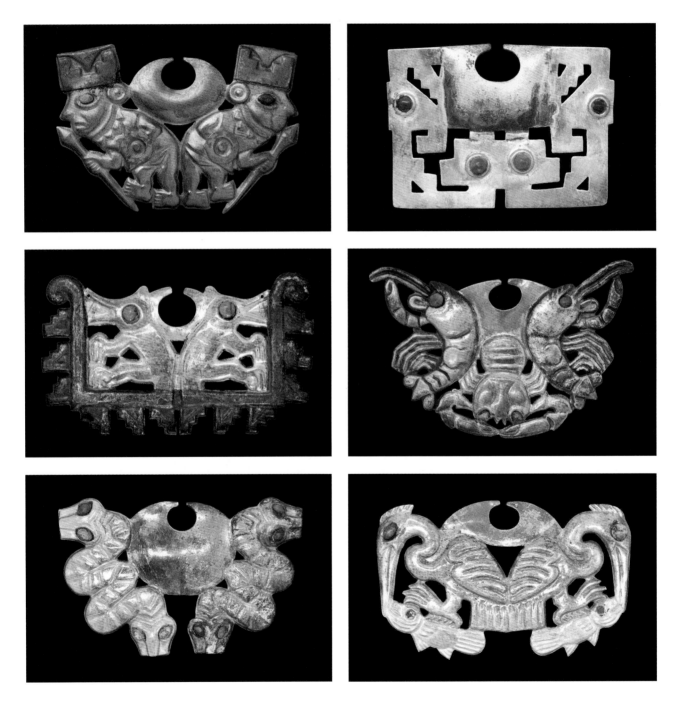

to represent a stylised version of one of the headdresses used by the mythical figure of the great Moche hero. Although this is an isolated example, it reflects that this woman must have assumed certain leadership roles that were typically taken on by men.

RITUAL BATTLES AND SACRIFICE OF PRISONERS

One of the most common scenes in Moche art is the ritual battle, followed by the sacrifice of prisoners (fig. 5.6). The scenes exhibit hand-to-hand combat between pairs of opponents, following certain conventions: the attacker tries to defeat his adversary by hitting his head with a club to knock off his headdress, then grabs him by the hair and finally takes away his weapons and clothing. The naked captive warriors, with ropes around their necks as a sign of submission, were led in a procession towards the warrior chiefs (figs 5.13–5.15). Later on, the prisoners were tortured and sacrificed in several ways.[12] In the Moche mythical cycle, the battles and human sacrifices are linked to two key moments. The first is the beginning of the period of chaos and disorder – the dry season, which is dominated by the nocturnal gods, the Owl and the Moon. The second is the restoration of cosmic order and the celebration of the beginning of the rainy season, where the image of the sun and the direct intervention of the hero prevail. In both situations, the sacrificed prisoner's blood was thought to be consumed by the gods and goddesses.

This last episode has been depicted in fine-line painting on several exquisite ceramic vessels, as well as in a polychrome mural found at the Pañamarca site in the Nepeña valley.[13] Another similar scene has been carved on a more unusual piece: a bone spatula in the form of a fist, with the middle finger slightly raised, producing a similar profile to that of a five-peaked mountain (figs 5.16–5.17). The spatula's flat surface was probably used for the preparation and consumption of some sort of substance. The carved images represent a human sacrifice carried out under the care of the owl god, and repeated motifs of warrior clubs and felines flank a prisoner next to a pair of cacti, probably the San Pedro variety, a species used in shamanic rituals due to its potent psychoactive effect.[14] As part of the ritual aspect, which was directly related to the agrarian myths and seasonal changes, Moche leaders, dressed as divine creatures, were in charge of administering human sacrifice. Although there is no conclusive proof of blood ingestion, skeletal evidence shows young men having endured violent trauma, which relates to similar practices to those observed in scenes of Moche art. The discovery of

around a hundred bodies in two of the upper courtyards of Huaca de la Luna is evidence of these practices.[15] The treatment and trauma traces seen on the bodies reveal blood extraction from neck cuts, as well as signs of flaying and being thrown from a rocky outcrop next to the square, practices also represented in Moche art.[16]

Although death by exsanguination is the most well-documented form of sacrifice among the Moche, it is highly probable that member mutilation may have had a greater relevance as a method to obtain blood without resorting to the slaughter of prisoners.[17] Some sculptural vessels, including those called *huacos retrato*, represent figures with foreign traits who have some sort of mutilation, especially on the nose or lips.[18] This type of practice would not only have fulfilled the need for blood, but would also have enabled the Moche to take advantage of the survivors and use them to carry out tasks controlled by the state.

Most of the battle scenes depict warriors who display similar attributes and weapons on both sides, indicating that the fighting was often between different Moche groups (figs 0.5 and 5.18). However, there are also various scenes where the groups fighting are differentiated by their clothing (particular headdresses, disc-shaped earrings, vests and loincloths, sacks for carrying coca) and physical appearance (height, fringed hairstyles, the use of moustaches and beards, specific facial painting designs), as well as by their body language and the use of weapons and fighting techniques (slings, stones, and truncheons with star-shaped or spherical heads, among other forms).[19] This last group seems to represent non-Moche peoples, especially those who inhabited high valleys and the neighbouring mountains of La Libertad and Áncash, among them the people of Recuay. These ethnocultural distinctions seem to suggest that the blood of the prisoners would have come from different peoples. This sheds light on the Moche's situation when we consider the region's historical background, and especially the high-Andean migrations that occurred in the centuries before the rise of the Moche state.

In this respect, ritual battles might have responded not only to a calendar structure with a mythical background, but also to strategies of integration and social cohesion. The inclusion of the figure of the Other, as well as its eventual capture and sacrifice, must have strengthened the Moche identity as a group. Even though the Moche had a broad geographical distribution, having a strong presence even in border areas like Alto Piura, the interethnic relationships probably had marked regional differences, which were, in turn, reflected in the culture and the variations in the iconographical themes represented in art.

Once the combat finished, the vanquished warriors were stripped of their clothes and headdresses, and each had a rope attached to his neck. The naked prisoners were then transported to a ceremonial space, where they were handed over to the priests for sacrifice. Their blood was extracted and presented as offerings to the main deities. The sacrifice rituals took place in the mountains or on the islands off the coast.

FIG. 5.13 (ABOVE LEFT) Vessel in the form of a high-status prisoner
Moche AD 100–400
Pottery
H. 23 cm, W. 12.1 cm, D. 21 cm
Museo Larco, Lima, Peru, ML002043

FIG. 5.14 (ABOVE) Vessel in the form of a prisoner in front of an officer
Moche AD 500–700
Pottery
H. 23 cm, W. 12.1 cm, D. 20 cm
Museo de Arte de Lima, Peru, IV-2.0.2139
Prado Family Bequest

FIG. 5.15 (LEFT) Prisoners in procession, line drawing from a ceramic vessel held by the American Museum of Natural History. Moche Archive, Dumbarton Oaks, Trustees for Harvard University, Washington, DC, PH.PC.001_0008

This spatula was probably used in the preparation and consumption of ritual powder substances. The motifs carved into its surface present a scene directed by a Moche god, half human–half owl, with a naked prisoner about to be sacrificed. Motifs of war clubs, felines and sea creatures depicted in different divided sections remind us of the painted murals that decorate the ceremonial buildings where these rituals actually took place.

FIG. 5.16 Spatula in the shape of an arm
with carved mythical scene
Moche AD 100–700
Bone with turquoise inlays
L. 20.8 cm, W. 3.5 cm, D. 3.2 cm
British Museum, Am,+.6383
Donated by Augustus Wollaston Franks

FIG. 5.17 Design on the bone fist, line drawings
by Thomas Athol Joyce, from *A Short Guide to the
American Antiquities in the British Museum, with 12
Plates and 48 Illustrations*, London, 1912, figs 41
and 42

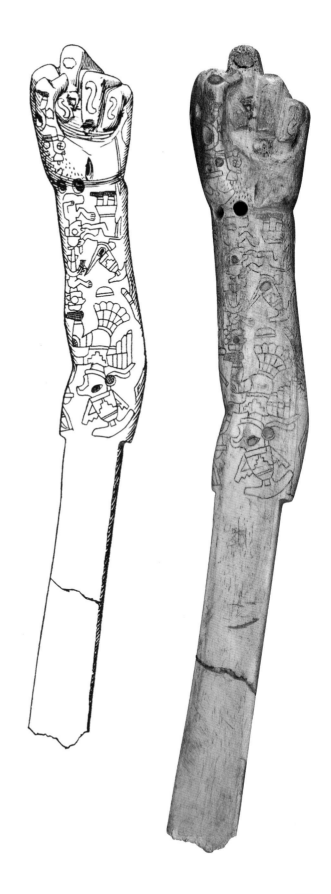

Combat was an important ritual for the Moche and depicted on objects spanning the course of over 500 years. Recent archaeological findings suggest that the events illustrated indeed took place in reality, requiring large amounts of resources. The combat scenes began with finely dressed warriors bearing clubs and shields, ready to take on their opponents. The confrontation usually involved two warriors engaged in hand-to-hand combat. All evidence seems to suggest that the objective of this combat was not to kill the enemy, but to capture them for the purposes of ritual sacrifice.

FIG. 5.18 (RIGHT) Vessel depicting a sleeping warrior wearing a nose ring and ear spools
Moche AD 100–600
Pottery
H. 24.4 cm, W. 12.5 cm, D. 20 cm
British Museum, Am1909,1218.15
Donated by Henry Van den Bergh through the Art Fund

FIG. 5.19 (BELOW) Crescent-shaped nose ring with discs and stars attached
Moche AD 100–600
Turquoise and gold
H. 3.4 cm, W. 12.7 cm, D. 0.2 cm
Museo Larco, Lima, Peru, ML100851

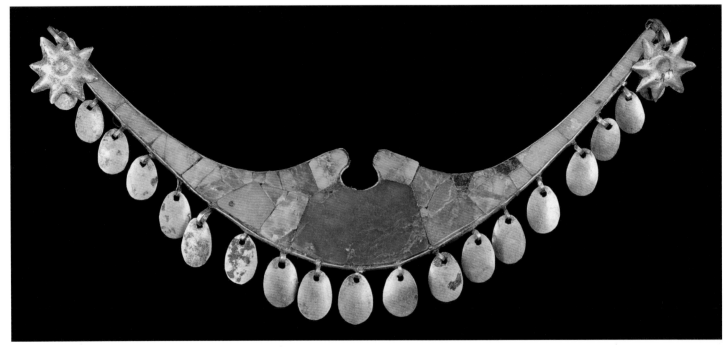

Despite the demarcation of new territorial borders, the Moche seem to have negotiated strategic alliances with their neighbours. The production and exchange of goods, practices also seen in Moche visual art, might have included the participation of foreign agents.

MUSIC AND DANCE

Music and dance had a major role in the celebration of rites of passage and invocation; they were represented in art by human beings and hybrid characters, anthropomorphised animals or plants and the deceased. The individuals wearing warrior or priest clothing, or with similar headdresses to those worn by divine characters, stand out among the human figures. Some dancers even wear masks, adopting the facial appearance of certain characters or animals, but also men either mutilated or with a corpse-like appearance. This might suggest that dance and music were integrated into commemorative rituals. Some researchers relate these celebrations to the end of a given cycle of battles and ritual sacrifices.[20]

One interesting case is a male figure sitting playing a flute, who we can identify by his clothing as one of the participants in a scene at the textile workshop (see figs 2.19 and 5.21). In other representations, which seem to refer entirely to events in the Moche mythical world, the association between music and death is reaffirmed in scenes from the land of the dead, where cadaverous figures, among them men, women and children, dance holding hands to the beat of the drums (*tinyas*), flutes (*pinkullos*), horns (*q'epas*), panpipes (*antaras*) and sticks of jingle bells.[21] The ceremonies themselves, by means of sound and movement, created multisensory experiences where the participant could encounter the sacred and come into contact with forces or entities from diverse worlds and times. Among the Moche's wind instruments, it is worth noting the use of *Strombus galeatus*, a marine species of conch found in equatorial waters, which was transformed into potent resonators known as *waylla q'epas* or *pututos*. These were used for different occasions, including ritual battles and the capture of prisoners. Besides having a sonorous function, the meaning and value of these seashells adopted a transcendental role in the trope of the hero figure trading them during a trip to eastern lands (see page 127).

PRODUCTION AND EXCHANGE

The Moche rulers controlled the specialised production and exchange of luxury goods.[22] In sites such as the Huacas de Moche and Pampa Grande (Lambayeque valley), workshops were located inside the urban fabric, close to the residences of the elite or temple areas.[23] Through these activities, the Moche established relationships with other ethnic groups. There are sculptural vessels that represent characters with foreign traits carrying textile garments decorated with Moche designs (fig. 5.20); some of these vessels have been found in graves at the Huacas de Moche.[24] Working under a regime controlled by Moche elites, these workshops would have been tasked with the manufacture of garments displaying the symbols and aesthetics of their new patrons.[25]

One fine-line painted bowl, possibly found in the Chicama valley, presents a weaving scene at a textile workshop (fig. 5.21).[26] The workshop is organised around a quadrangular patio, where the weavers perform their tasks on stools covered by mats.[27] Poles made of carob, a tree native to the north coast of Peru, are used to hold the waist looms. The weavers sit in front of each pole, wearing girdles that allow them to secure the loom to their bodies. Next to each one, there are many spindles with skeins of yarn, probably of different colours, which are used in the production of garments. Two types of garments produced at this workshop are identifiable: vests and headbands decorated with Moche symbols. Very few Moche textiles have survived the test of time, mainly due to conservation issues. However, pieces such as this decorated vessel allow us to reconstruct the methods and environment of production. Although it is hard to determine the gender of these artisans, the use of long, loose hair is evident, with the exception of one individual who wears it short. Both styles can be observed in Moche representations of warriors and captives from the Andean highlands.

Another interpretation of this scene is that the artisans are supervised by figures of the Moche elite.[28] In two annexe areas of the workshop, some figures are presenting or exchanging vessels laden with food. Among the products you can identify fish, chillies and the *cañán* (lizard), a reptile that even today is a part of the northern culinary tradition, especially in the Jequetepeque valley. One of these figures, sitting on a covered bench, is wearing a large tunic, its sleeves decorated with small quadrangular details and with fringes along the chest, which fastens at the waist. Additionally, he wears a turban-style headdress with a veil that covers the back of his head, as well as a headband decorated with geometric themes that folds around the head. Significantly, the garment of this figure is similar to the one worn by the flute-playing figure mentioned earlier (see fig. 2.19).

The Moche bowl opposite depicts the most complete image of textile weaving known in pre-Columbian art. The scene takes place in a workshop, where eight weavers are working with waist looms alongside ceramic vessels, spindle whorls and textile samplers. These might have served as guides for the techniques and motifs that they had to achieve. Male figures, in charge of supervising these activities, are depicted exchanging goods.

FIG. 5.20 (LEFT) Vessel depicting an individual holding a shirt
Moche AD 100–800
Pottery
H. 19.5 cm, W. 14.7 cm, D. 18.3 cm
British Museum, Am1930,Foster.7
Donated by Walter K. Foster

FIG. 5.21 (OPPOSITE) Flaring bowl with fine-line drawing depicting weaving scene
Moche AD 100–800
Pottery
H. 18.7 cm, W. 33.9 cm, D. 34.2 cm
British Museum, Am1913,1025.1
Donated by Herbert Gibson, 1st Baronet

FIG. 5.22 (ABOVE) The painted scene on the bowl, line drawing. Moche Archive, Dumbarton Oaks, Trustees for Harvard University, Washington, DC, PH.PC.001_0026

This vessel depicts a *coquero* holding a lime container. *Coqueros* were officers in charge of the chewing of coca, a practice that consisted in placing in the mouth a wad of leaves together with lime powder in order to help extract the drug from the leaves. Still practised by Andean communities, the chewing of coca leaves act as a mild stimulant to suppress hunger and tiredness, in addition to its symbolic use in special offerings.

FIG.5.23 (RIGHT) Vessel depicting an officer holding a lime container
Moche AD 200–600
Pottery
H. 18.8 cm, W. 13 cm, L. 18 cm
Museo Larco, Lima, Peru, ML001064

FIG.5.24 (BELOW) Lime container
Moche AD 200–600
Copper alloy
H. 17.2 cm, W. 7.3 cm, D. 15 cm
Museo 'Santiago Uceda Castillo' – Proyecto Arqueológico Huacas de Moche, PHL-PL I-039

The main character in the Moche mythical narrative is Ai-Apaec, a name derived from 'Aipæc' (Muchik for 'the maker', according to Fernando de la Carrera's 1644 text, *Arte de la lengua Yunga*). He takes part in scenes of violent confrontations, exchanges of goods, sexual exploits and human sacrifices.[29]

One of these episodes takes place in eastern lands beyond the Andes, where he meets with characters that perform a *chacchado de coca* ritual when the rains begin.[30] The celebrants wear long tunics decorated with geometric themes and a chequered pattern, headdresses and ornaments that differentiate them from Moche warriors and priests (fig. 5.23). In their hands, they carry containers known as *caleros* and some small sticks to extract the lime, which later on they will mix with the coca (*Erythroxylum coca*) leaves they are chewing. The lime helps to activate alkaloids from the *bolo de coca*, transforming it into a stronger stimulant. The hero takes part in this event, for which he receives the appropriate garments and accessories: special headdresses, disc-shaped earrings, a sack for the coca leaves, the *caleros* (fig. 5.24) and a hanging metal dress in the shape of a feline (fig. 5.25). Once under the rain, the hero looks up and, putting his hands together, he witnesses how the great two-headed serpent appears across the sky (fig. 5.26). Ai-Apaec places the serpent around his waist, harnessing in this manner the fertilising power that allows him to produce rain and fill up the rivers.

This encounter with the *chacchadores* allows the hero to establish an exchange of goods; he gives them a set of *pututos* (*Strombus galeatus* shells), which he obtained during a voyage to the ocean. Like other ancient heroes, Ai-Apaec will manage to return home after a long trip through the Andean-Amazonian world, carrying with him a series of exotic goods: in one hand, seashells, and in the other coca leaves and plants from the Amazonian area (*Nectandra pichurim* and *Guarea grandifolia*).

FIG. 5.25 Vessel depicting Ai-Apaec in a mythical scene, surrounded by a bicephalous serpent
Moche AD 200–600
Pottery
H. 25 cm, W. 13 cm, D. 17.7 cm
Museo Nacional de Arqueología, Antropología e Historia del Perú, C-54667

FIG. 5.26 Coca ritual with Ai-Apaec under a bicephalous arch, line drawing from a ceramic vessel held by the Linden-Museum, Staatliches Museum für Völkerkunde, Stuttgart. Moche Archive, Dumbarton Oaks, Trustees for Harvard University, Washington, DC, PH.PC.001_0099

FIG. 5.27 (PAGE 128, WITH DETAIL)
Ritual cape in the form of a feline
Moche AD 200–600
Cotton, copper, resin, semi-precious stones and feathers
L. 67 cm, W. 29.5 cm, D. 11 cm
Museo 'Santiago Uceda Castillo' – Proyecto Arqueológico Huacas de Moche, PHL-PL I-149

Importantly, some of the archaeological finds made at Huaca de la Luna in the Moche valley relate to Ai-Apaec's mythical journey described above. A number of elite graves include metallic funerary objects that coincide with various objects in the hero's story, particularly a hanging cape with feline shape (fig. 5.27) and a lime container (fig. 5.24).[31] These objects must have had ceremonial functions linked to the *chacchado de coca* and the celebration that marks the beginning of the rainy season. They were probably used by the people who reenacted the Moche hero's character in rituals.

THE SEA AND ITS MYSTERIES

The regional networks of exchange and interaction enabled the Moche to access the resources of diverse ecosystems. Since the dawn of Andean civilisation, the sea has been a primary resource for the survival of coastal societies. The ancient fishing villages developed appropriate technologies for gathering resources, for both shore and deep-sea fishing. For the latter, the fabrication of boats made from *junco* or *totora* (*Scirpus* sp.) was essential. These reed-like plants are cultivated even today in the wetlands adjacent to the sea in several coastal regions.[32] The production of *caballitos de totora*, as the boats are traditionally known, dates back at least 3,500 years, according to finds uncovered at Pampa Gramalote, the site close to the present-day town of Huanchaco.[33] The demand for these boats was probably determined by numerous human and geo-environmental factors, from an interest in deep-sea species, to the necessity of crossing the strong break of waves at the shore, to curiosity about the small islands close to the coast.[34]

In Moche iconography, the sea and islands were places that evoked dark forces, death and the transition to the underworld. Ai-Apaec himself had to wander the vast ocean, following the path taken by the Sun and overcoming several difficulties, including fierce battles with various marine creatures. Finally, he would arrive on an island, where, near to death, he would be prepared to enter the land of the dead. Notably, the hero was not the only one to turn to the islands. The moon goddess, escorted by a sea god, arrived there in a boat made of *totora*, bringing her captives along with her (fig. 5.28). On the islands they would perform sacrifices honouring the owl god, the powerful god of night. Likewise, sea lions were also hunted on the islands. All these events were part of the sequence of episodes related to the period of chaos and disorder when the Sun was a prisoner in the underworld. In this way, the islands fulfilled an important role within the Moche cosmovision. Seen as some kind of small mountains rising from the sea, they created a space where life

and death were brought together. From the northern coast, within the area inhabited by the Moche, one could see various islands and islets, such as Lobos de Tierra (Piura), Lobos de Afuera, Macabi, Guañape y Chao (Lambayeque), Corcovado and Santa (Áncash).

The exceptional discovery of a group of wooden objects on the Macabi Islands, situated opposite the coast of the Chicama valley, confirmed the symbolic value that these figures possessed for the Moche. These include three ornamental sceptre tops, one with the image of the owl god playing an *antara* (fig. 5.32) and two representing prisoners wearing headdresses of this nocturnal creature and ropes around their necks (figs 5.34–5.35). Of these, one wears a vest of metal plaques while the other does not and has his hands tied. Another carving is a sculptural vessel in the form of a completely naked prisoner with a rope around his neck (see fig. 5.58). This figure displays a mark shaped like an inverted V at the front part of the hair, which appears to be left by the intentional cutting of a lock of hair. This type of hair lock was typical of foreign warriors from the Andean highlands.

Another of the excavated objects corresponds to the upper end of a typical club head of a Moche warrior (fig. 5.31). Although truncheons were used mainly as attack weapons in ritual battles, in some scenes they were also used to hunt deer and sea lions. But possibly the most outstanding objects of this unusual discovery are the two wooden sceptres with complex carvings on the top sections. One of them presents a scene where minor creatures surround the main character, who is located in the interior of a structure (fig. 5.36). The other piece depicts a principal character sitting on what seems to be a throne, with steps surrounded by animals such as birds and sea lions (fig. 5.37). Both pieces include decorative owl heads. Even though there is no precise data concerning the original context from which the wooden sculptures originated, it is highly probable that they were part of human sacrifice rituals similar to those at Huacas de Moche. There, archaeologists found sculptural vessels, depicting naked prisoners with their hands tied, surrounding many of the bodies. A number of vessels were broken intentionally at the site, probably representing the symbolic death of any prisoner depicted on these vessels.[35] For the Moche, the similarity in the functions of the islands and the mountains – both spaces that produced life and death – transformed them into sacred places of worship. The supremacy of the political and ideological Moche regime, intrinsically linked to the manifestation of their distinctive visual art and beliefs, came to an end towards the close of the first millennium AD, making way for renewed ideologies and forms of regional government, such as Lambayeque and Chimú.

Moche myths tell us that once the battle had ended the vanquished warriors were taken to the islands in boats, where they were offered in sacrifice to the gods. Although this has not been confirmed by excavations on the islands, important ceremonies might have taken place in these outdoor spaces.

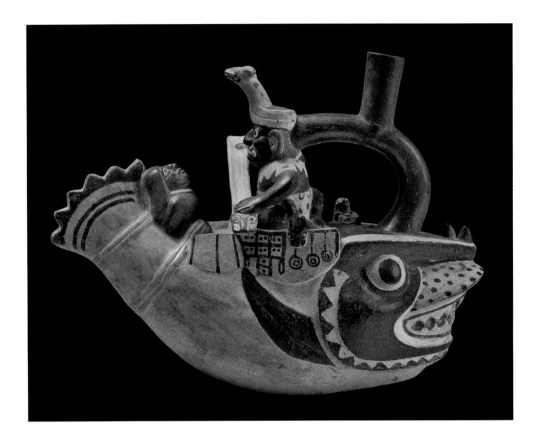

FIG.5.28 (LEFT) Vessel depicting semi-divine figures taking prisoners to the islands
Moche AD 100–600
Pottery
H. 21.8 cm, W. 29.3 cm, D. 9.7 cm
Museo Larco, Lima, Peru, ML003202

FIG.5.29 (BELOW) Prisoners taken to the islands in anthropomorphic reed boats, line drawing from a ceramic vessel held by the Art Institute of Chicago (1957.379). Moche Archive, Dumbarton Oaks, Trustees for Harvard University, Washington, DC, PH.PC.001_0005

FIG.5.30 (OPPOSITE) Vessel depicting a human figure in a reed boat
Moche AD 100–800
Pottery
H. 20 cm, W. 22.2 cm, D. 9.8 cm
Ethnologisches Museum, Staatliche Museen zu Berlin, V A 17582

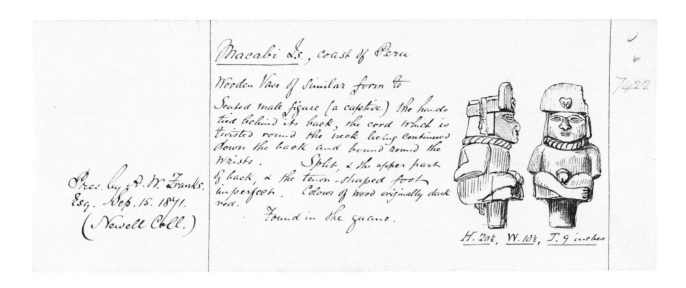

FIG. 5.31 (ABOVE) A handwritten slip recording
the acquisition of the wooden figure shown
opposite, 1871

FIG. 5.32 (FAR LEFT) Club head
Moche AD 100–800
Wood
H. 31.5 cm, W. 13.2 cm, D. 14.6 cm
British Museum, Am.7435
Donated by Augustus Wollaston Franks

FIG. 5.33 (LEFT) Humanised owl playing panpipes
Moche AD 100–800
Wood
H. 25.2 cm, W. 10.7 cm, D. 4.6 cm
British Museum, Am.7430
Donated by Augustus Wollaston Franks

These extraordinary wooden sculptures, depicting officers, mythical beings and naked prisoners, were found off the coast of Moche territory on the Macabi Islands, along with other objects such as ceramics, textiles and shells. They were discovered during the late 19th century buried in layers of guano (bird excrement) when it began to be widely exported as fertiliser.

FIG. 5.34 (LEFT) Figure depicting a bound prisoner with rope around his neck
Moche AD 100–800
Wood
H. 49.5 cm, W. 24.6 cm, D. 24.6 cm
British Museum, Am.7422
Donated by Augustus Wollaston Franks

FIG. 5.35 (BELOW) Figure depicting a bound prisoner with a headdress and rope around his neck
Moche AD 100–800
Wood
H. 49.5 cm, W. 22.8 cm, D. 19 cm
British Museum, Am.7420
Donated by Augustus Wollaston Franks

The Macabi Island wooden sculptures

Caroline R. Cartwright

The wooden objects discovered deep in the guano deposits of the Macabi Islands are some of the most fascinating creations from Moche culture. In order to gather more information about the Macabi Island objects in the Museum's collection, tiny wood samples were taken from already-damaged areas of seven objects (figs 5.32–5.37 and 5.58). In this analysis variable pressure scanning electron microscopy (VP SEM) was used to identify the type of wood. Due to the three-dimensional nature of wood anatomy, each sample was sliced to show transverse, radial longitudinal and tangential longitudinal sections. Examination of samples and reference specimens was undertaken using a scanning electron microscope.[1] The resulting magnifications were up to 600 times larger and working distances ranged from 10 mm to 20 mm; 3D mode was selected to maximise diagnostic features for identification, which revealed all seven objects to be algarrobo wood (*Prosopis* sp.). Although it is probable that *Prosopis pallida*, which is found in dry forests, was the source of the wood, it may be safer to adopt a cautious approach to identification until current taxonomic disputes have been resolved. Microscopy also showed that the wood structure is very brittle and friable (fig. 5.38), presumably as a consequence of burial of the carvings in the islands' deep guano deposits.

Prosopis pallida, a thorny tree in the Fabaceae family, is native to Peru, Bolivia, Colombia and Ecuador. In some of its native habitats the tree is over-exploited, whereas it is regarded as invasive in other regions to which it has been introduced in order to combat soil erosion. Algarrobo trees can access water sources deep underground through long taproots, so they survive well in dry environments. These long-living trees produce dense, hard, resinous, reddish-brown wood used for tools, charcoal and firewood.

Further scanning electron microscopy was coupled with energy-dispersive X-ray spectroscopy (SEM-EDX) to investigate inorganic chemical elements present on the seven carvings. The analysis revealed peaks on the wooden figures for Hg (mercury) and S (sulphur), thus indicating the use of cinnabar (mercury sulphide) to give a red appearance. This scientific research has shown that red colours had significant importance for Moche people: they used reddish-brown algarrobo wood to carve the sculptures, which were then painted in cinnabar – despite it being toxic to handle – in order to make them bright red.

FIG. 5.36 Staff depicting an officer in an architectural structure
Moche AD 100–800
Wood
H. 44 cm, W. 13.5 cm, D. 13.5 cm
British Museum, Am.7431
Donated by Josiah D. Harris

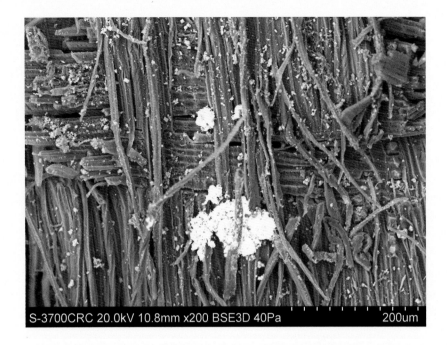

S-3700CRC 20.0kV 10.8mm x200 BSE3D 40Pa   200um

FIG. 5.37 (LEFT AND DETAIL) Staff depicting an officer
in an architectural structure
Moche AD 100–800
Wood
H. 73.5 cm, W. 14.8 cm, D. 13.6 cm
British Museum, Am.7432
Donated by Augustus Wollaston Franks

FIG. 5.38 (ABOVE) A VP SEM image of a radial
longitudinal section of a *Prosopis* wood (*algarrobo*)
sample from fig. 5.37, showing the fragile and brittle
cellular features. The white particles show the red
pigment cinnabar.

Recuay and their neighbours

George F. Lau

People of the Recuay culture (*c*. AD 100–700) flourished at the foot of Peru's Cordillera Blanca mountain range, which includes Huascarán, the range's tallest snowcapped summit (6,768 metres above sea level). They lived in fortified villages near their fields of potatoes, maize and quinoa, and they had pastures for their herds of camelids. They made pottery vessels decorated with colourful painted geometric and zoomorphic designs (fig. 5.39). Rare modelled jars show scenes of noble life: lordly celebrations; well-attired women and men; descendants worshipping ancestor mummies; ritual offerings of camelids; and the trading of drink (probably maize beer) and valuables, such as metal pins and weapons, pottery and cloth. Carved monoliths graced tomb buildings and depicted warriors, ancestors and mythical feline–serpent creatures (fig. 5.40).

The Recuay interacted closely with the Moche peoples of the Pacific coastal valleys. Both cultures shared religious symbols, including a mythical supernatural being shown as a rampant feline-like animal with a crest on its head. Interestingly, both also shared a fascination for the otherness ('alterity') of their neighbours. Some Moche potters depicted warriors defeating Recuay-like enemies, identified by their highland-style costumes and weapons (fig. 5.41); they also copied Recuay pottery shapes and themes, while using their own materials and techniques. Recently, exquisite earspools of gold foil and mosaic inlay, typical of Moche metalwork, were found at a Recuay site in the mountains. Like many nations, peaceful relations and trade with neighbours may have occasionally deteriorated into tense conflict. The Moche may have seen their Recuay enemies as prey (identified by their painted face spots and forelocks), to be captured, stripped and humiliated by the victorious (see fig. 5.13). Both the Moche and Recuay constructed their group identity through the Other.

Later, the Recuay had close dealings with emissaries of the powerful Wari state, who expanded outwards from Ayacucho in the South-Central Andes. During this period, Recuay craftspeople were inspired by Wari pottery, textiles and even their religious imagery. Some vessels made by the Recuay show dignitaries in four-cornered hats typical of the Wari (see figs 6.9–6.11). Some Wari are shown as captives; others are offering goblets and drink. Being part of the Wari network enabled Recuay peoples to benefit from the exchange of coastal, jungle and highland products: rare goods (metals, obsidian, salt, coca and hallucinogens) and dazzling luxuries (vessels, seashell, tapestries and feathers) were especially valued by provincial leaders and their noble families.

FIG. 5.39 Vessel in the form of a female figure, with a mythical being painted on the reverse
Recuay AD 100–700
Pottery
H. 13.8 cm, W. 11.4 cm, D. 11.5 cm
British Museum, Am1896,-.1230

FIG.5.40 (RIGHT) Monolith in the form
of a human figure
Recuay AD 100–700
Stone
H. 31.5 cm, W. 16 cm, D. 23 cm
British Museum, Am1986,02.1

FIG.5.41 (BELOW) Ritual battle between the Moche
and the Recuay, line drawing from a ceramic vessel held
by the Ethnologisches Museum, Staatliche Museen
zu Berlin. Moche Archive, Dumbarton Oaks,
Trustees for Harvard University, Washington, DC,
PH.PC.001_0507

Chimú: the earthly kingdom of the sea

Gabriel Prieto

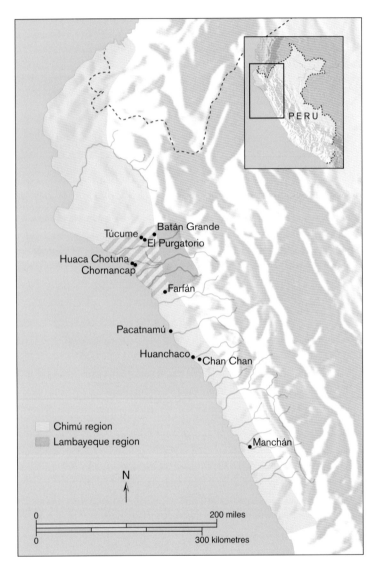

FIG. 5.42 Map of the north coast, showing the extension of the Chimú territory around the 15th century AD

The Chimú kingdom was a coastal civilisation in northern Peru that developed between the tenth and fifteenth centuries AD. It spanned from present-day northern Lima in the south to the border between Peru and Ecuador in the north, stretching for almost 850 kilometres along the Pacific coast (fig. 5.42). Despite more than 148 years of Chimú archaeological studies there is no consensus on exactly how big this kingdom was.[1] Archaeological evidence found in

the highland adjacent to the Moche valley suggests that the Chimú controlled territories in the Carabamba and Huamachuco basins, which were rich in crops, minerals and camelid herds. They possibly went as far as the Marañón river, where they gained access to Amazonian products such as chonta wood (*Bactris gasipaes*) and ishpingo seeds (*Nectandra* spp.), and a variety of exotic and polychrome feathers (from, for example, *Ara ararauna*) for embellishing their clothing (fig. 5.43). Their presence is also found in the region of Huancabamba, in the highlands of Piura towards the Mountain Forest of the Jaén basin, confirming an active interaction with highland and even Amazonian societies.[2]

CHAN CHAN

The jewel in the crown of the Chimú kingdom was the city of Chan Chan, built in the centre of a newly created artificial valley named the Valle del Chimo (according to colonial Spanish accounts), located at the northern end of the original Moche valley (fig. 5.44). During its height, Chan Chan grew to more than 24 square kilometres, larger than any city in Europe at the time and with an estimated population of 50,000 to 75,000 inhabitants, not counting the numerous satellite towns in its hinterland.[3] Chan Chan was a cosmopolitan city, whose residents came from across the Chimú territory. The diverse population intertwined their own cultures, fashions and tastes with the official Chimú artistic and ideological canons. The brown colour of Chan Chan's adobe brick walls probably served as the perfect background for the beautiful polychromatic cotton and camelid-fibre textiles masterfully woven and embellished with feathers, embroidery and paint by expert weavers and artisans (see figs 2.20 and 5.51).

Around AD 1450–70 the Chimú were engaged in a long-term war with the Incas, the coeval civilisation rising in the southern highlands of Peru who rapidly expanded their political and territorial control over the majestic Andean mountains, but also penetrated into the fertile and heavily populated coastal valleys. It seems that both Chimú and Inca peoples had a particular interest in controlling Pachacamac, a prestigious pilgrimage and ceremonial centre situated on the central coast of Peru. Towards the beginning of the

sixteenth century, the Incas had absolute control of Chan Chan and the Chimú kingdom.[4]

Spanish looting during the sixteenth and eighteenth centuries has deprived us of enjoying the scientific excavation of the contents of the once-intact royal mausoleum built on the rulers' palaces of Chan Chan. Indeed, epic legends and disturbing accounts in the archives of the colonial city of Trujillo reveal the splendid treasures taken from these rich tombs, which surpassed in gold and silver three or four times the mythical ransom – one room full of gold and two rooms full of silver objects and jewellery – paid by Inca Atahualpa to Francisco Pizarro during the siege of Cajamarca in 1532–3.[5] The Chimú were renowned for a long-established tradition of goldsmiths on the north coast of Peru. Previously, the Chimú had conquered other societies such as the Lambayeque (AD 750–1300/50).[6] Chimú goldsmiths perfected their metallurgical abilities by resettling many specialist artisans from their territories, forcing them to live and work in Chan Chan. That was possibly the fate of skilful Lambayeque goldsmiths who now had to craft jewels and ritual paraphernalia for the Chimú elite (fig. 5.49). The traces of these forgotten metal artists are still visible in the ruins of their workshops and ingots left behind in the *barrios* of Chan Chan (fig. 5.50).[7] Glowing gold cups and silver bowls were displayed to reflect the sun's and the moon's rays in splendid ceremonies that now are just a whisper in the abandoned palaces and temples of Chan Chan.

The visual impact of these radiant and precious artefacts had a double effect: a shiny quasi-supernatural perspective for the spectators; for their immediate users, the symbolism conveyed by the marine deities engraved onto their surfaces (fig. 5.54). According to recent studies, the size and orientation of an object's design were closely related to the size of the architectural space in which it was used.[8] Therefore, one would expect that metal bowls were exclusively used by the Chimú priests in small settings like the so-called *audiencias* (U-shaped structures with niches in their walls), which were profusely decorated with marine motifs.[9] Metal bowls and goblets could have been held aloft to toast the ancestors in festive events hosted in the Chimú palaces' large plazas. These fabulous events were immortalised – much like present-day 3D animations – in curious wooden architectural models, plazas packed with musicians and dancers, and a plethora of other figures within and outside the sacred precinct, worshipped the dead bodies of the Chimú rulers (figs 5.45–5.46).[10] Toasting with brewed maize beer or *kótzo*[11] created a communion with the spirits of the earth and the sea.[12] The mediators between the real world and the pantheon of goddesses and gods were the mummified bodies of the Chimú rulers carefully brought to life in elaborate ceremonies, in which their descendants emphasised their legacy, spiritual and demi-divine roles. These events served for the royal lineage descendants to legitimise their inherited status within the extremely hierarchical and

competitive Chimú society; like in European courts, they were also charged with political symbolism and opportunism ran rife.

As coastal peoples, Chimú artists were fascinated by the sea and its fauna. The interior walls of Chan Chan's palaces were decorated profusely with waves, fish, seabirds, crabs and lobsters and more everyday scenes such as fishermen casting their nets from reed boats. The sea was an essential resource for the emergence and consolidation of early civilisations in the coastal Andes.[13] The Chimú's predecessors, the Moche, represented elaborated reed boats in their art (fig. 5.30), demonstrating that this kind of vessel, still in use at Huanchaco (a traditional fishing village 5.6 kilometres north of Chan Chan), has existed for thousands of years in this region. The people from Huanchaco claim a direct link with the Chimú that goes beyond reed boats and marine subsistence; some of these fishermen's surnames are direct

evidence of the intricate social dynamics that took place in the past. For example, when Chan Chan was under Inca control, its last ruler had a surname that still exists in Huanchaco today, the Huaman-Chumo family (see page 18).[14]

It is currently widely accepted that the Chincha kingdom, a contemporaneous state on the south coast of Peru, was the only civilisation to navigate and trade along the Peruvian and Ecuadorian coasts.[15] Indeed, large wooden oars (or perhaps *huaras*) have been found at many sites along the Chincha coast (fig. 5.47). But people in Huanchaco claim that they also sailed along the north coast of Peru, and that their ancestors founded many modern fishing towns such as Huanchaquito in the Chimbote bay and Santa Rosa on the Lambayeque coast.[16] Have these claims been handed down through generations' reminiscences of a Chimú system of coastal trade once active along the coasts of Peru and Ecuador? There are several other grounds for claiming that the Chimú, as well as the Chincha, played a prominent role in marine trade in the past. One piece of direct evidence is that hundreds of

FIG. 5.44 (OPPOSITE) The *audiencias* sector of the Tschudi palace (also known as Nik-an, or the 'house of the sea') in Chan Chan, Huanchaco, Peru

FIG. 5.45 Architectural model of a ceremonial palace in Chan Chan
Chimú AD 1440–1665
Wood, resin, bone, semi-precious stones, clay
H. 40.5 cm, W. 41 cm, D. 48.5 cm
Museo 'Santiago Uceda Castillo' – Proyecto Arqueológico Huacas de Moche, PHL-PL I-012

FIG. 5.46 Some of the figures on the architectural model, line drawing. Museo 'Santiago Uceda Castillo' – Proyecto Arqueológico Huacas de Moche

When this Chimú model was recovered from a looted tomb at Huaca de la Luna, it became one of the most important discoveries in the history of Peruvian archaeology. Made out of carved wood with shell inlays, the space pays homage to its makers' ancestors. Inside there are musicians, hunchbacked figures preparing *chicha* (maize beer) and a group of funerary bundles. Reduced-scale models found inside the model itself seem to be a clear indicator of their possible function as a context within which activities were presented to ensure that practices remained in the collective memory. Based on the layout of the space and the ornamentation of its walls, the piece has been associated with the greater ceremonial palaces of Chan Chan, where similar ceremonies were carried out.

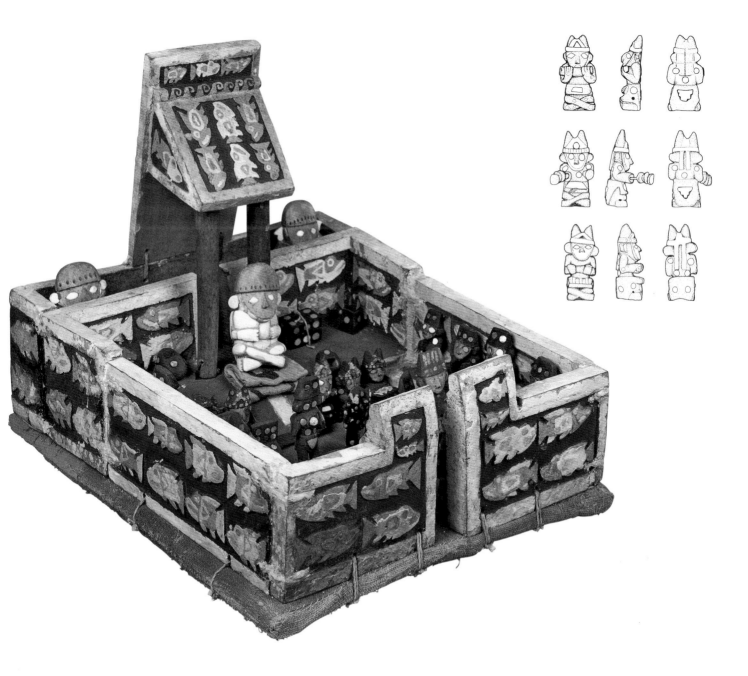

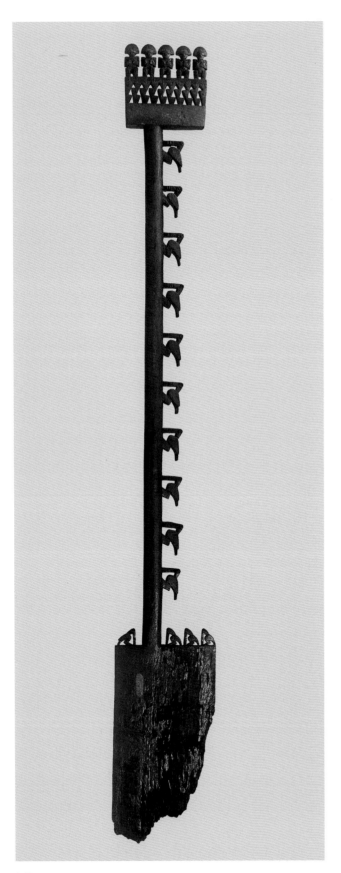

Spondylus shells, a type of spiny mollusc from the Ecuadorian coast, were found complete or fragmented in looted cemeteries at Chan Chan and more recently in scientific excavations at Huanchaco. Beyond being exotic and visually appealing, these shells were considered sacred among Andean societies and were associated with rainfall and fertility.[17] The Chimú controlled the distribution of these shells on the north coast of Peru for several centuries and they became an important tool for trade as highly valued objects, as well as central offerings in their official religious acts. Chan Chan and its immediate surroundings have more complete *Spondylus* shells and derivative objects than any other archaeological sites in the Central Andean region. These shells were so precious that they are represented in beautiful ceramic vessels, metal ornaments and even mural art (fig. 5.56). More recently, excavations have discovered hundreds of *Spondylus* shells alongside what were mass child and camelid sacrifices: their significance is yet to be explained, but could relate to the promise of fertility that these shells embodied. Meanwhile, the Pacific shore's almighty waves are still resonating with the glorious past of a forgotten civilisation that, in the middle of the fertile deserts of the Peruvian north coast, made the sea sacred.

FIG. 5.47 Paddle with figures
Ica–Chincha AD 1100–1400
Wood
L. 165.5 cm, W. 21.8 cm, D. 4.2 cm
British Museum, Am1938,1017.13

FIG. 5.48 (OPPOSITE) Headdress
Central Coast AD 1470–1532
Cotton and feathers
H. 70 cm, W. 51 cm, D. 48 cm
British Museum, Am1914,0731.67

This headdress was probably produced for the Chimú–Inca elites during the period of expansion to the Central Coast region. It is made from plain cotton weave with small feathers adhered to the main body and long feathers attached at the top. Towards the back of the cap there is a panel with a sea-creature motif that has been depicted in green, orange and yellow feathers, arranged between colourful geometric panels.

The Chimú conquered other northern societies such as the
Lambayeque, who were skilful goldsmiths and craft artists. In order
to improve their own metallurgical capabilities, the Chimú forced
the Lambayeque to resettle in Chan Chan, where they were obliged
to produce sumptuous objects and ritual paraphernalia for the
elites. Traces of their workshops have been found in lower-class
neighbourhoods.

FIG. 5.49 (LEFT) Earplug depicting
a mythical figure
Lambayeque AD 900–1300/50
Wood, mother-of-pearl, shell
H. 10.5 cm, W. 8.8 cm
British Museum, Am1960,06.1

FIG. 5.50 (ABOVE) Double spout and bridge
bottle with four human faces
Lambayeque AD 900–1300/50
Silver
H. 24.2 cm, W. 23.7 cm, D. 9.7 cm
British Museum, Am1947,20.1

FIG. 5.51 Tapestry featuring
anthropomorphic birds
Chimú AD 900–1470
Camelid fibre, cotton
H. 38.5 cm, W. 88 cm
British Museum, Am1896,-.509
Donated by Augustus Wollaston Franks

Spondylus: the sacred thorny oyster

Cecilia Pardo and Julio Rucabado

> [They] *offered sea shells, which they call* mullu. *And they offered them to the fountains and springs, stating that the shells were daughters of the oceans, mother to all the waters … they used these shells in almost every different way of sacrifice, and even today, they throw some ground dust of* mullu *in the* chicha [maize beer] *as superstition.*[1]
>
> José de Acosta, 1590

FIG. 5.52 A modern *Spondylus* shell

Access to exotic sumptuary goods through long-distance exchange routes dates back to pre-Ceramic times in the Central Andes. Semi-precious stones such as turquoise brought from Ecuador or lapis lazuli from the southern Andes (modern-day Chile) were highly valued and used in the production of fine personal adornments, as inlay decorations and offerings specially made for elite burials. Exceptional finds from sites such as Kuntur Wasi, Sipán and Sicán in the northern Central Andes offer some extraordinary examples.[2] But certain marine conch shells, like the *Strombus galeatus* and more importantly the *Spondylus* bivalve, locally known as *mullu*, were among the most desirable in this system of imported goods.

Commonly known as the thorny oyster and found in different oceans worldwide, *Spondylus* is a spiny bivalve with unique colour tonalities ranging from white to orange, red and purple (fig. 5.52). In South America the main known species are *Spondylus princeps* and *Spondylus calcifer*.[3] *Spondylus* was a very highly valued material for Andean societies during the pre-Columbian period: among other potential reasons, it was regarded as a symbol of fertility. Under normal atmospheric circumstances, the bivalve can be found in the warm seas of the Pacific Ocean, from the Gulf of California down to the coasts of Ecuador. However, during El Niño events, once every four years warm waters would reach the coasts of northern Peru and consequently result in a large proliferation of *Spondylus* shells.[4] Divers were trained to remain under water for an extended period of time to collect these sacred offerings from the sea, which normally dwell in depths between 15 and 30 metres below sea level. Warm water would also bring rains, instrumental for agrarian societies living in coastal deserts. Moreover, recent studies suggest that the flesh of the *Spondylus* would act as a hallucinogenic substance that Andean peoples would consume so that they could interact with their ancestors in the spiritual realm.[5]

The earliest examples of the use of *Spondylus* in the Andean region date back to the pre-Ceramic period, with a few found in early sites such as Real Alto in Ecuador and Caral in Peru.[6] These isolated discoveries mark the starting point of a long history of this symbolic mollusc in the Andes. In the centuries that followed, its growing importance is perceived in the iconography carved in the stone sculptures and walls of Chavín de

Huántar. The conch shell appears in the Tello Obelisk, as well as in a slab which shows the image of a deity holding a *Spondylus* in one hand and a *Strombus* in the other (see fig. 2.10). This relationship has been interpreted as a possible symbol of dualism, where the shells are associated with opposite and complementary features.[7] Although it was broadly used by coastal societies, archaeological evidence of *Spondylus* has been spread across different regions: for example, in the sacred spaces of the Nasca, where the massive geoglyphs were drawn. In the pampas of Palpa, a group of offerings was found in ceremonial mounds located in a trapezoidal geoglyph, which included pendants made from *Spondylus* and conch bivalves, alongside fine polychromatic pottery vessels, maize rolled up in textiles and remains of crabs.[8] Although the Nasca lived on the south coast of Peru – 1,750 kilometres away from the northern oceans where *Spondylus* were found – it seems that it was imperative for them to walk for weeks in order to offer the sacred oyster in the ceremonies carried out by these coastal societies.

At around the same time, the Moche used *Spondylus* to produce fine personal adornments, such as breastplates made from small beads.[9] Images depicted on vessels suggest that during their early periods *Strombus* was more popular than *Spondylus*. The snail mollusc played a major role in myths, said to be collected from the ocean by Ai-Apaec, the main deity of the Moche, to be then used as a form of ritual exchange with highland communities who would give coca leaves in return (fig. 5.25). However, towards the final stages of Moche, interest in *Spondylus* seems to have increased. According to studies, this would have happened as a result of a long-distance exchange system that developed into a wider network during the later periods.[10] It is worth noting that this increase coincided with a series of El Niño events around AD 600, which would have disrupted the climate in the region significantly.

Although there is some evidence of the use of *Spondylus* during the Wari period, it became widespread during the influence of the Lambayeque and Chimú on the north coast (AD 900–1470). This is testified by the diversity of its representation in ceramics, metal vessels, mud friezes and inlay decorations, as well as the presence of the shell itself at archaeological sites (figs 5.53 and 5.56).[11] This evidence reflects the enduring networks between Andean societies from Peru and Ecuador, and also a major shift in the belief systems of the northern cultures, who began to focus their attention on the marine world. In the Lambayeque ceremonial centre of Chornancap, a high-status male figure was buried holding a *Spondylus* bivalve in each hand, while twenty other shells were arranged close to his body. Locally known as the 'Lord of the Spondylus', he could have been the human embodiment of a mythical figure related to shell harvesting, represented on silver vases and friezes in other temples, such as Huaca Las Balsas in Túcume (figs 5.54–5.55).[12] During colonial times, Spanish chroniclers documented that the dust of ground *Spondylus* was spread to purify the path where the deities walked. A myth registered at the site of Túcume describes the arrival of Naymlap and Ceternic, founders of the Lambayeque lineage, and mentions the presence of a special retainer known

FIG. 5.53 Stirrup vessel with moulded *Spondylus* shells
Chimú AD 900–1470
Pottery
H. 16.7 cm, W. 17.2 cm, D. 10.1 cm
British Museum, Am1956,+.3

FIG. 5.54 (ABOVE) Bowl with engraved motifs
of divers with *Spondylus* shells
Chimú AD 900–1470
Silver alloy
H. 3.9 cm, Diam. 13.8 cm, D. 13.7 cm
Museo Larco, Lima, Peru, ML100754

FIG. 5.55 (RIGHT) Line drawing of bowl with engraved
motifs of divers. Museo Larco, Lima, Peru

as Fonga Sigde, meant to be in charge of spreading the sacred red dust along the path of his lord.[13]

Offerings of *Spondylus*, along with other reduced-scale gold and silver objects, were found associated with the ceremonial sacrifices of young children, forming part of a ritual known as Capacocha, dating to the later Inca period.[14] Some of these shell goods were probably produced in workshops managed by the empire, such as those found at Cabeza de Vaca in Tumbes, a major provincial administrative centre located along the Qhapaq Ñan (road system).[15] Importantly, Incas developed close relationships with the coastal kingdom of the Chincha, who established a major long-distance exchange system based on the circulation of shells and metals that connected populations between Manta (Ecuador) and the Collao (Bolivia).[16]

Although the symbolic value of *Spondylus* decreased with the passage of time, it is still present in many aspects of Andean society today. Beads and carved fragments are still used as inlays to decorate contemporary jewellery, and the bivalves can still be found in the local markets, along with other symbolic objects that are still used in shamanistic practices, demonstrating that some cultural aspects have endured the course of time.

FIG. 5.56 *Paccha* with representations of *Spondylus* shells
Inca AD 1400–1532
Pottery
H. 23.7 cm, W. 23.5 cm, D. 24.6 cm
Museo de Arte de Lima, 2007.16.70
Donated by Petrus and Verónica Fernandini

Death, killing and human sacrifice

Jago Cooper

Around AD 1450, a few kilometres outside the city walls of Chan Chan in northern Peru, more than 140 children aged between eight and thirteen years old were killed by having their hearts removed in a small number of mass-killing events.[1] Extremely well preserved due to the desert environment, the children are carefully laid out together in rows, their cotton tunics stained with blood and excrement, a sight that brings to life the fear and reality of death in an extremely powerful and emotional way. Visiting the site today and seeing their meticulously careful recovery – in advance of the urban expansion of the town of Huanchaco – provokes existential questions, because how people treat their dead reveals a lot about a society's beliefs and values relating to life (fig. 5.57). Death is a deeply emotive subject and often difficult to write about. Human awareness of our own mortality generates enormous empathy for the dead, no matter when and where the person died. It is an area of human behaviour that most quickly highlights cultural difference and the contrasting moral judgements of right and wrong, which are so deeply entrenched in different belief systems. Even the term 'human sacrifice' commonly provokes reactions of horror, incredulity and shock, and these responses can quickly develop into moral judgements of the protagonists as brutal, savage or uncivilised.[2] However, such cultural contrasts are best addressed with informed discussion, reflection and thought. The gaze of moral certainty and judgement is rarely turned on one's own cultural practices and can often be driven by a lack of understanding or empathy for another's.

Today, the responsibility of those in the present to those living in the past and future is commonly distant and detached. But in the Andean world the interconnectedness of past, present and future did not hold such abstraction from reality, and death, killing and human sacrifice are commonly represented in the iconography and objects of all cultures. Human actions had an immediate impact on past and future, which was why they had to be so very careful with each act undertaken, so respectful of the delicate balance between time and space and between order and chaos.

FIG. 5.57 Archaeological excavations at Huanchaco carried out by Gabriel Prieto's team in 2018 reveal a large number of child sacrifices

MOCHE SACRIFICE: CASUALTIES OF BATTLE

In the early Middle Ages in Europe, the idea of war was to ride into battle to massacre as many of the opposing force as possible. Most of the soldiers would have suffered terribly from their wounds, often dying slowly over hours or days. Traditionally, whoever had the most soldiers left standing on the field of battle was declared the victor, stories of glory would be told, and the spoils of war would be taken. Such a scene of wanton murder, human suffering and lack of care for the dying would have been abhorrent to many Andean societies. Warfare in the Andean world was violent and bloody, but killing the enemy on the battlefield was not always the primary objective.

The archaeological evidence for warfare can be difficult to interpret and there is much discussion surrounding the nature of combat in all Andean societies. Nonetheless, there are clear indications of ancient Andean attitudes to death and killing that emerge. The archaeological evidence from the region identifies fluctuating levels of internecine violence throughout the last 5,000 years as well as the prevalence of ritual homicides and bodily mutilations.[3] However, the cultural frameworks within which death and killing were understood require elaboration. In terms of warfare, the aim of Andean battles was often to punish and capture individuals by force in order to publicly subjugate them to the will of their captors. Andean warfare was often first and foremost a public spectacle. The narrative iconography on Moche ceramics and ethnohistorical documents about Inca battles reveal that Andean battles often began with drinking, feasting and formal ceremonies carried out by opposing warriors, priests and musicians. There could be many days of culturally prescribed ceremonies, music and dancing before any act of violence would occur. This is one of the many reasons given to explain how arriving European soldiers overcame larger Inca forces in battles during the early years of colonial encounter, because the European soldiers simply were not playing by the same rules or objectives of engagement.[4] Opposing sides in Andean warfare would wear clothing and adornments to identify status and signify rank. They would meet to fight with weapons primarily aimed to injure in hand to hand combat rather than kill outright or massacre from afar. Indeed, death in the fight could be considered a consequence of violence rather than the stated aim of the physical engagement. Within societies such as the Moche, a selection of people from the losing captives would be taken back to the Moche city to be paraded, bound and trussed, and would occasionally have their penises or hearts removed in public to signify their defeat.[5] In many ways, the main focus of Moche warfare was the post-battle taking of the life force of individuals in a public spectacle. This was the way in which battle were publicly demonstrated to be won, and these narratives were then told with objects and public art to ensure that the social memory of victory was preserved (fig. 5.14). As a result, the common use of iconography and public displays of killing in Andean art has a broader meaning than brutality and savagery: in the case of the Moche, it is a demonstration of power and indication of the value of the life force of those killed.[6] There is much debate among scholars about the relationship between the narrative scenes of ritual warfare and human sacrifice in Moche imagery.[7] However, recent archaeological discoveries have highlighted the correlation between representation and archaeological fact.[8] The Huacas de Moche site has two large adobe brick pyramids with a series of palace complexes and workshops. More than seventy individuals who have been identified as captives of battle have been ritually killed and buried at the site.[9] Scientific analysis suggests their throats were slit and their bodies were then sometimes mutilated and dismembered before being publicly displayed. Human crania were sometimes transformed into drinking vessels, with associated ceramics indicating that priests drank the blood of the victims as part of the sacrificial ceremony. The bodies were then placed in pits within the building structures, acting as a physical connection with the social memory of the dramatic acts of killing. These same narratives were then reinforced in the visual record of painted murals and painted ceramic vessels used at the site; the socially sanctioned justification for killing was therefore constructed around a wider context of violence and death.

Iconography of deliberate killing was prevalent in Andean society – whether it was the trussed and bound warriors of the Moche, the decapitated trophy heads of the Nasca (fig. 5.59),[10] the sacrificed children of the Chimú or the mummified remains of children killed on the mountaintops by the Incas, all reflect that killing had a central role as a form of power and control.[11] These examples are referred to as 'human sacrifice', but in essence they were homicides for socially accepted reasons. Each diverse Andean society had different motivations for their selection of who was killed and by what means, but they all reflect the cultural norms within their own social context. When they are compared with European warfare, the context

for justifying murder is different. In medieval Europe, killing an unarmed warrior after a battle was won was culturally unacceptable; it was against the principle of chivalry.[12] However, the killing of an armed man on the battlefield was both expected and celebrated. In Moche society, the opposite was the case: killing on the battlefield was a waste of valuable life force, because the correct place for killing was after the battle and back in the Moche heartland. The two acts are the same – murder – and it is only the context and rationale that change. A number of studies suggest that fewer people were killed as a percentage of the population in warfare in societies in the Americas than in comparable conflicts in Europe during the same period.[13] In the Andes, the losing side would return to their homes and continue their own way of life, albeit from a position of subjugation, with the required tributes of material goods and food made to the victors. Therefore, the justification of killing requires careful thought and reflection before judgements are made. The striking image of a person tied in ropes and about to be killed as a 'human sacrifice' is shocking to modern cultural sensibilities, not because of the difference in human behaviour but because of the contrast in justification. In today's media, these rituals are often sensationalised and Andean cultures are characterised as overly violent and savage, contributing to the Othering of their beliefs. But in reality this exposes a cognitive dissonance in how killing is socially sanctioned and justified in the West.

CHIMÚ SACRIFICE: POLITICS OF CONTROL

The children killed outside the walls of Chan Chan in the fifteenth century lie on top of a rare congealed layer of wet mud, indicating the impact of a recent El Niño-driven storm in this usually rainless environment. The evidence carefully excavated by archaeological director Dr Gabriel Prieto and his team suggests that the children were killed in order to stop an extreme weather event and as a political act of decisiveness in the face of a common threat to the Chimú way of life. Chimú concerns about the threat of extreme weather brought about by climate change are an interesting point of comparison with those widely felt today in the twenty-first century.[14] There is a shared belief that human actions and activity will directly influence the likelihood of climate change and the frequency of extreme weather events. There is also a shared understanding that actions as individuals will not be enough to effect change and therefore we are forced to rely on those in power to take the necessary steps to remedy the situation. This deferment of decision-making responsibility is done in the knowledge that such actions may adversely impact the quality

FIG.5.58 Figure of a naked and bound prisoner
Moche AD 100–800
Wood
H. 32.7 cm, W. 18 cm, D. 13.8 cm
British Museum, Am.7424
Donated by Josiah D. Harris

the future, this is culturally understood because those deaths are in the future and thus envisaged as indirect and abstract.[15] Within this way of understanding time, it would be completely unacceptable for any government to kill people in the present to save more people in the future. The relationship between present deaths and future deaths and between cause and effect are underpinned by a Western linear understanding of time. We sacrifice the lives of people in the future to avoid the immediate death of people in the present. Even if it could be logically argued, based on saving more people overall, the premise of cause and effect happening at the same time is not accepted. Because of this, today's solutions are situated as ambitions for the future with aspirations to cut emissions by a given deadline and hopes that we will later start to see a downward trajectory in CO_2 production.

In contrast, within Chimú culture, the origins and solutions of climate change and extreme weather are all in the present rather than the past and the future respectively. Time in the Andes was not linear but cyclical and interactive, so actions in the present immediately impacted the lives of those in the past and future. Therefore, in terms of a threat there is a direct responsibility and immediate need for action and political pressure to protect lives. Human actions and cultural acceptance of justified deaths are entirely contingent, and, in this case, divided by an understanding of time.[16] As anthropologist Johannes Fabian writes, 'To a large extent, Western rational disbelief in the presence of ancestors and the efficacy of magic rest on the rejection of ideas of temporal coexistence implied in these ideas and practices.'[17] The cultural logic of how life should be valued is rooted in the sense of time that determines the immediacy of action required. It does not mean that life itself in the Andean world was not valued – in fact, sacrifice can sometimes be a cultural statement of just how highly life is valued.

REVERENCE FOR THE DEAD

One reason we know so much about Andean societies is their exceptional reverence and care for the dead. They believed that the dead were in fact still alive in a parallel realm.[18] The earliest mummification in the world happened around 9,000 years ago in the Central Andes, and the careful preparation, wrapping and burial of the deceased reflects their beliefs in continued life. The ability to converse with the dead and even bring them out to participate in important decisions reflects this different attitude to death. Europeans recording Indigenous practices in the sixteenth century could not understand why mummies were brought out at significant

of life of individuals within society. Among the Chimú, and across the world today, there is an awareness that the decisions made by those in power will be closely bound up with political complexity related to retaining power, doing the 'right thing' and behaving according to accepted cultural beliefs and public opinion. Today it is widely believed that a failure to change people's behaviour will directly lead to more extreme weather, environmental disasters and the deaths of a significant portion of the population – the Chimú feared the same consequences.

However, a crucial difference between Andean cultures and contemporary Western cultures is in relation to their concepts of time and death. Around the world today, people can often distance themselves, and their leaders, from personal responsibility when it comes to climate change and extreme weather events. The origins of the problem are seen as being in the past, linked to historic events such as the Industrial Revolution or the invention of the combustion engine, while the expected impacts and window of opportunity for solutions stretch away into an unknown future. Even though people know that inaction now will lead to the deaths of people in

moments and were often asked to contribute to important decisions and moments of change. Such was the active role of the dead in Andean society, there was even a social hierarchy for the physical remains of the dead. The wrapped cadavers of the Inca elite were known as *mallki*, revered dead who actively participated in Andean life and whose power to influence the living remained. *Mallki* would often be brought out into public spaces or important meetings in Inca society as a physical representation of the continued involvement of the individual. This relationship with the dead, particularly in the form of mummified remains, reveals a complex understanding of death based on this connection between the living present and living past (see fig. 6.15). A prepared death was considered a passage into a parallel realm of time and space. Sometimes the *mallki* or dead could transform into stone, becoming a *waq'a*, which is why certain stones in the landscape can be identified as *wallqi*, a Quechua word for 'brother of brother', to refer to the permanence of the dead in the landscape of the living.[19]

Among Incas, this realm of *tirakuna* (powerful beings) dwelt in *waq'as* (sacred stones) or on *apus* (mountaintops). Special places such as mountaintops were sites where the dead, living and unborn came together. At the tops of many of the highest mountains in the Andes, the highest archaeological sites in the world have been found and excavated by high-altitude archaeologists.[20] Some of these sites include the remains of Inca children, who have been found killed on top of the mountains in order to be with the *tirakuna* on the *apus*, an Inca practice known as *Capacocha (see page 176).*[21] Scientific analyses reveal that the preparation of these children took many years. Those fated to be killed in the *Capacocha* ceremony as teenagers were often taken into special care from the age of four and prepared for their fate by religious practitioners. Isotopic evidence taken from their hair and teeth has revealed that more than a year before their death in their mid-teens, they would be taken on a tour of the Inca nation, reinforcing this sense of death as a public spectacle. They were fed a special diet, had parts of their hair ritually cut more than six months before death, were given coca to help them climb at high altitude and then killed on top of the mountain to remain there for centuries, often perfectly preserved in the ice. The differences in who was killed, where and how in Inca society when compared with the Moche examples discussed earlier highlight some of the cultural differences between Andean societies, but many of the principles that underpin their understandings of death, killing and sacrifice are linked. There is a connection between the act of killing and the carefully chosen location in the landscape; the intricate

relationships between time and space; and the ability of deceased individuals to move between parallel realms. The shared ideas of sustaining the world that supports life through death are concepts crucial for understanding the Andean world.[22]

ACCEPTING DEATH

All cultures have justifications for death, killing and sacrifice: it is the different social contexts and exceptions, rather than a dissimilarity in behaviour itself, that provokes our moral reaction. In most countries today, death can happen only in a limited number of legally defined ways: natural causes, unlawful killing, lawful killing, suicide, and accident or misadventure. These distinctions do permit the killing of others for a number of legally defined reasons, such as self-defence, defence of others and government-approved war. In many cultures, sacrifice is often rewarded, socially accepted and even celebrated. Military honours reward the taking of opposition soldiers' lives and commend commanders who make the difficult decision to send troops into situations where they are likely to die. In fact, the main difference between using the word 'sacrifice' instead of 'killing' or 'death' is the implication of the assumed ideological reason for the act of 'sacrifice'. Therefore, the key question is how a society decides what justifies death and killing: what do people accept it is worth dying or killing for? Be it swearing to God to kill for the Queen in the UK,[23] or swearing to Ai-Apaec to kill for the Moche rulers in ancient Peru, the ideological distinctions between death, killing and sacrifice in different cultural frameworks are not always as clear as they may first seem.

The act of looking at death through a different cultural lens of time can radically change and challenge our own cultural perceptions. Is the nature of relationships between the dead, living and unborn thoughtfully understood in today's society? Should the relationships between cause and effect, human action and impact, and life and death be considered in a different light – and if they were, would our cultural understanding of what constitutes acceptable sacrifice change? All too often with judgements of human behaviour, if something is outside the accepted norm, it is deemed wrong, savage or uncivilised. A rejection of the Other, of anything that strays beyond our own societal boundaries, means that our capacity for alternative understandings is limited. If we take the time to understand the Andean worldviews represented in this book, our imaginations can be opened up to different judgements of the past and alternative ideas for the future.

FIG. 5.59 Vessel depicting an individual holding a severed head
Nasca 100 BC–AD 650
Pottery
H. 16.8 cm, W. 15.2 cm, D. 17 cm
British Museum, Am1954,05.808
Donated by the Wellcome Institute

6 Empires in the sky: Waris and Incas

The rise of empires: Waris and Incas

Andrew James Hamilton

The Incas hold an unrivalled place in Peruvian cultural history. They are the only Andean civilisation that has really gained international, popular recognition. This stands in contrast to, say, Mexico, where both the Aztecs and Mayas have become widely known, and where Teotihuacan is visually familiar to many.[1] This awareness allows Mesoamerican culture history to be understood as long and sequential. However, within cultural perceptions of Peru, the Incas' singular reputation affords them outsized importance but also eclipses their many predecessors. Around the world, many people may be unaware that these famous builders of Machu Picchu were merely the culmination of a cultural tradition spanning thousands of years, as this book so richly details. But the Incas' hegemony also impacts scholarship. Inca ideas, beliefs and terms – especially ones elaborated upon in colonial chronicles – are often projected backwards on to earlier cultures, 'Inca-ising' them, when in reality the cultural influence flowed in the opposite direction.

Indeed, Inca culture and art were both predicated on the achievements of their forebears and a deliberate reaction to them. Their empire may have lasted only a little more than a hundred years: perhaps rising in the late 1300s before being dramatically cut short by Spanish invaders, beginning in the 1530s. There is evidence that the Incas were self-conscious of their relative newcomer status. When they first founded their capital Cusco at the junction of two rivers in a high intermontane valley in southern Peru, they had only recently migrated to this area (fig. 6.4). Their mythologies, in part, positioned themselves as the inheritors of a much older and greater cultural tradition to the south-east, a mammoth pilgrimage centre called Tiwanaku that was built on the shores of Lake Titicaca in Bolivia from as early as 200 BC and which reached its peak between AD 500 and 900. As Juan Diez de Betanzos and other sixteenth-century Spanish chroniclers recorded, Incas believed that their creator deity Viracocha formed humans from the clay and stones around the edge of the lake.[2] And when Inca masons constructed Cusco, they may have sought to create visual reminders of this heritage by emulating the dressed stone walls of this powerful predecessor – at that point already in ruins (fig. 6.1). However, scholars who have studied the technical relationship between Tiwanaku and Inca stonework have cast doubt on the idea

that there was any kind of direct lineage, concluding that there was only a superficial similarity.[3]

In fact, the Incas' capital was not actually located within former Tiwanaku lands; rather, it occupied what had been the territory of their equally impressive contemporaries, the Waris, whose empire had centred around the citadel of Wari to the west of Cusco (fig. 6.2). It is currently thought that the Waris and Tiwanakus coexisted peacefully.[4] The two shared many elements of material culture but had very different architectural styles (fig. 6.3). While Tiwanaku was designed as a public complex, employing architecture of mass and volume such as stepped pyramids and walled plazas to receive large numbers of people, Wari was a warren of passageways and mid-sized rooms. Its most significant temples, which had a D shape, were fairly small and could accommodate only limited numbers of people. It is hard for us to make fair comparisons between Wari and Inca architecture because so much of Cusco was obliterated under colonial rule; but, surviving Inca ceremonial architecture may bear a greater resemblance to Wari structures in terms of their scale and accessibility.

Another significant connection between the Inca and Wari empires had to do with the ways they recorded information. The Incas used fibre, the most important technology of the Andes, to create a notational system of branching knotted cords, called a *khipu*, which means 'knot' in Quechua (figs 6.5–6.8). The Wari used fibre to create similar devices, but they employed a number of different structures, such as cords tied in loops and segments of cords wrapped with finer, more colourful threads. Many Wari *khipus* do not even contain knots – which raises the questions of what their makers would have called them and how scholars should refer to these devices if not by their later Inca name. Because we cannot yet fully decipher either Wari or Inca *khipus*, unfortunately we cannot establish how closely related their notational systems really were.[5]

Incas and Waris also shared an affinity for fine textiles, especially tunics, garments that were typically worn by men in Andean cultures. The most accomplished Wari tunics were woven in tapestry weave, were longer than they were wide, and had motifs that – to Euro-American eyes – might seem highly abstracted and geometricised (fig. 6.12). A Wari jar in the form of a man bears a painted representation of one of

PAGE 156 The walls of the Inca site
of Sacsayhuamán, with the city of
Cusco in the background

FIG. 6.1 An Inca street in Cusco

FIG. 6.2 Map of the Wari Empire

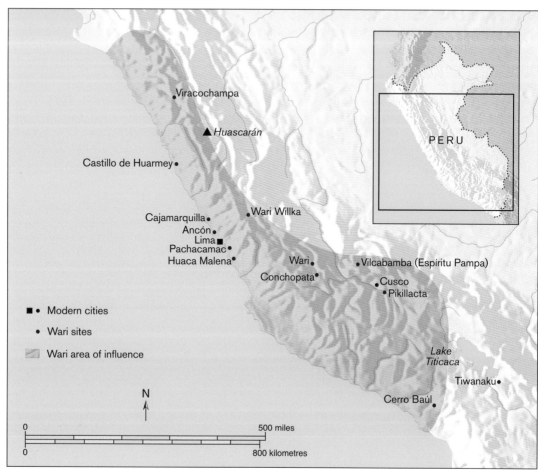

- Viracochampa
- ▲ *Huascarán*
- Castillo de Huarmey •
- Cajamarquilla •
- • Wari Willka
- Ancón •
- Lima ■
- Pachacamac •
- Huaca Malena •
- Wari •
- • Vilcabamba (Espíritu Pampa)
- Conchopata •
- Cusco •
- • Pikillacta
- *Lake Titicaca*
- Tiwanaku •
- Cerro Baúl •

PERU

■ • Modern cities
• Wari sites
░ Wari area of influence

N

0 ————————— 500 miles
0 ————————— 800 kilometres

these tunics that helps us understand the images the weavers wove (fig. 6.9). One half of each motif is a face in profile, while the other half is a stepped-fret pattern, a long-standing Andean design (see pages 46–7). This particular Wari tunic was actually excavated in Ancón (just north of Lima, on the Pacific coast), quite far from the Wari capital, indicating the great extent of Wari power and suggesting why Incas may have been so keen to embrace their legacy.[6] The finest Inca tunics were very similar, in that they were also tapestry woven, longer than they were wide, and tended to feature motifs that seem abstract (fig. 6.14). As a consequence, scholars grapple with how to refer to the designs (such as this one, dubbed 'the Inca Key'), which was likely worn by certain Inca officials. However, Wari and Inca tunics were fundamentally different in other ways. Wari tunics were usually constructed from two panels that were seamed together along the centre of the chest and down the middle of the back. Inca tunics, in contrast, were generally one solid panel. This meant that they would have been made on looms of totally different dimensions. On the whole, Wari tunics also tended to be of finer fabrics with higher thread counts – although this may be a consequence of differential preservation. (Many fine Inca tunics may have still been in use at the time of the Spanish conquest, and were worn throughout the colonial period until they were eventually worn out; the very finest Inca tunics, belonging to the emperor, were ritually burned.) Thus, while Incas may

have been reinventing or visually referencing their formidable ancestors, what they were doing, what ultimately allowed their empire to expand and unite more territories across the Andes than ever before and in such a short period of time, was something wholly new.

Indeed, as Cusco grew, the Incas fell into a conflict with their neighbours, the Chancas, sometime in the 1430s and eventually proceeded to conquer them.[7] It is as if this set off a chain reaction. From that point forward, each Inca ruler after the next added more and more communities and territories to their burgeoning empire – which they called 'Tawantinsuyu', meaning the four parts united – until it stretched along the spine of the Andes from southern Colombia to the middle of Chile. As they did so, they not only continued to reflect their mighty predecessors, but also absorbed traits of the many contemporaries they conquered. For example, when Inca Emperor Túpac Inca Yupanqui defeated the powerful Chimú kingdom on the north coast of Peru, possibly in the 1470s, he was duly impressed with their riches, especially objects made of precious metals. As the Spanish chronicler Pedro Cieza de León recounted, Túpac Inca Yupanqui rounded up the Chimú goldsmiths and brought them to Cusco to create such works for the Inca state.[8] Thus, it is possible that many gold and silver 'Inca' objects, such as the reduced-scale llama (see fig. 0.2), reduced-scale figures (figs 6.26–6.28) and *tupu* pins in this book (see figs 7.21–7.27), may actually have been made by Chimú hands.

FIG. 6.4 Map of the Inca Empire, showing its influence and extent

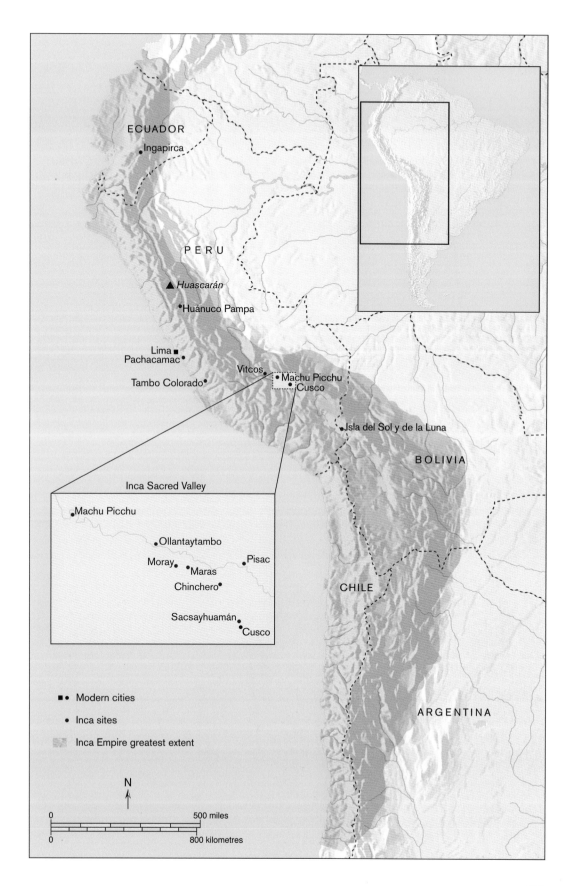

ECUADOR
• Ingapirca

PERU

▲ Huascarán
• Huánuco Pampa

Lima ■
Pachacamac •
Vitcos • • Machu Picchu
Tambo Colorado • Cusco

• Isla del Sol y de la Luna

BOLIVIA

Inca Sacred Valley

• Machu Picchu

• Ollantaytambo
Moray • • Pisac
• Maras
Chinchero •

Sacsayhuamán •
• Cusco

CHILE

ARGENTINA

■ • Modern cities

• Inca sites

Inca Empire greatest extent

N

0   500 miles
0   800 kilometres

Andean civilisations used string devices to record information, which Incas called *khipus*. Wari examples often featured cords tied in circles and cords wrapped with colourful threads. Inca *khipus* lacked these traits and bore a greater variety of knots. Colonial sources suggest that Incas used *khipus* as accounting devices, as well as for recording narrative information. Unfortunately, scholarly knowledge of how to read *khipus* remains limited. In the 1920s, L. Leland Locke deciphered the system of knots that Incas used to inscribe numbers. However, numerous *khipus* bear knots that do not follow this system. The significance and relevance of other traits – like colour, knot directionality and branching structures – remain unclear.

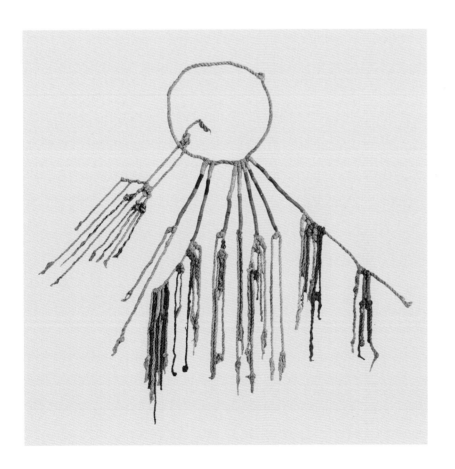

FIG. 6.5 (LEFT) *Khipu*
Wari AD 600–900
Cotton, camelid fibres and natural dyes
L. 26.5 cm, W. 7 cm
Fundación Temple Radicati, 2007.16.2 (TR12Q8)

FIG. 6.6 (ABOVE) 'Chief accountant and treasurer, Tawantin Suyu Khipuq Kuraka, keeper of the *khipu*', illustrated by Felipe Guamán Poma de Ayala in *El primer nueva crónica y buen gobierno*, 1615, p. 360, drawing no. 143. The Royal Library, Copenhagen, GKS 2232 4°

FIG. 6.7 (RIGHT) In *khipus*, numbers were inscribed vertically within each hanging cord. In this example, the knots clustered around the middle record the 'units' digits, while the knots embedded in the upper half of the cords signify the 'tens' digits.

Khipu
Inca AD 1400–1532
Textile cords and knots
L. 45 cm, W. 34 cm
British Museum, Am1937,0213.84
Donated by John Goble

FIG. 6.8 (BELOW) Hypothetical cords show how Incas would have recorded various kinds of numbers, both through different types of knots and their placements

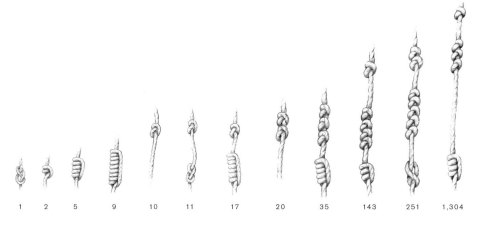

| 1 | 2 | 5 | 9 | 10 | 11 | 17 | 20 | 35 | 143 | 251 | 1,304 |

In the Wari Empire, elite men often wore four-cornered hats that complemented their finely woven tunics. The squarish hats were shaped by knotting. Their makers formed the intricate designs by adding short lengths of brightly dyed fibre, creating a pile like a minute carpet. The resulting hats were quite small and would have been worn on top of the head rather than actually encompassing it. These accessories were clearly an integral part of Wari male costumes, as they were regularly recreated in ceramic figures and vessels shaped like figures – such as the one on the facing page, which likely originally held two staffs.

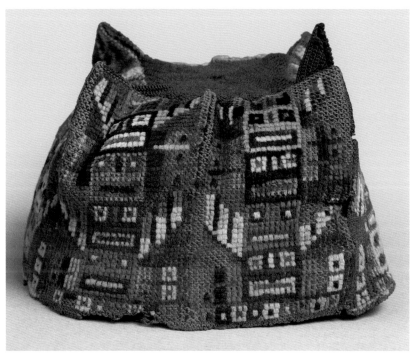

FIG. 6.9 (OPPOSITE) Figure of an elite male wearing a ceremonial shirt and a four-cornered hat
Wari AD 600–900
Pottery
H. 28.7 cm, W. 23 cm
Museo Amano, FMAC-000020

FIG. 6.10 (TOP) Four-cornered hat
Wari AD 600–900
Camelid fibres, cotton
H. 10 cm, W. 17 cm, D. 15 cm
British Museum, Am2006,Q.1

FIG. 6.11 (BOTTOM) Four-cornered hat
Wari AD 600–900
Camelid fibres, cotton
H. 10 cm, W. 13 cm, D. 13 cm
British Museum, Am1951,14.1

This elaborately woven tunic covered the exterior of a Wari mummy. The deceased was excavated around 1870 from a sprawling burial site discovered at Ancón, just north of Lima. Although the dig was led by two German volcanologists, Wilhelm Reiss and Alphons Stübel, it was one of the first systematic archaeological excavations conducted in Peru. The numerous artefacts were brought to Berlin and extensively studied at the Königliches Museum für Völkerkunde, now the Ethnologisches Museum. Reiss and Stübel collaborated with painter Julius Fiebiger and lithographer Wilhelm Greve to illustrate the artefacts lavishly. Between 1880 and 1887, they serially published *The Necropolis of Ancón in Peru*, a multi-volume set of elephant folios with nearly 150 images of over 1,000 artefacts.

FIG. 6.12 (LEFT) Tunic worn by a mummy
Wari AD 500–800
Camelid fibres
H. 140.2 cm, W. 120.2 cm
Ethnologisches Museum, Staatliche Museen
zu Berlin, V A 7468

FIG. 6.13 (ABOVE) A funerary bundle displaying the Wari tunic. Wilhelm Greve, 'Plate 16, Sumptuous Mummy Pack', lithograph from Wilhelm Reiss and Alphons Stübel, *The Necropolis of Ancón in Peru: A Contribution to our Knowledge of the Culture and Industries of the Empire of the Incas, being the results of excavations made on the spot by W. Reiss and A. Stübel*, Berlin: A. Asher & Co., 1880–7, vol. I, p. 64. British Museum, fKUU [REI-]V.1

FIG.6.14 Tunic
Inca AD 1450–1532
Camelid fibres
H. 88 cm, W. 70 cm
Ethnologisches Museum, Staatliche Museen
zu Berlin, V A 31526

What has been less often observed, however, is that as this occurred, Incas may have adopted or adapted the royal Chimú funerary rites that utilised these objects. A reduced-scale model of a Chimú burial or scene of ancestor worship may materially record such an event (see fig. 5.45). Even at these small dimensions, we can appreciate the pomp and circumstance that may have inspired Inca rulers to supposedly invent, as Diez de Betanzos alleged, a new royal funerary rite they called the Purucaya that Túpac Inca Yupanqui first performed to observe the death of his father Pachacuti.[9] Ultimately, Incas did not bury their deceased kings and queens; rather, their mummified bodies continued to reside with the living in their palaces, being fed, dressed and feted – possibly in a similar manner to Chimú rulers (fig. 6.15). Thus, as Incas appropriated these many skills, practices and belief systems, they seemingly recast them as 'Inca'.

What the Chimú example makes clear is that the Incas were not just co-opting certain objects and rituals but, above all, diverse peoples. Incas were expert amalgamators. Certainly, their armies were essential in this; but the real mechanism that allowed their empire to grow with such alacrity was their administration and infrastructure. Similar to how they relocated the metal workers, Inca administrators would uproot whole groups of newly conquered peoples and transplant them to staunchly loyal regions of their empire with a similar climate and topography, then move new batches of Inca settlers into the vacated areas. These acts of dislocation and reconfiguration meant that conquered peoples could only remain united with their satellite communities through the political enterprise of the Inca Empire. Inca administrators were able to move such large populations because they built an extensive network of roads, the Qhapaq Ñan, connecting distant parts of their empire.[10] Given the extremely mountainous terrain, they also excelled at engineering suspension bridges to traverse deep chasms. And, just as they moved people along these roads and bridges, they also moved goods. When they conquered new lands, they set aside a portion of them for state use. The harvests from these plots were, among other things, used to fill the state's system of storehouses. In them, administrators stockpiled goods and supplies from across the empire that could be redistributed to these many peoples when crops failed or natural disasters such as El Niño occurred. Inca administrators were able to achieve all these roads, bridges and agricultural work by requiring all denizens of the Inca Empire to complete an annual amount of labour for the state.

But perhaps one of the greatest and most lasting creations of Inca workers – still visible throughout the highlands, whether seen from the window of a bus or explored virtually

FIG. 6.15 A mummy bundle being ceremonially carried on a litter. 'La fiesta de los defuntos', illustrated by Felipe Guamán Poma de Ayala in *El primer nueva crónica y buen gobierno*, 1615, p. 258, drawing no. 100. The Royal Library, Copenhagen, GKS 2232 4°

through Google Maps – are the omnipresent scars of disused terraces arrayed across the mountainsides. Because of the steep topography, wide open fields were few, and Incas laboured to terraform the slopes with vast cascades of agricultural terraces (see fig. 6.37). Brilliant feats of engineering, the terraces kept rich topsoil from being washed away; and, during deluges, they forestalled mudslides. Because this region is so close to the equator, growing zones are not actually determined by latitude, but rather by elevation. By creating protective microclimates, terraces extended the areas where warmer-growing crops could be cultivated. Some of the most famous Inca terraces are at Moray, just north-west of Cusco (see fig. 6.39). Rather than being arranged in parallel lines, these were built in striking concentric circles that descend into the ground. Their unusual shapes help us recognise that this proliferation of terraces was not just a tool for farming: Incas constructed them with significant aesthetic intentions. These sprawling earthworks were like a kind of land art, re-sculpting the mountains according to Inca principles. They effected a cultural idealisation of the natural world as discernible and unique as a formal French garden or a rambling English park.

At the same time, it is important to realise that for the Incas the natural world was indivisible from the supernatural. For example, in their battle against the Chancas, Incas claimed that an army of boulders named *pururaucas* decided to animate and come to their aid. Incas also believed that rocks could grow tired and even cry. The natural world, thus, had to be worshipped and celebrated so that it might look kindly on those who depended on its bounty. Spanish chroniclers and extirpators recorded various rituals that Incas performed to fructify their fields. To make libations of maize beer, Incas may have used a vessel shaped like a foot plough or *chakitaqlla*, an ear of corn, and a reduced-scale version of another typical Inca vessel called an *urpu* (see fig. 6.43). This trinity might seem peculiar, but it was almost certainly meant to represent the agricultural cycle in its totality: the foot plough that planted the kernel, which grew into a corn stalk and produced an ear, which in turn was fermented into maize beer stored in *urpus* (see figs 6.40–6.42), which finally was poured back into the ground as an offering to bless the kernel.

The movement and flow of irrigating liquid was a powerful force in Inca beliefs.[11] Thus, Incas created many ritual objects called *pacchas* that were designed to feature the flow of liquid, either pouring into a stream or running through channels (see fig. 7.28). Other *pacchas*, often made of stone, were shaped like basins and seemed to emphasise the collection or containment of liquid (fig. 6.16; see also fig. 7.29). This large *paccha* with handles was carved with coiled and writhing snakes, perhaps symbolically drawn to the cool, refreshing liquid inside the vessel, and of ritual significance. Given that they were made of stone, such objects may have referenced the pooling and puddling of rainwater on exposed rocks, whether boulders or bedrock. One of the largest and now most famous *pacchas* is a boulder at a temple complex called Saywite, west of Cusco, that Incas carved with a reduced-scale landscape flush with cisterns for holding water and chutes for releasing it (fig. 6.17). The Saywite Stone was most likely activated by rain and may have been used in rituals to try to coax the rainy season's return or convince it to cease. Finally, Incas also made ceremonial wooden cups, called *keros*, for drinking toasts of maize beer – likely extending these notions of the sacred flows of liquids to the human body and its functions (see fig. 7.18).

Not only was this reverence of the natural world evident in formal rituals and state-level practices, but also in peoples' everyday lives. Incas took care of hearth deities called *conopas*, which they believed were responsible for the productivity of their crops and herds. *Conopas* could be made from a variety of materials – most often unusual or colourful stones. Although they could be iconic or aniconic, the ones most commonly recognised in scholarship are shaped like rotund and fleecy llamas. Households might make offerings of llama fat to their *conopas*, placing it in a well or depression in the animals' backs, in the hope that they would ensure prosperity for the family's actual herds. Clearly, the object was not a sculpture or a vessel, but an animate being. As colonial documents show, *conopas* could have names, could feel happy, dejected and seemingly even lonely – such that human caretakers might offer their *conopa* a wife for company. Although most camelid *conopas* manifest diverse colours and shapes, a subset were carved from solid black rock in a standardised and stylised form (see figs 6.32–6.33). Highly polished, these may have been a type of imperial Inca *conopa*, possibly serving as gifts to regional lords and officials in order to indoctrinate communities in this Inca practice.

Of course the most well-known – but not necessarily well-understood – facet of Inca culture is Machu Picchu (see page 172). Popularly, some may assume that this was the only settlement of its kind that the Incas built. In fact, it was and is not singular. Machu Picchu was a royal estate – like Balmoral Castle or the Sandringham Estate. Thought to have belonged to Emperor Pachacuti, it was built at a lower elevation than the capital to take advantage of warmer temperatures, especially during the cold nights of the dry season. It was likely continually inhabited by a small community of caretakers and agricultural labourers, and only periodically visited by Pachacuti and his royal court. Pachacuti seemingly had numerous other royal estates and presumably would have divided his time between them. In fact, tourists who visit Machu Picchu by train usually depart from another of his estates, Ollantaytambo. And, just beyond Machu Picchu – currently reachable only by a multi-day hike – is the far larger royal estate of Choquequirao (fig. 6.18). While Machu Picchu is marketed to tourists as a one-of-a-kind destination, the real wonder is how many other, similarly impressive, Inca archaeological sites still exist and can be visited.

A final misconception about Machu Picchu – which in fact originated with one of its first foreign visitors, the explorer Hiram Bingham – was that this site was 'the lost city of the Incas' and the settlement that they eventually retreated to after the Spanish invasion. This is incorrect.

FIG.6.16 Container with snakes
carved on the sides
Inca AD 1400–1532
Volcanic stone
H. 17.5 cm, W. 62 cm
British Museum, Am1991,Q.4

FIG.6.17 The upper surface of the
Saywite Stone in Apurímac, west of
Cusco, was carved with scores of humans,
animals and architectural features, as
well as numerous cisterns, chutes for
conducting liquid and holes for draining
it. Incas likely used the intricate reduced-
scale landscape in rituals to attempt to
beckon or quell rains.

Saywite Stone
Inca AD 1400–1532
Andesite (volcanic stone)
H. 2.5 m, W. 2.5 m, D. 3 m
Saywite, Apurímac, Peru

FIG.6.18 The Inca royal estate
of Choquequirao

That site, originally called Vilcabamba, has been identified as yet another ruin now called Espíritu Pampa. History books often state that the Spanish conquest took place in 1532; but, from an Inca perspective, it lasted some four decades. Driven from Cusco, Inca kings continued to rule at Vilcabamba until 1572. During this time period, Inca makers persevered in creating fine tunics while incorporating subtle European influences (see fig. 7.14). They also developed new artistic styles, using, for example, colourfully pigmented mopa mopa

resin to elaborate *pacchas* and *keros* (see figs 7.19 and 7.20). But perhaps most importantly, Indigenous intellectuals and artists such as Felipe Guamán Poma de Ayala and a number of other anonymous illustrators set out to learn European textual traditions and graphic styles so that they could take active roles in documenting the history of their people in order to counter Spanish narratives (figs 6.6 and 6.15).[12] For scholars today, these Indigenous accounts have become among the most important sources for understanding Inca history.

Machu Picchu

Cecilia Pardo

Very few places in the world spark people's interest and curiosity like the sacred citadel of Machu Picchu. Attracting over 4,000 tourists daily, it is a worldwide landmark and the symbol of a culture that was indeed much more than one site. Machu Picchu was one of several palaces built by Incas in a place known as the Sacred Valley of the Incas, 60 kilometres north-west of Cusco, the empire's capital city.[1]

With a name that means 'Ancient Mountain', Machu Picchu is located within a secluded cloud forest, 2,650 metres above sea level, and surrounded by a deep meander generated by the course of the Urubamba river through the southern Andean highlands of Peru. It was built in the fifteenth century during the reigns of Inca Pachacuti and his son, Túpac Inca Yupanqui.[2] The site is comprised of around two hundred buildings – built with polished stone walls in the classic Inca architectural style – which were strategically adapted to fit the landscape. The urban sector is surrounded by agricultural terraces where crops were grown to feed the local inhabitants. Temples, residential compounds, large plazas, stairways and water channels are among the diverse elements of architecture that one can encounter when visiting the site. Its builders wisely modified the topography, creating a system of artificial mounds and terraced pyramids in order to obtain multiple pieces of level terrain. Granite rock, abundant in local quarries, was carefully cut so that the pieces could fit together without the use of mortar when building the magnificent tall walls.

While Machu Picchu's main function is still under discussion, it is very likely that it was built to establish an administrative and ceremonial palace on the outskirts of Cusco, as a means of expanding the agricultural boundaries during the peak of the empire, and thereby establishing a link between the highlands and the Amazon. By standing at the top of Machu Picchu one can establish visual contact with a long chain of mountains, a group of which are still considered to be *huacas* (sacred places). In Andean traditions, these powerful *huacas* exercised control over the fertility of animals and agriculture and over the protection of local populations. Incas took advantage of the many resources growing in the tropical forests of the Amazon, including fruits, vegetables, medicinal and ornamental plants, and other herbs used in rituals. Although they never conquered the peoples of the eastern region, known as *ch'unchus* or *antis*, they established connecting routes for the exchange of goods. Machu Picchu and other sites might have functioned as strategic hubs: evidence for this can be found in the many roads that connect the mountain site with neighbouring regions.

While Machu Picchu is mentioned by early Spanish chroniclers in the sixteenth and seventeenth centuries, and documented later on by nineteenth-century European explorers, it was Hiram Bingham (1875–1956), a professor at Yale University, who brought it to worldwide attention.

FIGS 6.19–6.20 Machu Picchu
1938
Photographs
H. 23 cm, W. 17 cm (each)
British Museum, Am,B53.5, Am,B53.6

FIG. 6.21 (OPPOSITE) A present-day view of the Inca site of Machu Picchu

In 1911, Bingham embarked on an exploration of the southern Andean region in search of the lost city of Vilcabamba, thought to be the last Inca bastion of Indigenous resistance during the first decades that followed the arrival of the Europeans.[3] However, on his way to Vilcabamba, and thanks to the information provided by a local named Melchor Arteaga, he stepped into a place that astounded him. When Bingham arrived at Machu Picchu on 24 July, two local families were living at the site. Over the next four years Bingham uncovered a series of buildings hidden under growing vegetation, which had been ignored by researchers and authorities. At the time, the reignited worldwide interest in Machu Picchu motivated the local intellectuals in Cusco to rediscover Inca culture, encouraging the ideology behind the Indigenismo movement of the 1920s – which, among other principles, claimed the revival of the Inca image in modern culture.

The popularity of Machu Picchu continued to grow throughout the twentieth century (figs 6.19–6.20), and it was declared a UNESCO World Heritage Site in 1983. In 2007 it was named as one of the New Seven Wonders of the World, a recognition that was reaffirmed by the New Seven Wonders Foundation in 2019. Today, Machu Picchu has been reimagined and romanticised in various guises as 'the' archaeological site of Peru, and is constantly presented as the symbol of the country. But Peru is so much more than this distilled image of a single place, and Machu Picchu itself is so much more too (fig. 6.21). Its relevance as one of the Incas' greatest architectural achievements – immersed in a remarkable, secluded environment at the convergence of highlands and tropical forest – and its key historic function as a hub for social interaction are just some of the reasons for our attraction to such an iconic site.

An analysis of coca leaves

Caroline R. Cartwright

In Andean cultures the chewing of coca leaves for their stimulative, medicinal and digestive properties can be traced to pre-Columbian times. The genus *Erythroxylum* (Erythroxylaceae family) contains 259 currently accepted species (some with subspecies), but few of these species contain sufficient alkaloids to be chosen for chewing as a stimulant.

In the Department of Scientific Research at the British Museum, I used variable pressure scanning electron microscopy (VP SEM) in order to identify camelid and cotton fibres in six Paracas and Nasca embroidered textiles. The inside of one of these textiles, a bag (fig. 6.23), was sampled for any traces of coca leaves. Tiny particulate material was found and examined using a scanning electron microscope.[1] The resulting magnifications were up to 600 times larger and the working distances ranged from 10 mm to 14 mm, and 3D mode was selected to maximise diagnostic features for identification. Present-day coca leaves were used for comparative reference. The VP SEM examination of the small specks of material from inside the bag revealed sufficient diagnostic features to identify some of the material as fragments of *Erythroxylum* sp. coca leaves (fig. 6.22). Also present were stem segments of *Erythroxylum* sp. and tiny lumps of calcium. The presence of calcium is particularly intriguing: some published archaeological data interprets it as evidence for early cultures baking calcium-bearing rocks to produce lime. This would in turn help them to extract alkaloids from the coca leaves in order to enjoy the stimulating effects.[2] It is fascinating to discover that with the use of scanning electron microscopy we can analyse such tiny specks of material to confirm the function of this textile as a coca bag.

FIG. 6.22 (LEFT) One of the specks of material found inside the textile bag (fig. 6.23), showing a fragment of coca leaf (*Erythroxylum* sp.) with tiny white calcium particles and other detrital particles on its surface. This image was created using variable pressure scanning electron microscopy (VP SEM).

FIG. 6.23 (ABOVE) Coca bag
Inca AD 1400–1532
Camelid fibres
H. 52.5 cm, W. 19 cm
British Museum, Am1921,0312.12

According to ethnohistorical records and scientific studies, these bags were probably used to carry coca leaves, as part of the *chacchado* (coca chewing). This practice, still in use by Andean communities, consists of chewing and keeping a cud of coca leaves in the mouth between the cheek and jaw, so that the liquids can be absorbed.

FIG. 6.24 Coca bag
Wari influence AD 800–1000
Camelid fibres
H. 34 cm, W. 31 cm
British Museum, Am1954,05.525
Donated by the Wellcome Institute

FIG. 6.25 Coca bag depicting two zoomorphic figures
Nasca–Wari AD 600–800
Camelid fibres
H. 43 cm, W. 16 cm
British Museum, Am1954,05.495
Donated by the Wellcome Institute

Capacocha rituals

Andrew Hamilton

Scale played an important role in the Inca intellectual tradition. The Inca people commanded an ethnically diverse empire in which numerous different languages were spoken. Scaled relationships offered non-verbal ways of communicating complex ideas, beliefs and meanings. As a result, they created numerous miniature or reduced-scale objects that conjured the concept or significance of their referent objects – for example, the Saywite Stone, the *paccha*, and numerous *conopas* (see figs 6.32–6.33 and 7.27–7.29). Incas also made many reduced-scale gold, silver and *Spondylus* shell figures (figs 6.26–6.28). They dressed them in painstakingly woven reduced-scale garments, where even the embroidery stitches decorating the selvages were minutely recreated (figs 6.29–6.30). Far from toys, these were potent offerings used in a variety of rituals. In fact, they played a central role in the most solemn of all Inca ceremonies: the Capacocha. In Capacocha rituals, children – who were likely perceived to be reduced-scale embodiments of all Inca people – were sacrificed with other reduced-scale offerings to ensure the wellbeing of society as a whole. Capacocha ceremonies took place throughout the Inca Empire, often to mark important occasions such as the coronation of a new ruler, royal weddings and royal deaths. It was felt that by sacrificing the thing that was desired – healthy, young children who symbolised the bounty of the empire – the empire would reciprocally receive that bounty on a greater scale. In recent decades, archaeologists have excavated a number of Capacocha burials located on high mountain peaks, the most significantly scaled points within the landscape, in distant corners of the Inca Empire where they had remained undisturbed for centuries.[1]

FIG. 6.26 Reduced-scale figure
Inca AD 1400–1532
Gold
H. 5.7 cm, W. 1.6 cm, D. 1.2 cm
British Museum, Am1927,1007.6
Donated by Col. F. H. Ward

FIG. 6.27 Reduced-scale figure
Inca AD 1400–1532
Gold
H. 5.8 cm, W. 1.6 cm, D. 1.7 cm
British Museum, Am1847,0527.2

FIG. 6.28 Reduced-scale figure
Inca AD 1400–1532
Gold
H. 5.7 cm, W. 1.5 cm, D. 1.9 cm
British Museum, Am.7082
Donated by Augustus Wollaston Franks

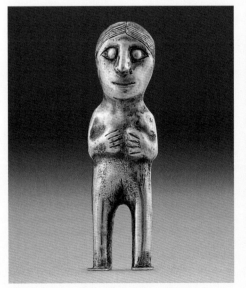

FIG. 6.29 (RIGHT) Half of a miniature shawl
with cord and shawl pins
Inca AD 1400–1532
Camelid fibres; cotton and metal
H. 15.3 cm, W. 8.3 cm (shawl); L. 12 cm (cord and pin)
British Museum, Am1862,0611.2; Am1862,0611.4.a–b
Donated by William Bollaert

FIG. 6.30 (BELOW) Miniature tunic
Inca AD 1400–1532
Camelid fibre, cotton
H. 16.7 cm, W. 16 cm
British Museum, Am1923,1208.2
Donated by Countess Elena Donoughmore

Conopas

Bill Sillar and Amelia Perez Trujillo

Inca art includes very little figurative or realistic imagery, most ceramics, textiles and architectural embellishments appearing to our eyes to be abstract or geometric. However, a major exception to this are small carved stone figurines depicting crops and animals, particularly llamas and alpacas with hollows in their backs. These objects are referred to as *conopas* in early colonial documents that explain how native Andean people used them in the preparation of offerings, which are very comparable to aspects of animism practised in the Peruvian Andes today (fig. 6.31).

Many people in the Andes understand the world as a multitude of sentient places, objects, plants and animals that communicate with each other. Landscape features such as particular mountains, lakes, rocks, fields and houses are named living beings that are capable of transmitting vitality. Humans are a part of this animate world, with responsibilities to care for and work with it, including making offerings to feed the earth. Preparing offerings of coca leaves and libations of *chicha* beer (derived from maize) can be a daily occurrence, but special offerings at specified times of the year involve a more complex sequence of materials and gestures using ritual objects, such as *conopas*, that participate in the preparation of these offerings.

The offerings process is a careful choreography of meaningful and animate materials. Bringing ingredients together and verbal evocations activate and direct the offering. Objects that feature in household rituals today include small carved stone animals that are inherited or acquired at annual pilgrimage sites, as well as various 'found' objects such as unmodified stones and pieces of glass. These objects, referred to in Quechua today as *enqa* or *illa*, are considered to be living entities that support animal and crop fertility. *Illa* and *enqa* are described as children of the mountain deities (*apus*), or as emerging from the caves or springs of *ukhu pacha* (the inner world). Mountain peaks are understood to be the most powerful entities in the animate landscape of the Andes. The mountains are considered to be ambivalent earth beings or deities, which can either protect or threaten the endeavours of Andean people, and are referred to by the Quechua word for a lord or authority (*apu*).

The modern community of Raqchi, to the south of Cusco, is a village of agriculturalists and artisans living next to the Inca site of Cacha (see page 181). At least once a year they prepare their household offerings, during which coca leaves are dedicated to a named recipient (for example, specific houses, fields, pastures, paths, roads and market places) before being sent to the *apus* by being burnt. Making these offerings expresses a commitment to work with the land and herd the animals. During these rituals, the carved animal *illa* are said to drink the *chicha* and chew the coca, while they communicate the beneficiaries of the offering to the mountain *apus*.[1]

Conopa is the word most commonly used in early colonial documents (and still used in the Apurímac region today) to describe these ritual objects

FIG. 6.31 A modern offering being prepared in the Andes

(figs 6.32–6.33). In 1621 the Spanish Jesuit missionary Pablo José de Arriaga explained that a *conopa* could be a found stone or other natural material with an unusual colour or shape, but also stones carved in the form of llamas, maize or potatoes.[2] Stone is a particularly evocative material within Andean cosmology, associated with the origins of people and animals as well as the powerful mountains. As with modern *illa*, colonial sources state that *conopas* were carefully preserved as family heirlooms, passed from father to son, and protected 'as the most precious thing that their parents had left them'.[3] Arriaga describes *conopas* as being the focus of intimate household rituals that were held in private at particular times of the year, such as before going on a journey or sowing crops.[4] He lists the use of coca, maize, animal fat and *chicha* within the offerings, as well as describing blowing over the coca and burning the offering in order to dedicate these ingredients.[5] *Conopas* were not part of the offering and were kept safe by the household to be brought out for future rituals: 'Rare are those who do not have them, for they are the principal inheritance of the family, and sometimes they have two, three, or four of them.'[6] Some colonial-period *conopas* are described as being vessels with bowls hollowed out in their backs. Anthropologist Jorge Flores-Ochoa observed modern herders, who described the indentation in the back of a *conopa* as a *cocha* (pond/lake) which they filled with animal fat during rituals.[7]

Fat (*vira*) is considered a vitalising force, and placing the *vira* in the *cocha* may have been considered a way to feed or animate the *conopa*. During a trial in 1656 a native Andean, Hernando Caruachin, described being given a black stone *conopa* in the form of a man's face with an indentation in the back which he filled with llama fat and a small coin to supplicate for good fortune.[8] Combining the vitalising llama fat with a coin (the new method of exchange that was transforming Andean economic relationships) would have been highly symbolic. The llama fat placed into the *cocha* of the *conopa* would have had an energising role. The Inca name for the animating force is Viracocha, sometimes personified as a man who walked over the earth and brought people and animals out of the land at various places of origin. It is likely that the stone (and earth source) of the *conopa* was just as important as its camelid shape in making a link between the llamas and the Earth Beings that care for them. The simple act of placing camelid fat into the hollowed-out space of these small carved stones may have been as transformative and meaningful as a Catholic priest holding aloft a small circle of bread.

Jesuit priests such as Arriaga were seeking to locate and eradicate Indigenous Andean religious practices: they sought to destroy objects they considered idolatrous and punished those involved. For instance, Arriaga reports that between February 1617 and July 1618, Hernando de Avendaño hunted down and destroyed 3,418 *conopas*.[9] This aggressive Spanish extirpation of idolatry made it perilous to be found with *conopas*, and so the care of these objects and their associated ritual practices became confined to the private and protected space of the family home. Perhaps for this reason, at around this time, in the former Inca site of Qotakilli in Cusco a group of thirteen *conopas* were buried and hidden in the corner of a domestic house near to where the colonial chapel had just been constructed.

Across the Andes many people adopted Christianity while still protecting aspects of their worldview, which included a commitment to the animate landscape. The *conopas* used in family rituals provided a vehicle through which native Andean cosmologies and cultural values could be maintained. Carved *conopas* were, and are, just one component of a wider understanding that the land, animals, plants and people are all living and interdependent beings, and a care and concern for these underpins many Andean cultural practices, even as the material, symbolic and ritual aspects may vary in different regions or change through time.

Inca architecture and the temple of Viracocha at Raqchi

Bill Sillar and Amelia Perez Trujillo

Incas rapidly established the largest pre-Columbian empire of the Americas. By the time of the Spanish conquest in 1532, they had incorporated territory stretching from Colombia to Chile. But the Inca state had not emerged until the mid-thirteenth century, long after the decline of Wari and Tiwanaku. It was formed through alliances between local ethnic groups in the area around Cusco. The Cusco region is where the finest examples of Inca architecture can be found: here they drained, constructed terraces and rebuilt the earlier Killke community (c. AD 950–1200), which resulted in a capital with impressive stone buildings, streets paved with stone and massive plazas in which they could hold state rituals. Many of the most famous Inca archaeological sites – such as Chinchero, Pisac and Ollantaytambo – are within one to three days' walk from Cusco; these were private estates of the ruling families, where they hosted diplomatic parties and conducted ceremonies.

Inca workers used stone, wood and bronze tools (rather than draft animals or iron) to create constructions that are justly famed for the quality of their close-fitting stonework, landscape engineering and beauty. Although the stonework is the most representative surviving element of Inca building, adobe (mud shaped into bricks) was used extensively and early Spanish observers also marvelled at the quality of the thatched roofs. Each Inca building is site-specific, built into the landscape with views framed through trapezoidal windows and doorways, and designed to direct people's movements into more open, dramatic spaces for religious activities and public festivals. Incas did not just conceive individual buildings: by creating outside spaces such as courtyards, alleyways, terraces, stairs, water channels and fountains, they worked with the living landscape, which was a focus of their religious devotion. The landscape settings of Machu Picchu and Choquequirao may appear hard to access, but construction at these specific points placed Incas at the centre of powerful mountains, rivers and solar alignments in order that they could express their command over the Andean cosmos.

As an example of Inca architecture, we can look at the large temple constructed at Cacha (modern-day Raqchi), 110 kilometres south of Cusco (fig. 6.34). At first sight this rectangular building may appear to have little more sympathy for its landscape setting than a large warehouse (fig. 6.35). But it is not meant to be seen in a photograph – it was built to be experienced from the ground. The central wall, with over 2 metres of fine, close-fitting, polygonal stonework at its base, has a further 10 metres of adobe mud bricks rising above. This wall formed the central partition and roof support for a 92-metre-long rectangular building. At the far end of the building, Incas constructed a shallow pond with two sets of Inca 'baths', which were fed from an underground spring. The *mestizo* chronicler

FIG. 6.34 The central support wall of the Temple of Viracocha, Raqchi

Garcilaso de la Vega (1539–1616) explained that this building was a temple dedicated to the Andean creator god Viracocha.[1]

The animating deity Viracocha is said to have created people at Tiwanaku, sending them underground to each ethnic group's designated place of origin (*paqarina*). As Viracocha walked towards Cusco, he called people to emerge from their *paqarina*. However, the people at Cacha emerged from the *paqarina* with their weapons and attacked Viracocha. In response, Viracocha caused a volcano that showered the people with fire until they supplicated him in order to be saved. Many of the sites associated with the Viracocha legend, such as Tiwanaku, Isla del Sol and Pachacamac, had been significant during the earlier period of Tiwanaku and the Wari Empire. This also includes Cacha, which had been a major Wari administrative and ritual centre, and where a large statue had become a focus of worship by the time of the Incas. When the Inca ruler Huayna Capac saw the statue at Cacha and was told about Viracocha and the volcano, he 'decided that the remembrance of this event should be greater and ordered the erection of a large building near the burned hill'.[2]

Unusually for an Inca building, there is an early colonial account of how people moved inside this structure:

> On entering the temple by the main door, they turned right down the first passage until they came to the wall at the right-hand side of the temple; they then turned left down the second passage and went on till they came to the opposite wall. There they turned right again down the third passage, and by following the series of passages in the plan … they came to the twelfth and last where there was a staircase.[3]

FIG. 6.35 (OPPOSITE) The Inca site at Raqchi, in the Cusco region. The central wall of the Inca temple can be seen in the foreground. The red roof tiles are a modern addition to protect the adobe wall.

FIG. 6.36 Diagram of the section of the Temple of Viracocha, drawn by Bethan Davies

Two lines of pillars supported beams running from the central apex to the outer walls (today, visitors entering the remains of the building by the surviving doorways have their progress blocked by these pillars). As participants walked around these pillars towards the outer wall and then back to the openings in the central wall, they traced the zigzag path that Garcilaso described and walked in twelve different directions before arriving at the far end of the building (fig. 6.36). Climbing stairs to look out from this end of the temple would have provided a spectacular view of the volcano reflected in the waters of the artificial pond. Garcilaso's description suggests that this is where the ancient statue of Viracocha had been relocated to by the Incas.[4] Perhaps for the pilgrims who came to, and through, this building, they were literally walking back in time to meet their origins at the *paqarina* of Cacha. This vast structure was a powerful intervention in the landscape and history of Cacha, reclaiming it as a centre for Inca ritual and power.

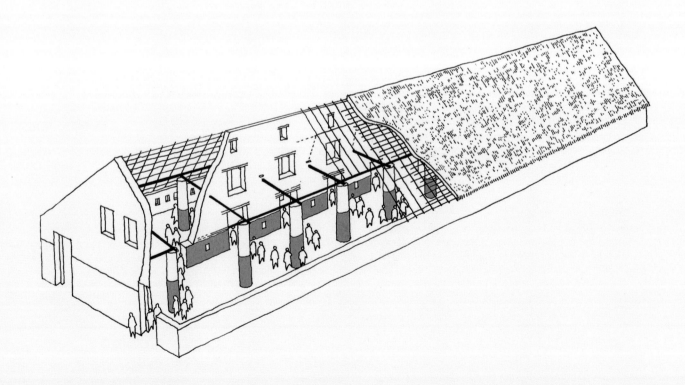

Andean engineering:
the power of water and stone

Jago Cooper and Thomas A. Cummins

The magnificent landscapes of Peru are a stunning visual record of thousands of years of technological innovation and human ingenuity. The striking sight of terraces covering the slopes of the steep Andean valleys represents not only an ongoing collective effort of labour to maintain them but also an insight into the intrinsic relationship between the people and the landscape (fig. 6.37). At the time of European arrival in Peru, more than two million acres of terraced agricultural land had been dug out from the high mountainous terrain of the Andes. It often surprises Peruvians to discover that scholars believe more land area was cultivated in the country during pre-Columbian times than today.[1] This enormous scale of landscape engineering was also applied along the coast, with verdant green swathes created in the desert using ancient irrigation systems to capture the water flowing off the mountains and foster new life in the arid sands. These feats of earth removal embody millennia of cultural knowledge and shared ideas about the reciprocal responsibilities of people and environment. Indigenous engineering has been described by the academic Carolyn Dean as an elegant and integral element in the ongoing dialogue between inhabitant and inhabited earth.[2]

Stone, earth and water have always been revered by Andean communities. This means that working with them is more than technological engineering: it is spiritual interaction with living beings.[3] A journey through these landscapes today provides an opportunity to better understand Andean values and cultural approaches to communal projects that echo through time – from Waris to Incas, to contemporary communities today. Many researchers also acclaim the development and expansion of engineering innovations and large-scale projects as underpinning the rise of particular societies and explaining the reasons for their relative successes.[4]

IRRIGATION

A single 200-kilometre transect drawn from the Pacific coast to the Amazon includes more than thirty-four distinct environmental zones over the Andes. As the temperature drops about 1° C for every 100 metres of altitude gained,

the range of microclimate habitats changes extremely quickly, so that managing agricultural land and access to water can be very challenging and requires ingenious solutions. This same transect also ranges between some of the driest places in the world in the west to some of the wettest in the east. The process of moving water from where it is – the river valleys flowing down from the highlands – to where it is needed – the deserts on the west coast – in order to grow and sustain human communities is complex. This vertical environmental diversity and local climatic variability is what drove Andean peoples to conceive of adaptive engineering projects and innovative technological solutions.

These ancient water management systems can be found in each of the major river valleys coming west out of the Andes (fig. 6.38). Over time, the complexity of the engineering technology increased both in the highlands and along the coast, beginning with the Paracas and Nasca cultures expanding the natural springs and building lined wells and reservoirs, followed by Waris and Incas developing complex irrigation canals, aqueducts and hydraulic systems. The scale of the pre-Columbian engineering is impressive, with many irrigation canals and aqueducts still in use today. In the Moche valley alone, more than thirty ancient canals extend through the desert landscape near the coast. These are more than a thousand years old and range in length from 0.6 to 7.8 kilometres, diverting water away from the river water source to bring water to human settlements. These irrigation systems helped transform a waterless desert into a fertile living environment that could support populations of tens of thousands of people during the Moche era.[5] Complex social organisation and cooperation was required to develop these large-scale engineering projects, to manage agricultural land and to control water. It has long been argued that such coordination helped create the system of social organisation and cooperative labour that underpinned these societies and acted as a catalyst for the development of more large-scale and complex societies.[6]

TERRACES

The initial creation of the terracing systems extends back at least 5,000 years and is likely to date back even earlier.

FIG. 6.37 Inca terracing in the Colca Canyon, near Chivay, Arequipa, Peru

They can be hard to date archaeologically, as terraces have often been maintained, rebuilt and improved over millennia. The success of many highland cultures is frequently linked to their building terracing systems across their territories and the consequent rapid expansion of available agricultural land. This was how the Wari and Inca peoples in particular were able to support such high population densities in their mountainous heartlands.

The pre-Columbian stepped terraces that cover large parts of the Andes were created with different techniques, but most commonly by building a stone enclosing wall that followed the contour of the side of the mountain. This retaining wall was normally built on carefully constructed and often deeply excavated stone foundations in order to prevent subsidence. It was then in-filled with rocks, sand and topsoil to create a flat agricultural surface. The stone terrace walls have thermodynamic benefits at higher altitudes, providing some frost protection as they maintain and then emit some solar radiated heat during the night. The composition of the soil was adjusted to suit local climatic conditions, plant requirements and the need to increase drainage or retain moisture. The best topsoil, commonly transported in from a nutrient-rich river valley, was piled up to 1 metre in depth on top of another metre or so of sandy gravel mixture, which in turn was placed on top of larger stones to create soil stability and drainage.

The horizontal projections of the terraces also helped to prevent soil erosion and water run-off, increasing the amount of land available for cultivation. The terraces were sometimes specially irrigated; this was most commonly done by siphoning off water from the closest river, often high up in the mountains. A water channel would then be carefully built in stone or lined earth, perfectly following the contour of the mountain to maintain the right gentle level of fall, often channelled via aqueducts built over depressions or ravines, in order to be transported to where the water was needed. The sheer scale of pre-Columbian terracing and irrigation systems in the highlands helps explain why population densities were commonly much greater in
pre-Columbian times in these regions than they are today.

The site of Moray, located about 50 kilometres north-west of Cusco, beautifully demonstrates the use of both terracing systems and controlled microclimate adaptation, which helped to manage and extend the altitude at which certain crops could be grown. The three circular and concentrically enclosed terraced depressions at Moray are up to 120 metres in diameter and up to 35 metres in depth from top to bottom (fig. 6.39). The microclimate variation

FIG. 6.38 Baño de la Ñusta ('The bath of the princess')
Ollantaytambo, Cusco region
1938
Photograph
H. 23 cm, W. 17.5 cm
British Museum, Am,B53.32

in temperature difference can be as much as 10° C between the top and bottom. The terrace stone walls heated up by the sunshine, combined with natural protection from the wind, create a favourable microclimate that enables crops to grow above their usual range of altitude. The understanding and management of local environmental conditions, using techniques to protect against frost damage and nutrient-rich irrigation methods, is what enabled Andean communities to grow crops up to 4,000 metres above sea level, far higher than the natural range of the plants grown.[7] The highest permanently occupied settlement in Europe is the village of Juf in Switzerland at 2,126 metres above sea level.[8]

Conversely, the majority of the estimated ten million inhabitants of the Inca Empire in the Andes lived higher than 3,000 metres above sea level. Even today the villages around the Ticlio mountain pass, at an altitude of 4,700 metres above sea level, remain the highest inhabited settlements in the world.[9] The ability to thrive so successfully at these high altitudes and across such mountainous terrain is largely due to the complex terracing systems and microclimate adaptations. The labour requirements for these large-scale engineering projects were met through the Andean system of shared labour, *mink'a*, in which people came together to work on communal projects that benefited their community.

ENGINEERING PRINCIPLES

Ingenious traditional ecological knowledge is still valued today: the same systems continue to be maintained and in some cases entirely restored.[10] Since the 1980s, internationally funded projects to restore long-abandoned irrigation systems and agricultural terraces have highlighted the successful ingenuity of Indigenous approaches to landscape management.[11] A series of projects to dig out pre-Columbian irrigation channels and restore integrated irrigation and terraced agricultural systems, sometimes abandoned for centuries, have had great successes (and some failures) over the years.[12] In the ensuing discussions, one key factor has been the need to persuade people, and governments, of the value and efficacy of Indigenous engineering techniques.

Many of these restoration projects have had to navigate sociological dynamics in order to demonstrate the comparative benefits of locally adapted ancient engineering techniques over and above the popularity of modern technologies developed in other parts of the world and applied to the Andes despite their unsuitability.[13] Such projects highlight the common failure to appreciate the deep environmental knowledge of Indigenous peoples in the Andes and the technological ingenuity of pre-Columbian engineering solutions. Their success was demonstrated by various cultures over millennia before the impact of colonialism and subjugation of Indigenous practices denied them the respect and revitalisation they deserve.[14]

The social principles intrinsic to the relationship with and responsibility for the management of the landscape closely align with Andean principles of reciprocal relationships between people. Andean peoples often create an implicit connection between the earth and human life, language anthropomorphising the landscape and highlighting that culture and nature are indistinguishable from one another. The soil is described as flesh and stone as bones,

FIG. 6.39 The Inca site of Moray

and so an agricultural terrace becomes the body.[15] The terrace structure harnesses life from the flesh and stability from bone, making it a living being to be tended and cared for in order to mutually sustain plants and people. The built environment provided stability and fixed points of temporal connection: people and beings could turn into stone and the life force of someone powerful could be held in stone, fixing their past ancestral presence in the present. This is why offerings to carved stones, a practice common throughout the highland Andes today, is a sacred act of respect and honour for the life force of the landscape they represent.

In the Andes, engineering projects were practical, aesthetic and religious at the same time. The shaping of earth, stone and wood into large-scale projects combined technological, creative and spiritual viewpoints, and this relationship with the landscape connected ancestors, descendants and powerful spiritual beings through time (figs 6.40–6.43). It was by channelling this approach to the living landscape that pre-Columbian Andean peoples were able to undertake these extraordinary engineering projects. Canal cleaning, terrace reconstruction and road maintenance were all cyclical acts of labour repeated each year, echoing a sense of continually connected time materialised in the landscape.[16] Such human effort was the obligation of all individuals, or personal 'sacrifice', that was necessary to sustain the landscape and environment, which in turn sustained their society. The technological innovation and ingenuity of Andean peoples, which exploited the region's unique environmental conditions, was the basis of their success – and this approach continues to thrive in the region today.

Urpus were traditional vessels used to carry *chicha* (maize beer) or water. The typical Inca form, with a pointed base, extended spout and loops for taking rope at the sides, lends itself to being filled on the ground and then transported on the individual's back without the liquid spilling.

FIG. 6.40 (ABOVE) *Urpu*
Inca AD 1400–1532
Pottery
H. 17.9 cm, W. 14.2 cm, D. 10 cm
British Museum, Am1938,1017.10

FIG. 6.42 (RIGHT) *Urpu* in the
form of a person carrying an *urpu*
Chimú–Inca AD 1400–1532
Pottery
H. 15.6 cm, W. 15.4 cm, D. 11.6 cm
British Museum, Am1927,0307.8
Donated by Mrs J. E. Birch

FIG. 6.41 (TOP RIGHT) *Urpu* bearer
Inca AD 1450–1550
Pottery
H. 19.5 cm, W. 11.3 cm, D. 16.8 cm
Ethnologisches Museum, Staatliche
Museen zu Berlin, V A 19105

FIG. 6.43 (OPPOSITE) Vessel combining
representations of an *urpu*, a maize ear
and a plough tool
Chimú–Inca AD 1400–1532
Pottery
H. 42.3 cm, W. 22.6 cm, D. 13.6 cm
British Museum, Am1947,10.39
Donated by Mrs E. H. S. Spottiswoode

7 The Andean legacy: enduring traditions

Textiles of the Andes:
techniques, traditions and cultures

Elena Phipps

The earliest surviving examples of Andean textiles exhibit an extraordinary mastery of artful skills. From the preparation and spinning of fibres into yarns, to colouring them with sources from nature, to the interlacing of complex structural motifs and the creation of significant and symbolic representations in the designs, Andean weavers excelled in their artistic practice. We can see that the earliest material evidence, such as that from the Guitarrero Cave (*c.* 8000–4500 BC) or the coastal middens of Huaca Prieta (*c.* 2500–1800 BC) – preserved in the intermontane highlands, in the form of basketry and netting, ropes and cloth – addressed the basic survival needs of human civilisation, providing the means to gather, carry and store foods, to form protective shelter and to make clothing.[1] But these early examples – among some of the oldest preserved worldwide – and those that followed also demonstrate that from the very beginning, the practice of making and using textiles contributed to and engaged with the religious, social and political power structures of the Andean world. These textiles are notable for the especially complex nested symbolic designs of supernatural beings and deity figures, as well as raptors, coiled snakes within condors or fanged caiman, whose images were woven into the very structure of the cloths rather than added to their surface.

The process of making complex textiles formed an underlying conceptual matrix of knowledge and value systems as active, creative expressions of art, culture and identity. Textiles were highly valued and deeply embedded in every facet of life in the Andean world: they embodied the interface between an individual and their place in society, and between the formation of a local identity of one cultural group and that of another. The materials and their construction as woven objects are linked to the visual and conceptual understanding and experience of the people of the region, and the textiles that have been preserved today enable us a glimpse into the magnificence of the art that developed through millennia (fig. 7.1).

TEXTILE MATERIALS AND METHODS

Textile traditions evolved within all the diverse environmental zones of the region – from dry coastal deserts to high snow-capped mountains and, from the interface of the two, through the fertile river valleys that traverse from the highlands westwards, to the Pacific Ocean, and eastwards, to the tropical wetlands of the Amazon. Here cultures thrived and developed particular regional approaches to the use of materials and techniques. The materials available from these various regions and the methods of production – whether resulting in sheer lightweight cotton cloths from the coast or densely woven garments made from animal hairs from the highland camelids – together contribute to the fingerprint of the cultures that produced them. Their significance goes beyond the physical as the materiality of cultural identity. Cotton, *Gossypium barbadense*, originated in the coastal valleys, while the camelids – llamas, alpacas, guanacos and vicuñas – thrived in the highlands. Peruvian cotton is a long-stapled and fine quality species which gives it a shiny and pliable character. It also grows naturally in a range of colours, including white, cream, beige, brown, pinkish and greenish hues, especially from the north, although white and brown were certainly the colours most commonly found throughout the expansive coastal region (fig. 7.2).

RAW MATERIALS: CAMELID FIBRES, COTTON AND DYES

Camelids served many roles in Andean society: beasts of burden for carrying goods throughout the region; precious

PAGE 190 Señora Quintina Huanca, from the Asociación de Tejedores Munay Ticlla de Pitumarca–CTTC, weaving in 2021

FIG. 7.1 Detail of a plain weave cloth with tapestry section. Supe, Peru, *c.* 1800 BC. Division of Anthropology, American Museum of Natural History, New York, 41.2/5517

offerings to appease the gods; suppliers of warmth and protection, with their pelts and hairs for furnishing and clothing for daily and ritual life; and sustenance as a food source. Their hairs, shorn for textile use, ranged from stiff and straight to soft, almost silk-like and supple, and also, like cotton, they had their particular natural colour palette. These colours ranged from white through to dark brown, light brown, warm brown, black and eventually greys, often found mixed within a single animal. The length and quality of the hair – notably in its fineness – was clearly differentiated by artisans and nobility alike, and for those animals that were domesticated these physical qualities and colours were selectively cultivated through animal husbandry, especially for the llamas and alpacas. The wild species – the vicuñas and guanacos – had the finest of hairs and, with their distinctive light brown colour and silkiness to the touch, they were most highly prized (fig. 7.3).

These colours inherent to cotton and animal hairs provided the weaver with a natural palette. At the same time, colourants from nature in the form of mineral pigments and dyestuffs sourced from plants and animals were used by skilful and knowledgeable artisans, creating an even wider range of colours.[2] Inorganic earth minerals, such as irons and ochres, mercury and lead sulphates, provided ancient textile makers with brilliant reds, oranges and yellows, especially used on cotton. Organic reds, used primarily on the animal hairs, come from plants such as the madder-like roots of the *Relbunium* genus shrub, found in the early textiles, especially those made before the third or fourth centuries AD (see fig. 4.12).[3] Cochineal, a brilliant crimson red dye coming from a small insect that lives on the *Opuntia* cactus, became the predominant source of red textile colour in the centuries that followed. Beginning in the sixteenth century, cochineal from the Americas was of great interest (only second to gold and silver) to the Spanish, and it became a highly prized commodity for global trade. Its bright red colour soon was found in Spanish woollen cloth, British embroideries, French tapestries, Italian silks, Turkish velvets and Chinese bed hangings. Cochineal remains, to this day, a contributor to the Peruvian economy (fig. 7.4 and see fig. 5.51).[4]

Brown colours, coming from plant-based tannins such as the pods of the *huarango* trees (genus *Prosopis*) or other leaves and barks were among the earliest dyes used, along with indigo. Indigo blue coming from the leaves of the tropical *Indigofera* plant(s), sourced mostly from the selva region of the Amazon, was used as early as 4000 BC and notably discovered in Huaca Prieta, perhaps providing the earliest evidence of trade between the ecological zones.[5] Coastal species of

FIG. 7.2 Raw, unspun balls of cotton in their natural colours. North coast of Peru, 1981. British Museum, Am1981,19.234.b

FIG. 7.3 Thomas Bewick, *La Vigogne, c.* 1753–1828. Graphite with brown wash. H. 8.9 cm, W. 9.5 cm. British Museum, 1882,0311.1646. Donated by Isabella Bewick

FIG. 7.4 Crushed cochineal, used to make textile dye

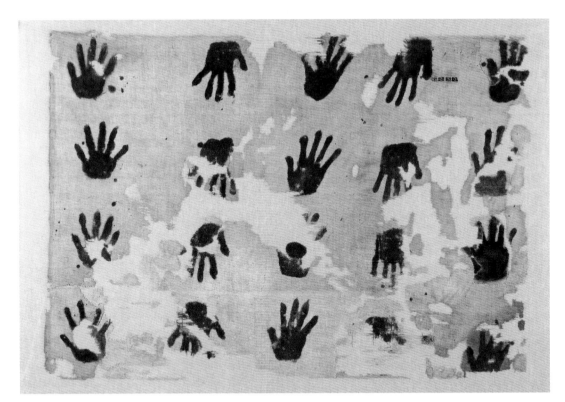

FIG. 7.5 Textile with handprints
in shellfish purple
South coast of Peru, 100 BC AD 100
Cotton
H. 61 cm, W. 91.4 cm (approx.)
Houston Museum of Natural Science

shellfish provided a special purple colour used on cotton cloth: due to its chemical nature, the yellowish liquid colourant is often milked from the shellfish and placed directly onto the cotton cloth, where in the presence of air it turns to a deep reddish-purple colour. In the Ocucaje area of the Ica valley on the south coast of Peru, artisans from *c.* 150 BC sometimes applied this liquid to their hands and then onto the cloth, leaving direct handprints – perhaps the only personal clue to the generally anonymous ancient Andean artists (fig. 7.5).[6]

LOOMS

We can glean aspects of the weavers' identities, however, through their choices of materials and techniques – from region to region and time period to time period, artisans developed characteristic methods of production. Among these telltale cultural features are, for example, the spin direction of the yarns (whether twisted to the left or right), and whether they are used singly or plied together to create a combined yarn of two or more strands.[7] The yarns are used to form the warps (the first set of yarns placed on the loom) and the wefts (the second set, interlaced perpendicular to the warp), ordered and organised in a variety of ways, distinctive from culture to culture.

Weaving tools, notably the looms, also are of particular types, tailored to the character of the cloth to be woven.

Looms in the Andes are composed generally of a set of sticks that hold the warp in place. The backstrap or body tension loom is tied at one end to a fixed post and, at the other, around the weaver's waist. This type of variable tension loom was used to create, among other types, the loosely woven and patterned plainweave and gauze cloths created on the coast. The backstrap loom was a fundamental tool throughout the Americas, notably from Mexico to the southern regions of South America, until the Spanish arrived with their foot-pedalled constructions, and the backstrap loom continues to be used today (fig. 7.6). One extraordinary Moche ceramic from the north coast of Peru is one of the rare depictions of pre-Columbian artisans with their looms (see fig. 5.21). Appearing to be a kind of weaver's workshop, we can see each weaver seated with their tools, including the loom tied to an architectural post at one end and strapped round their back at the other. One can also see the small sticks with yarns wound on them ready to be used, likely indicating the multiple weft colours the weaver would use to create the designs, whose model appears above.

In contrast, the densely woven warp-faced patterned cloth of the highlands requires a stronger, fixed tension, and tends to be woven on looms that are staked out horizontally to the ground (fig. 7.7). The extremely fine tapestry weave, used by many cultures but perfected notably by Wari and Inca weavers, can be woven on various types of loom, but the finest – sometimes with over eighty yarns per centimetre of weaving – were likely to have been made on upright fixed looms (figs 7.8 and 7.9). These three types of loom – the backstrap loom, the horizontal ground loom and the upright loom – all remain in use today, as Indigenous weavers continue to pursue the art and craft of weaving.

All Andean textiles, with few exceptions, were woven as four-selvaged finished cloth. This process required advanced planning and thought to create a specific size and shape of textile for a specific function – whether for a man's tunic, a woman's mantle or dress, or a cloth to wrap coca leaves. Unlike the weaving traditions of other parts of the world, including Europe, Asia, Africa and North America, where cloth is woven in lengths that are then cut to form garments, the traditions that developed here are uniquely Andean. Cloth was used without cutting, respecting the integrity of the physical object itself, and was created with purpose and intent. In some highland ethnographic traditions, the finished edges have been described as forming the 'mouth' of the textile, which interacts with the outside world, and as a result edges are important for maintaining the boundaries, physically and conceptually, as defined by the cloth itself.[8] Most traditional weavers working today maintain this practice of creating four-selvaged cloth, following the method as it has been conducted for millennia, which retains the integrity of the intentionality and purpose of the woven cloth.

Weaving with yarns, organising them as single, double and even triple sets, resulted in some of the most complex textile structures known throughout the world. These woven fabrics were used daily as garments or in ritual and ceremony, and represent the broadest range of weaving traditions, qualities and designs of thousands of years of Andean history. While in some cultures patterning systems developed as part of the mechanical features of the loom, in the Andes the creation of designs relied on the imagination and memory of the weaver for their production: complex mathematical counting formed the basis for a number of textile systems that integrated sequences of hand movements with memorised patterns and designs. In a culture with no writing, the pre-Columbian weavers drew from traditional knowledge, passed down from generation to generation, through learning stages and practice.

WEAVING AND CULTURE

Some cultures excelled in specific ways of making textiles of specific qualities. Tapestry weaving, for example, facilitated the creation of especially pictorial and curvilinear designs,

FIG. 7.6 Backstrap loom with a partly woven textile attached
Chancay AD 1000–1470
Wood, camelid fibres
H. 34 cm, W. 40 cm
British Museum, Am1997,Q515

formed with the densely packed wefts, often with polychrome yarns (fig. 7.10). Others worked in geometric harmony within the gridded format of the woven cloth while patterning with a number of techniques such as openwork gauze (fig. 7.11) or densely packed float-patterning systems. Doublecloth and triplecloth were used to create strong contrasting designs. And in the highlands were the highly complex warp-patterned weaves (see fig. 6.23). The weavers' technical vocabulary developed over generations, and enabled artisans to create beautiful designs and structurally integrated textiles. Some cultures excelled in creating design effects through complex dyeing, as we see in the Nasca–Wari example of a discontinuous warp and weft, which is tie-dyed in multiple colour strips after weaving and subsequently re-organised into a chaotic creative burst of contrasting colour and pattern.[9]

Other cultures used needlework as their primary art form – such as the people who created the extraordinary

FIG. 7.7 A weaver using a horizontal ground loom, 1982

mummy bundles, with layers and layers of wrapped cloth, for the burials in the Paracas Peninsula, on the southern coast of Peru. Meticulously embroidered, row by row, they created complex supernatural creatures in a myriad of colours and variations that cover the sacred cloths used to accompany the honoured ancestors (see figs 4.11–4.12). In some of these elite burials, archaeologists have found complete matching sets of garments, evidence of the concerted efforts by the craftsmen and women who likely had devoted their lives to the production of such fine and complex works.[10] And in some cases, in the rush to complete the work for the funerary bundles in time for the ceremonial interment, unfinished work was also included, which provides evidence of the process by which the artisans worked, including the order of colours and designs (fig. 7.12).

The environmental conditions for textile preservation along the dry desert coast are prime for those textiles that have been left undisturbed in underground burials for centuries, and it is from these contexts that we have the highest number of textile finds. This has enabled the study of the sequence of cultures that occupied the region over millennia. Unfortunately, the moist climate in the highlands has not been so compatible in conserving the evidence of the rich textile traditions there. As a result, we know less about highland weaving practices, though we can study those examples that have found their way to coastal burials, through the exchange, trade and political waves that traverse these

distinctive regions. The exceptions are the beautiful textiles that were part of the Inca Capacocha ritual. Carried out in the highest altitude sites, in the frozen volcanic peaks of the Andes mountain range, the specially chosen young girls and boys were sacrificed to the gods in a solemn and sacred ritual carried out only in time of extreme duress. Their ritual garments, along with the small dressed figures, represent the finest Inca weaving traditions (see figs 6.29–6.30).[11]

Even when cloth may not have been preserved, however, we see evidence of its use depicted in other media. Drawn, for example, on Moche ceramic vessels, we can see the representation of elaborate cloth-formed headdresses and garments, palanquins and other ritual textile paraphernalia that was often covered with precious metals, shells or feathers (see figs 5.20 and 5.49). Cloth played a role in all ritual activities – whether worn as special emblematic garments or given as offerings. Sometimes ceremonial cloth itself was buried, such as the giant cotton textile estimated to be over 50 metres long found interred in its own deep burial trench near the vicinity of the largest ceremonial mound along the south coast of Peru, at the Nasca site of Cahuachi, by archaeologist William Duncan Strong in the 1950s.[12] Another extraordinary example of the importance of textiles in the Andean ceremonial world can be seen in the cache of ninety-six blue and yellow Macaw-feather-covered cotton panels found rolled up inside several large ceramic vessels, which may have been offerings accompanying an important Wari-period elite or human sacrifice in the Churunga valley on the south coast of Peru.[13] Specialist weavers used the colourful feathers of Amazonian birds and tied each one individually on to strings, which were then stitched onto woven cloth, forming impressive items that could shimmer in the sunlight (see fig. 5.48). In the absence of actual bird feathers, sometimes depictions of feathers were used in woven form, created in tapestry, and incorporated into garments as borders (see fig. 2.4).

Incas were renowned for their use of garments as tools of diplomacy, distributing tunics woven under royal auspices to regional authorities as a key method for negotiating social allegiance and fealty within the empire. Conversely, according to colonial sources such as Felipe Guamán Poma de Ayala (c. 1535–after 1616),[14] it is said that the Inca ruler would change into the clothing worn in a specific area that he was visiting when travelling, as a sign of respect to local lords. The Inca social organisation defined roles for the production of these special garments: they were made by women specially selected from populations throughout the empire, who were housed in special compounds in order to spin, weave and sew garments for royal requirements. Specialist weavers, the *cumbi camayos*, were extremely skilled and knowledgeable individuals who maintained the highest of standards for Inca weaving, notably the fine tapestry, *cumbi*, woven with over eighty yarns per centimetre.[15] This refined Inca weaving practice was drawn in part from earlier Wari/Tiwanaku cultural traditions. From a political perspective, the wearing of specific types of cloth – woven and designed according to social hierarchical rules – was part of all levels of Andean culture. Whether created for family, community or empire, the weavers and producers of textiles and garments developed extensive and unsurpassed artistic skills and their work was a cornerstone for the life of the region.

LEGACY

The legacy of centuries of weaving practice continues to thrive, while the lives of the weavers and their contexts evolve and transform in concert with the transformation of the social, political and economic realms of Andean life. From the time of the arrival of the Spanish in the early sixteenth century, major changes occurred that impacted the lives of the weavers and practice of their arts.[16] Under colonial rule, Andean weavers continued to create the garments and items used in daily life, although ritual behaviour was modified, or in some cases supplanted, with Christian practices, which also impacted the significance and role of certain textiles. Special textiles, such as those used to 'dress' *huacas* (sacred objects), were forbidden and confiscated as evidence of idolatry in the sixteenth and seventeenth centuries, and other cloths traditionally used in ritual processes as the *mesa* (surface),

FIG. 7.8 An upright tapestry loom in use, Villa Ribero, Bolivia, 1993

FIG. 7.9 The use of an upright loom. 'The Mercedarian friar Martín de Murúa abuses his parishioners and takes justice into his own hands', illustrated by Felipe Guamán Poma de Ayala in *El primer nueva crónica y buen gobierno*, 1615, p. 661, drawing no. 258. The Royal Library, Copenhagen, GKS 2232 4°

for the setting up of the curing paraphernalia used by local healers, now incorporated mantles and other daily textiles. The highly trained Inca royal weavers continued to produce textiles, including Inca-style garments that were used in new contexts, such as processions and other public events, and were worn by those who were substantiating their noble heritage. The weavers also applied their skills to create new forms modulated for Spanish taste, such as large wall tapestries and carpets, some created after European tapestry models, others entirely from the Andean imagination.[17] Steeped in generational methods of artistic practice, they continued the art of pattern-making in cloths used for garments, through the meticulous and measured hand processes they had used for centuries. These extraordinary weavers embodied the knowledge of the past while creating their future in utilising the language of Andean cloth.

Although changes have occurred in the fashion of dress in some regions of Peru up until the present day, some women, especially in some rural settings, continue to wear the *anacu* (wrapped dress) worn by Inca nobility as well as

the *lliclla* (shoulder cloth). And even the special belt of the *coya* (the Inca queen) that was made for the corn festival – so notable that it was documented by the Spanish friar Martín de Murúa in his 1590 manuscript *Historia del origen y genealogía real de los reyes Ingas del Piru* – is still woven today in the region of Huamachuco.[18]

While centuries of social and political upheaval have created unfathomable disjunctions – from the arrival of the Spanish in the sixteenth century, to the fight for independence in the early nineteenth century, and issues of agrarian reform and social identity in the twentieth century – the practice of spinning as well as weaving continues. For those who continue to live in traditional, rural communities, weaving is a necessity of everyday life for the family (fig. 7.15). For those whose extended reach has expanded to local, regional and international marketplaces, projects designed for newer interests and foreign customers have stimulated renewed commitment and engagement with the skills of the community. The great achievement of the Andean weavers can be seen in their aesthetic and technical prowess, but also in the knowledge and creativity expressed in the intersection between art and culture at its most diverse.

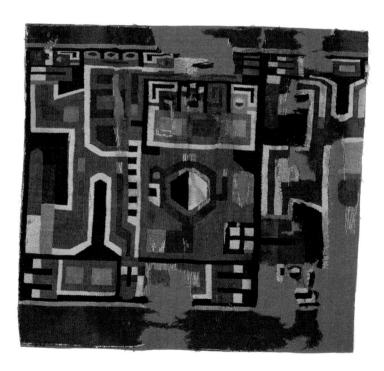

FIG. 7.10 Fragment of textile depicting a mythical being
Wari AD 600–900
Camelid fibre, cotton
H. 28 cm, W. 26.5 cm
British Museum, Am1954,05.482
Donated by the Wellcome Institute

FIG. 7.11 Detail of a patterned
gauze textile
Chancay AD 900–1430
Cotton
L. 74.5 cm (fragment)
British Museum, Am2006,Q.30

FIG. 7.12 Detail of a textile fragment
with unfinished embroidery
Paracas 500–1 BC
Camelid fibre, cotton
H. 22 cm, W. 30 cm
British Museum, Am1934,0714.6.b
Donated by Henry Van den Bergh
through the Art Fund

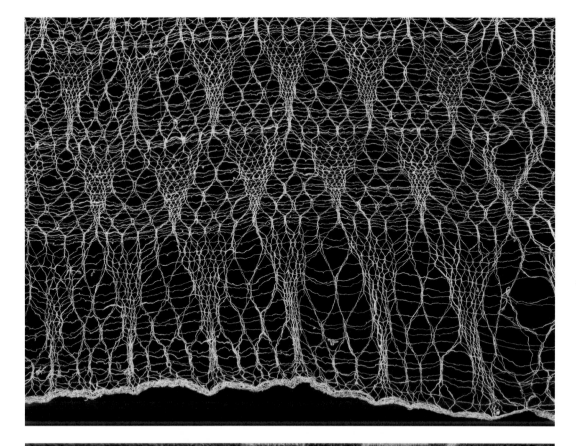

The Spanish friar Martín de Murúa's *Historia* of Peru is considered to be the first illustrated history of the Incas. The drawing shown here (fig. 7.13) is thought to be from the earlier of two known manuscript volumes, which includes over one hundred colour illustrations of the Incas, the *coyas*, ceremonies and traditions, which the Spanish documented during the first decades of their conquest. An example of the fine ceremonial tapestry shirts worn by Inca rulers, of which only a few examples survive, is illustrated here in immense detail.

FIG. 7.13 (ABOVE) Sapa Inca Sinchi Roca in Martín de Murúa, *Historia del origen y genealogía real de los reyes Ingas del Pirú. De sus hechos, costumbres, trajes, y manera de gobierno*, 1590. Ink, watercolour and other colourants on parchment. H. 32 cm, W. 25 cm. Private Collection

FIG. 7.14 (LEFT, AND REVERSE RIGHT) *Unku* with red textile on one side and blue on reverse
Colonial AD 1650–1700
Camelid fibres, cotton and embroidery
H. 80 cm, W. 73 cm
Ethnologisches Museum, Staatliche Museen zu Berlin, V A 4577

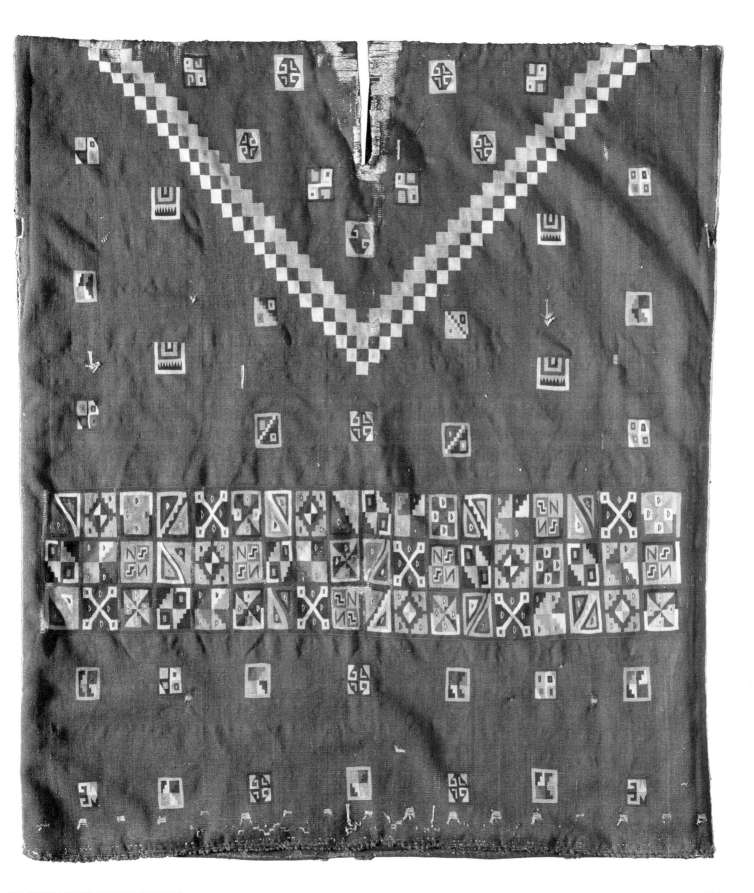

The two shawls displayed opposite come from the border region between Peru and Bolivia. Even though they were produced more than 300 years after the Spanish conquest, they show similar techniques and designs to those introduced by pre-Columbian societies. While one features natural dyes, the other shows traces of dyes based on chemicals – a result of Western influence introduced in the Andes during the 19th century. This painted shirt possibly belonged to the Yiné community in the eastern Amazon region in Peru. It has the typical ceremonial form of the *unku* linked to pre-Columbian times, but the painted designs relate to later traditions that continue to be in use in the present day.

FIG. 7.15 Ceremonial shirt from the Amazon
Yiné, AD 1550–1700
Cotton
H. 125 cm, W. 117 cm
British Museum, Am1904,1215.18
Donated by George Lomas

FIG. 7.16 Aymara textile shawl
Bolivia, late 19th–early 20th century
Wool
H. 102 cm, W. 95 cm
British Museum, Am1981,28.123

FIG. 7.17 Quechua textile shawl
Peru, early 20th century
Wool
H. 114.5 cm, W. 93 cm
British Museum, Am1982,20.71

Keros, pacchas, tupus and *unkus*: enduring Andean traditions

Ricardo Kusunoki

The Spanish conquest marked an abrupt and inevitable breaking point in the cultural history of the Andes. In the period immediately preceding this, the expansion of Tawantinsuyu (the Inca Empire) throughout the entire Andean region had permitted a coexistence between Inca worship and official practices – imposed as a sign of dominance – and a diversity of cultural forms. The incursion of Francisco Pizarro's armies in the early sixteenth century led to a radically different cultural order being imposed, but the construction and consolidation of this new colonial society was only possible through negotiating alliances with numerous sectors of the local elite. Early on, several regional leaders, members of the Inca royalty and Indigenous people in general, formed military collaborations with the invaders. A number of Incas rose to power after Atahualpa's death, either adopting a rebellious outlook or declaring themselves vassals of the Spanish Crown, until the last of them, Túpac Amaru I was decapitated in 1572 by order of the viceroy Francisco de Toledo.

When Peru was being reconfigured as a kingdom of the Spanish Empire, comprising numerous territories, each with its own laws and identity, the Incas' identity was key.[1] The old Tawantinsuyu sovereigns believed in a unified territory governed by a single person, a ruler who – in Atahualpa's case – would have finally yielded the legitimate governance from his domain to that of the Spanish monarch.[2] Objects and symbols of deliberately Inca provenance became more prevalent among Indigenous elites, who used them during very important public events to emphasise their 'imperial' Inca lineage while, at the same time, demonstrating their obedience to the authority of the king of Spain.

Colonial society would come to be defined by a division of crucial symbolic importance: the formation of two 'republics' based on legal differences between Spanish and Indigenous peoples.[3] Numerous objects of pre-Columbian origin remained relevant in this new set-up, becoming distinctively Indigenous when their use could serve other colonial functions. One example is the traditional Inca costume that the Indigenous elites wore during the most important public events, especially those that expressed their vassalage to the king of Spain.[4] The look of these garments was different from the ones worn prior to the conquest. Unlike their Inca precedents, which responded to clearly more prescriptive schemes, the colonial *unkus* display not only a greater compositional freedom – evident in the examples at the Ethnologisches Museum, Berlin (fig. 7.14) – but also demonstrate the desire to highlight pre-Columbian elements, which conveyed status and provided symbols of local difference.[5] Both the Berlin examples have waistbands composed using a larger number of *tocapus* (sets of squares with geometric decoration) than in the pre-Columbian examples. In addition, several of the themes shown in the waistband *tocapus* appear individually in other sections of both *unkus*.[6]

The *kero* is a ceremonial vessel thought to have originated around Lake Titicaca. Although it was important to the Incas, the earlier Waris and Tiwanakus also used them in ceremonies. One of the most important aspects of the *kero* is the role it played after the Spanish conquest as an enduring legacy of pre-Columbian tradition. These examples show both an original Inca style and a hybrid of Inca and colonial art, evidence that the traditional form continued under Spanish rule.

FIG. 7.18 (LEFT) *Kero*
Inca AD 1438–1532
Wood with silver studs
H. 21.1 cm, W. 18.7 cm, D. 18.7 cm
Museo de Arte de Lima, IV.2.3.0031
Donated by Pedro Ugarteche Tizón

FIG. 7.19 (ABOVE) *Kero* with painted scene
Colonial 18th century
Wood
H. 21 cm, W. 15.5 cm, D. 13.5 cm
British Museum, Am1923,0618.1
Donated by William George Buchanan

The variety of surviving colonial *unku* designs, with their emphatic display of *tocapus* and figurative or Western elements, shows a broad and diverse range of colonial expectations. These and other garments of pre-Columbian origin, such as *acsos* (folding tunics) and *llicllas* (wraps) made of fine tapestry, not only circulated among the descendants of the old Inca royalty, or the *curacas*, but became more widely available objects, which could now include individuals from other social or ethnic groups.[7] A similar process occurred with accessories associated with Indigenous clothing, such as *tupus* – pins worn by women to hold an *acso* at the shoulder or to secure a *lliclla* onto the chest (figs 7.21–7.26). In fact, the shape and style of the *tupus* underwent a more radical transformation than that of the garments: early on, a predominantly Western ornamental design was adopted. Some styles were still apparently current in the Andes at the end of the eighteenth century, such as a spoon-shaped model depicted in a painting that the viceroy Manuel de Amat y Junyent sent to Madrid in 1770 as part of a series of caste types.

Many objects of Inca origin continued to be used after the conquest, although the images they displayed, the ceremonies for which they were used, and even how they were created, were occasionally suspected of concealing 'idolatrous' cults. Examples include *keros*, vases made in pairs that were used to share *chicha* during rituals of alliance or reciprocity. The characteristic motifs on these vessels, and of Inca art in general, acquired different nuances during the decades after the conquest and underwent a radical transformation from geometric to more diverse figurative patterns.[8] The austere elegance of some *keros*, with motifs outlined with silver studs, might suggest that they were made in pre-Columbian times, but their design and technique are a colonial invention. The adoption of a figurative and openly narrative language enabled the makers to construct new interpretations of remembrance of the Inca past. This dramatic reinvention over time demonstrates that Indigenous peoples responded to colonisation with a determination to keep their own heritage alive. With the use of *mopa mopa*, a coloured vegetal resin that glazed the surface of wood, the *keros* could be employed as a medium for the depiction of figurative elements and scenes. These images strengthened the association between the vases and the pre-conquest era; they recreated the governance of Incas in an idealised manner and romanticised/celebrated their relationship with other communities, such as those of the Amazon.

In contrast to the various keros from the colonial period, a smaller number of colonial *pacchas* (ceremonial ceramic vessels) survive; the difference is probably due to the fact that the latter were explicitly related to rites involving water. Many *pacchas* were made with the same technique as *keros*, using lacquered wood, and consisting of a receptacle from which water is poured out of a hole to run along small channels before finally flowing out. Perhaps some distant affinity with purely decorative European jars explains their presence in the colonial Christian context. In fact, it has been suggested that many *pacchas* were disguised ritual objects that adopted the shapes of Western vessels associated with indoor water games.[9]

FIG. 7.20 *Kero* with painted scene showing a human figure wearing both Western and Inca attire
Colonial 18th century
Wood
H. 20.6 cm, W. 17.6 cm, D. 17.5 cm
British Museum, Am1950,22.1

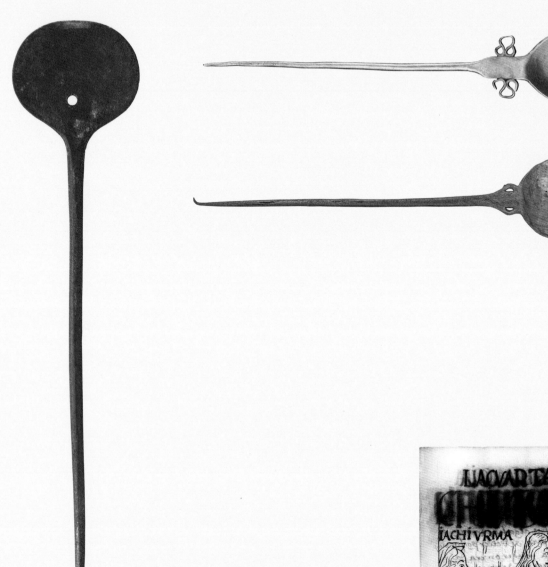

FIG. 7.21 (ABOVE) *Tupu* with perforated head
Inca AD 1400–1532
Copper alloy
H. 10.1 cm, W. 2.4 cm, D. 0.3 cm
British Museum, Am1937,0213.30
Donated by John Goble

FIG. 7.22 (TOP RIGHT) *Tupu*
Colonial 16th–17th century AD
Gold
H. 15.3 cm, W. 2.5 cm, D. 1 cm
British Museum, Am1928,0606.2
Donated by Henry Van den Bergh

FIG. 7.23 (ABOVE RIGHT) *Tupu*
Colonial 16th–17th century AD
Gold
H. 19.1 cm, W. 3.3 cm, D. 0.7 cm
British Museum, Am1972,07.19

FIG. 7.24 (RIGHT) 'The fourth *coya*, Chinbo
Urma Mama Yachi', from Felipe Guamán Poma
de Ayala, *El primer nueva crónica y buen gobierno*,
1615, p. 126, drawing no. 42. The Royal Library,
Copenhagen, GKS 2232 4°

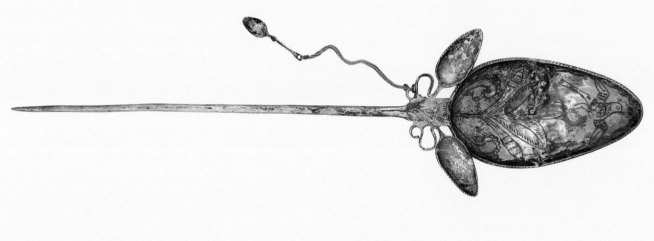

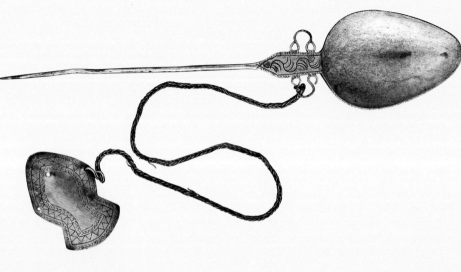

FIG. 7.25 (TOP) *Tupu* with depictions of flowers,
birds and leaves at each side
c. 18th–19th century AD
Silver alloy
H. 32 cm, W. 8.8 cm, D. 2.8 cm
British Museum, Am1995,13.1

FIG. 7.26 (ABOVE) *Tupu* with a medallion
attached
c. 18th–19th century AD
Silver
H. 28.8 cm, W. 1.9 cm, D. 6 cm (excl. medallion)
British Museum, Am1968,12.1.a–b
Donated by Mrs M. H. Whiteley

FIG. 7.27 (RIGHT) *Tupu* depicting symbol of
Peruvian flag
19th century AD
Silver
H. 25.5 cm, W. 9.3 cm, D. 1.3 cm
British Museum, Am1921,0723.1
Donated by Col. F. H. Ward

In the colonial period, the continued use of objects of pre-Columbian origin could only be permitted if they were stripped of any 'idolatrous' connotations and contributed to the assertion of colonial legitimacy. Following this logic, relics of the Inca period could be perceived as an expression of the Incas' own antiquity, of a pagan past – something akin to what the Roman Empire was for European Christians. The venture was so successful that throughout the eighteenth century, even images of the old rulers of Tawantinsuyu had acquired a key role in public ceremonies designed to acknowledge the authority of the Spanish monarch. In this way, the Indigenous elites could preserve those elements that presented them as 'natural lords' of the kingdom without questioning their Christianity. However, by the end of the century the idolatrous implications of that material universe were the least of the viceroyal authorities' concerns. A decisive moment would arrive after the Spanish defeat of Túpac Amaru II in 1781. As part of the reprisals against the rebels, the authorities ordered the destruction of many objects that evoked the Inca past. Fortunately for the preservation of cultural history, many of them survived this destruction and their manufacture and use still persists today in a variety of contexts across the Andes.

FIG. 7.28 *Paccha* featuring an animal as the bowl and a seated human figure as the spout
17th century
Wood
H. 15.2 cm, W. 52.6 cm, D. 13 cm
British Museum, Am1997,Q780

During the pre-Columbian period, different ceramic and wooden objects were associated with the worship of water, one of the most important religious practices of the Andean societies. These included *pacchas*, receptacles into which liquid was poured through a nozzle and then flowed through a series of channels. *Pacchas* remained in use during the colonial period, although they were adapted and transformed over time. After Peruvian independence, their use was limited to rural areas, where they continued to play a vital role in agricultural and livestock rites.

FIG. 7.29 *Paccha* with a human figure on top
Chimú–Inca AD 1438–1532
Pottery
H. 17.3 cm, W. 9.2 cm, D. 23.9 cm
British Museum, Am1921,1027.125

FIG. 7.30 *Paccha* in the form of a fountain with a man drinking from it
Inca AD 1450–1550
Pottery
H. 24.9 cm, W. 30.6 cm, D. 11.9 cm
Ethnologisches Museum, Staatliche Museen zu Berlin, V A 47569

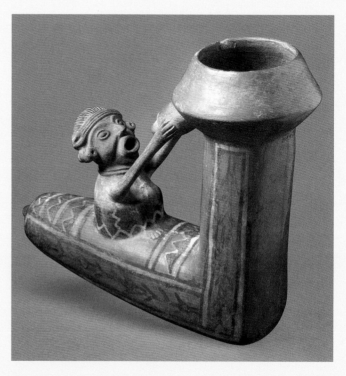

Approaches to conservation

Anna Harrison, Monique Pullan and Sophie Rowe-Kancleris

The archaeological objects displayed in this book and exhibition are remarkable in many ways, but foremost because they have survived the deteriorating effects of time. They may appear fresh and vibrant, but the intervening centuries have taken their toll, particularly on those objects made from organic materials such as textile, feather and wood. These have become brittle and weakened by their burial environment and the actions of temperature, humidity, light, pests and microorganisms, causing damage on both a structural and molecular level.

By storing and displaying these objects in controlled environmental and lighting conditions, we can now slow down some of the degradation processes. A careful observer will notice monitoring devices in museum display cases. Objects such as the Lambayeque ear spool (see fig. 5.49) benefit from tightly maintained temperature and humidity parameters, which protect the delicate mother-of-pearl inlay. Low light levels in the gallery minimise the damage caused by light, which is why many textiles are not on permanent display.

The careful mounting and positioning of objects on display can go a long way to reduce stress and strain, and help to provide the necessary support for fragile pieces. Textiles present particular challenges; although impressively colourful and complete, their fibres are weak and they cannot be hung, wrapped or draped. In the most part, these now must be displayed lying on low-angled boards. In a few instances, individually tailored support and mounting techniques such as near-invisible netting overlays allow objects, such as a long thin headdress or waistband (see fig. 2.16), to be displayed wrapped or coiled. This approach protects the objects while helping to give the museum visitor some insight into how they might have been worn.

Any conservation process is an intervention in the timeline of an object's 'life'. Conservators are mindful of the need to have as little impact as possible (the concept of minimal intervention) while at the same time working to safeguard the object's preservation. More intrusive stabilisation treatments tend to be carried out only when there is a particular risk, such as a loss of parts or decorative surface; and cleaning takes place only where there is the need to remove potentially harmful soiling or make the object more 'readable'. Thorough documentation of these treatments is essential. Conservators try not to impose values and aesthetics of the present day; more tangibly, they try not to introduce materials such as adhesives which may compromise future scientific analysis.

One of the joys of working as a conservator is the many hours spent in close contact with museum objects. Objects can reveal unexpected histories, taking us back to the lives of the people who created them, such as a beautifully decorated Inca beaker or *kero* (figs 7.31–7.33; see fig. 7.20). This has black resin applied to a crack, a repair made by those who used it, suggesting that it was broken then mended, and revealing it as a well-used and valued object – a wonderful insight and a timeless human connection.

FIG. 7.31 Conservator Sophie Rowe-Kancleris working on the *kero* (fig. 7.20)

FIGS 7.32–7.33 Details showing the black resin used to repair the *kero* (fig. 7.20)

Andean textiles in the Cusco region

Nilda Callañaupa Alvarez

In the Andes, the textile legacy of the pre-Columbian period has endured due to the formidable skill of master weavers – women and men who have continued the tradition of weaving on looms. The use of traditional waist and vertical looms has gone hand in hand with the application of age-old techniques, which include ways of colouring the fibres with plant-based, animal and mineral dyes. Textiles strongly represent Indigenous identities, and knowledge about weaving has been handed down through generations of Andean peoples. These traditions have persevered in spite of constant threats over a long period of colonial rule, but the twentieth century introduced a host of new problems. Globalisation and commodification have resulted in the proliferation of cheap materials, mass manufacturing and chemical dyes and synthetic fibres, which have become valued over traditional methods and labour. Another threat has been a general decline in knowledge, with younger generations not learning from their elders – which puts traditional practices at risk of extinction. Furthermore, racism against Indigenous peoples has provoked fear and shame when it comes to wearing traditional clothing.[1]

The Centro de Textiles Tradicionales del Cusco (CTTC) was founded as a non-profit organisation in 1996 by a group of Indigenous weavers from the community of Chinchero, as well as international supporters, the intention being to preserve the pre-Columbian legacy of weaving, maintaining it in the present and safeguarding it for future generations.[2] The Centre's mission is to promote the revitalisation and sustainable practice of ancestral textile traditions in the Cusco region, encouraging the empowerment of weavers in order to keep cultural identity and weaving traditions alive. This is carried out through both training and the promotion of the art of weaving, thus also improving the weavers' living standards.

The work of the CTTC focuses on the creation of groups of weavers from different communities within the region of Cusco (fig. 7.34). At present, there are ten associations made up of groups of elders, adults, young people and children, who use a variety of iconographical patterns, techniques and colours. Over more than three decades, the CTTC has encouraged awareness among the weavers about the cultural value of Andean textiles and the importance of their own identities by wearing traditional dress at important religious and political events of the community. Moreover, the Centre has been doing some research to recover pre-Columbian techniques through practical workshops carried out with local weavers from the rural community of Pitumarca, a town located in the Province of Canchis, 87 kilometres south-west of Cusco, near the highway that continues on to Lake Titicaca. Some of the pre-Columbian techniques recovered as part of this project are briefly presented below.

The CTTC seeks to promote a number of pre-Columbian and colonial weaving techniques. There are four that demonstrate particular styles and

FIG. 7.34 Weavers from Pitumarca creating the base structure for a textile, 2021

skills: discontinuous warp and weft weaving; double-cloth weaving; the cross-knit loop stitch technique; and the knotting technique.

To produce a discontinuous warp and weft pattern, the weaver manipulates the warp and weft into two or more separate and discontinuous blocks in order to create an effect of colours changing within the same layer.[3] In spite of its complex execution, this technique has been used in a diverse range of textiles, such as *unkunas* (medium-sized carrying cloths), blankets, ponchos and bags. Likewise, by means of collective work involving up to six women weavers, the CTTC has been able to replicate both the discontinuous warp technique performed by the Chimú and other techniques used by the Nasca to produce mantles.

The second method, the double-cloth technique, uses several heddles to allow the creation of double rows or double fabric. The double effect is created when two different sets of warps are interlaced with two sets of wefts to produce two different fabric structures.[4] Due to the increased number of threads in the warp, the textiles produced are more resistant than average. This technique was used during the pre-Inca as well as during the Inca period, and was developed mostly in coastal regions.

The third technique, the cross-knit loop stitch, was introduced towards the end of the Paracas period, its three-dimensional motifs decorating the borders of funerary mantles. Weavers from Pitumarca have been employing this technique, which is performed with a needle, in order to replicate figures of plants, animals and mythical beings featured in the original textiles; it is known to be one of the oldest traditions in the ancient world.

The fourth technique is a kind of knotting that has been implemented by the project's weavers to replicate the four-cornered hats of the Tiwanaku, Wari and Inca cultures (figs 7.35–7.36). Using mostly camelid fibres and needles, they have created the most visually striking specimens.

In addition to the recovery of pre-Columbian techniques, the CTTC has also been working to recover ancient techniques via several case studies. The first one was based on the miniature textiles found with the body of a young girl from the Inca period, known as the Girl of the Ampato. The find, part of a Capacocha sacrifice ritual performed by the Incas, was directed by anthropologist Johan Reinhard with the Museo Santuarios Andinos of the Universidad Católica de Santa María (UCSM) in Arequipa. The second study sought to replicate the colonial poncho of the famous liberator José de San Martín, which is currently housed at the Argentine National Historical Museum in Buenos Aires.[5]

Finally, the CTTC has also focused on reintroducing traditional techniques and designs that have fallen out of practice in recent years (figs 7.37–7.38). This is the case, for example, with the use of natural dyes, the extraction of fine threads and the perfection of the finish, projects that have been accomplished thanks to the patience and knowledge of the weavers. Even today, they continue to represent both aspects of their own lives and enduring weaving traditions through these timeless pieces. It is only by preserving and sharing these practices with younger generations that we will ensure the continuity and relevance of Andean textiles, which are without a doubt one of the richest traditions of the ancient world.

In partnership with the British Museum, CTTC weavers from the rural community of Pitumarca have created a new textile piece based on pre-Columbian and traditional techniques, an object which responds in many ways to the concepts addressed in this book (fig. 7.39). While Pitumarca has recently become an attraction due to Vinicunca – a site of geological beauty also known as the Rainbow Mountain, where the natural mineralogy and environmental conditions have created a marbling effect – it is above all known for its long-lived weaving tradition. While the community weavers stand out for their backstrap-woven traditional textiles, in recent years they have begun venturing into the revival of complex pre-Columbian techniques that were almost lost, such is the case of the discontinuous warp and weft technique, or *ticlla*. This form of weaving, introduced by the Paracas peoples around 2,000 years ago, is unique to the Central Andean region. It consists of changing the colour of the warp thread anywhere by inserting sticks into the warp. Other techniques frequently used by the Pitumarca master weavers are the complementary warp-faced weave and supplementary warp-faced weave and knits. Around forty adults and twenty-five young weavers travel once a week from the highland communities to Pitumarca and meet in the textile centre, where they spend time together weaving, knitting and braiding. Weavers in Pitumarca have focused on passing their knowledge to younger generations, a testament to the power of family and community when working together with respect to their past.[6]

The new commission, which is now part of the British Museum's collections, integrates four techniques belonging to different periods in the history of the Andean tradition (fig. 7.40). These include one tapestry technique in the Wari style (top left); one warp-faced Inca textile (top right); a replication of the colonial technique used in San Martín's poncho (bottom left); and finally a section that uses contemporary techniques from Pitumarca textiles (bottom right). A *chakana* or cross, made using the discontinuous warp-faced weaving technique, unites the different textiles as one.

FIG. 7.37 (BELOW) Señora Concepcion Chuquichampi, a weaver from Pitumarca, using a ground loom to work on part of the new textile commissioned by the British Museum in 2021

FIG. 7.38 (BOTTOM) A ground loom in use in Pitumarca, 2021

FIG. 7.39 (OPPOSITE TOP) Weavers working on the central section of the newly commissioned textile, 2021

FIG. 7.40 (OPPOSITE BOTTOM) The weavers of each section holding the finished textile commission: Gregorio Ccana Rojo (top left), Marina Maza Huaman (top right), Concepcion Chuquichampi (bottom left) and Alipio Melo Irco (bottom right)

Andean values and people power:
ayllu, *ayni* and *mink'a*

Jago Cooper

The ayllu *is a model whose reach stretches to almost all the Indigenous peoples of the Andean region: Colombia, Ecuador, Peru, Bolivia and Chile. It is* jatha, *the 'seed' from which civilisation and political structures such as Tawantinsuyu [the Inca Empire] were germinated. The* ayllu *remains today the unit that forms the fabric of social and political organisation.*[1]

Andean societies did not have a concept of personal ownership. Once this fundamental fact is grasped, the edifice of Western economic and political assumptions of how people organise themselves and how societies 'should' work begins to crumble away. The societal structures for people and power in the Andes emerge from a different framework of cultural values, based on social obligation and mutuality rather than the economic motivation and individualism that drive capitalist societies today.

A basic requirement of capitalism is that individuals and groups are able to own things and aspire to accrue capital. Such a system then necessitates the creation of laws to arbitrate ownership and documents to record it. Indeed, some of the earliest written texts in the Middle East are the tallies of harvested goods and records of land capital.[2] The invention of money – or in the early economies of the Middle East, rations representing a form of payment – resulted from a need for an agreed mechanism of financial control. In stark contrast, Andean societies shared a different view: the world was not seen as a set of resources that could be controlled and owned. Instead land, plants, animals, minerals and people were a living ecosystem that individuals and communities had an obligation to steward and sustain. This is why the invention of money was never required in the Andes. *Ayni* is a Quechua word that helps to define this perspective; it refers to the social expectation of reciprocal exchange and balance, of communal mutuality and compensation. This guiding principle of Andean life is that elements of nature give and receive to maintain balance and contribute to the harmony of the world.[3] It is connected with the Quechua term *mink'a*, which refers to the individual contribution and communal redistribution required to ensure *ayni*.

Mink'a often takes shape in the form of collective volunteer labour for communal projects, with people giving their time and effort to work together towards a shared goal.

These underlying cultural values mean that Andean societies had no reason to create a fixed and arbitrary monetary system. Value came from human communality of purpose, and value systems were based on the meaning of the materiality and process of creation rather than commodities. Things that were created through collaborative effort and time – such as agricultural terraces or an elaborate textile, which require many people working cooperatively for a prolonged period of time – had value not in an economic sense of hours worked but in a cultural sense of shared creation.[4] Trade and exchange networks should be thought of as negotiations of social obligation rather than commercial enterprises, even when operating on a large scale. This also explains why the individual ownership of land and material objects never occurred to Andean societies.[5] Individual and societal obligations were met through understanding and reciprocal obligation, established by the social expectations of the community. Occasionally they could be imposed and enforced through warfare, but this was not in the form of territorial ownership or economic servitude in the same way as in the Middle East and Europe during the same period. Therefore, this Andean world, without ownership and a monetary economy, provides a very different starting point for exploration. The notion of 'social capital' rather than 'economic capital' is a good place to begin.

AYLLU

Ayllu is a political, geographical and ethnic unit, but in its simplest form it is the basic unit of Indigenous community organisation. Today, each Andean village or town with ongoing Indigenous cultural practices has different *ayllus* to which people belong. Carlos Teodoro Rojas Capistrano lives in Tupicocha in the province of Huarochirí, and his *ayllu* is one of ten operating in his settlement. While they are not dependent on blood relationships, Carlos tends to describe *ayllus* almost like huge extended families, his *ayllu* being a community network of people he works with and has relied upon since childhood. Reflecting the role of dualism in Andean society, many smaller settlements have two *ayllus* or a series of paired *ayllus*. The *ayllu* is a lifelong obligation and is how most aspects of community work, *mink'a*, are organised within and around settlements.

The responsibilities of the land are shared out between *ayllus* and they are the organisms through which labour is structured and food is distributed (fig. 7.41). Through the *ayllu* the motivations of moral obligation and social expectation underpin the labour, trade and power structures of Andean societies. As sociologist Simón Yampara Huarachi writes, 'The *ayllu* is a systemic and holistic institution with four fundamental organisational pillars: a) management of territory; b) productive and economic system; c) the cultural system and the hierarchy of ritual spaces; d) the sociopolitical system and the hierarchy of authorities.'[6] Together, these elements maintain the balance of life in the *ayllu*.

Numerous studies have focused on the relative societal benefits of the *ayllu* system in providing social security for individuals as part of the collective. Their academic authors have frequently used Marxist, socialist or structuralist historical frameworks to build their arguments and interpretation of the *ayllu*, from the seminal work of José Carlos Mariátegui in the 1920s, to the anthropological adaptation of applying Indigenous principles to contemporary social theory in the 1970s by the likes of John Murra, John Howland Rowe and Reiner Zuidema.[7] Anthropologists have used these frameworks to demonstrate the vitality of Indigenous communities and to further ethnographic study into concepts that can reveal a uniquely Andean thought process. It is true that in many ways the *ayllu* acts as the universal social support network that provides for individuals relative to their needs. These historical systems of reciprocity and shared contribution are well documented in Andean ethnography and ethnohistory. More recent evidence from ancient DNA studies indicates that these community practices of the *ayllu* date back thousands of years.[8]

The ongoing contemporary relevance of these systems, both in practice and theory, has never been more important. Politically, these Indigenous principles and practices are powerful and commonly referenced in speeches by presidents of Andean countries. Historically, they also underpin the development of revolutionary movements such as the Movimiento Revolucionario Túpac Amaru (MRTA) and others that reference Indigenous resistance leaders in name and deed, as well as ambitions for Indigenous social justice that combine Indigenous principles with contemporary socialist ideologies in their manifestos. Consequently, the Indigenous past is still active and alive in the region's present, and found in the competing ambitions for Peru's future.

The *ayllu* fosters a system of exchange based upon the principles of *ayni* and *mink'a* and importantly they connect communities across the diverse Andean landscapes.[9] Each *ayllu* comprises land and individual members drawn from different environmental zones throughout the local region. This means that if one particular crop fails or harvest spoils, there is capacity in the *ayllu* redistribution system to provide food and avoid local famines and vulnerabilities to environmental hazards. This system of organisation has led some to describe Andean communities as 'vertical archipelagos' bound together by shared systems of social organisation and obligation.[10]

In some ways, this moral economy provides the best framework to understand the principles and values of Andean societies of both the past and present.[11] The arrangement is that people are obliged to contribute based on principles of responsibility, fairness, expectation and justice. The value of something is in the process of shared creation rather than the ownership of the material product in and of itself.[12] These Andean cultural values create their own structure for how power then functions within society.

POWER

Sébastien Rey and Irving Finkel, from the Department of the Middle East at the British Museum, recently identified and translated the world's oldest border marker. This stone pillar, written in cuneiform, was ordered by King Enmetena to be placed in the sand to mark the frontier of Lagash (modern-day southern Iraq), the Sumerian city-state he controlled 4,500 years ago.[13] On this earliest territorial marker, Enmetena justified his right to power over the land he owned, while also making pejorative comments about his rival in the opposing city-state of Umma on the other side of the valley. This is the earliest evidence of someone literally drawing a line in the sand to demarcate ownership and the geographical limit of their power.[14] However, this close tie between territorial ownership and individual control that underpinned the emergence of complex societies in the Middle East never happened in the Andes. There is little evidence of Andean societies ever creating a boundary marker or building a wall to delineate a territory of control and power. Those who gained power did not do so based on aggregated wealth and land; they did it by being focal points of moral obligation and arbitrators of social justice.

In the fifteenth century the power of Inca rulers stretched 4,800 kilometres from Ecuador to Argentina – a huge geographical area. This was not a territory of consistent ownership and control; it was a patchwork of negotiated obligations and shared goals. In fact, the Inca territory had lots of areas within it where peoples did not subscribe to the Inca system. Inca power stemmed from the desire of the people to be part of this system. To be part of the Inca

FIG. 7.41 (PAGE 218) Members of the local community harvesting salt at Salinas de Maras, north-east of Cusco. The salt pans are managed by surrounding *ayllus* and have been in use for over 2,000 years.

FIG. 7.42 This contemporary painting shows the *comuneros* holding a communal meeting in which they agree to remain united and help one another against the incursions of the Onqoy (terrorists) and the military, as both sides were disputing control over their territory. ADAPS, *Communal Meeting*, 1991. Acrylic on plywood. H. 80 cm, W. 120 cm. Museo de Arte de Lima. Donated in association with Vida Popular Arts of the Americas

PAGES 222–3 Mantle depicting human figures with feline mouth masks holding severed heads. Early Nasca 100 BC–AD 100. Cotton and camelid fibres. H. 142 cm, W. 286 cm. Museo de Arte de Lima, IV-2.1-0002. Prado Family Bequest. Restored with a grant from the Bank of America Art Conservation Project

Empire, communities did not have to change their identity, religion, language or any aspect of what people defined as 'their' own particular culture. This is one of the reasons that there is comparatively little Inca material culture in Peru. Those who chose, or were obliged through warfare, to join with the Incas were offered a better way of life. Incas built on the *mink'a* system of community labour within the *ayllu* by implementing *mit'a*, an expanded system of required work for the Inca state rather than just the local community. In return, Incas offered a way of living that included revolutionary technology (see page 185). They arranged an improved logistical network for the delivery of food and resources on newly built road systems. They provided goods, stability and security, and in return communities shared their resources, communal labour and specialist skills. This scheme of agreed participation in the larger system was completely normal for people in the Andes; it was built upon millennia of tradition in which power was rooted in shared responsibility and social obligation.

SOCIETY

In trying to understand Andean societies, some of which existed hundreds or even thousands of years ago, more knowledge often leads only to further questions rather than definitive answers. These societies were constructed within a different set of cultural values and based on responsibilities to a living world. However, the complex dynamics of cultural variability and adaptive change through time should never be overlooked. Historically, some scholars have interpreted these cultural values in a holistic way to discuss 'Andeanism', a romanticised and essentialised identity for all peoples of the Andes across time. But Andeanism is in fact part of a rich mosaic of national literature and culture produced within postcolonial contexts. As the anthropologist Mary Weismantel writes, the founders of the 1920s Indigenismo movement in Peru, such as Peruvian intellectual Luis E. Valcárcel, are the most critical sources of information about the *ayllu*. Their desire was to create powerful literature about their own ancestors and the history of the Andes.[15]

In this way, Andeanism can provide a context for shared social perspectives without denying the extraordinary diversity and dynamism of these cultures. The direct and brutal repression of Indigenous ways of life throughout the Andes over the past five hundred years, and the complexity of new sovereignties created during the birth of Peru, make the enduring legacies of Andean peoples an extraordinary testament to cultural resilience (fig. 7.42). Despite centuries of colonial oppression, the *ayllu* remains a common foundation for community organisation, Indigenous political activism, territorial land rights and even climate change response.[17] The vital role of Indigenous cultural principles, socio-economic structures and social values endure and help foster thought and reflection on the alternative ways in which all societies could be structured in the future.

List of lenders

The Amano Pre-Columbian Textile Museum, Lima, Peru
Complejo Arqueológico El Brujo | Fundación Augusto N. Wiese
Fundación Temple Radicati — Universidad Nacional Mayor de San
    Marcos, Lima, Peru
The Gartner Collection, Lima, Peru
Ministerio de Cultura del Perú
Museo de Arte de Lima, Peru
Museo Kuntur Wasi, Peru
Museo Larco, Lima, Peru
Museo Nacional de Arqueología, Antropología e Historia del Perú,
    Lima, Peru
Museo 'Santiago Uceda Castillo' — Proyecto Arqueológico
    Huacas de Moche, Peru
Private Collection
Staatliche Museen zu Berlin, Ethnologisches Museum, Germany

Note on dates and orthography

The many cultures in this book are dated according to the diagram on page 9, but there are a number of proposed date ranges accepted by scholars. New research and archaeological findings, which are uncovered as time goes on, continue to change and update the timeframes.

Similarly, the words in this publication can be spelled in different ways, which often depend on language and context. As pre-Columbian cultures did not use a formal writing system, there is no written record made by them of the languages they spoke, such as Aymara and Quechua.[1] Quechua words were recorded by the conquerors of the Incas, who used a Latin alphabet and adjusted the spellings according to their own interpretation of the pronunciation.[2]

From the 1970s onwards, scholars have been attempting to create de-Hispanicised spellings of Quechua words, such as writing 'Tiwanaku' rather than 'Tiahuanaco'. However, it is almost impossible to replicate a 'true' transliteration of these words, as the records we have are based on a sixteenth-century Spanish understanding of them, which does not necessarily incorporate glottal stops, accurate meanings or contexts, and the nuances of etymology. As a result, there are lots of variant spellings for these words and published works have different preferences. Some scholars have chosen to use variant spellings for places compared with cultures (such as 'Nazca' for the site and 'Nasca' for the culture).

This book uses 's' spellings for words such as 'Nasca' and 'Cusco', which are common in Peru today but less common in English-language publications. As a general rule, we have chosen to use 'w' and 'k' spellings for the most common words ('Wari' not 'Huari', 'Tiwanaku' not 'Tiahuanaco') – with a number of exceptions, including 'Inca' rather than 'Inka', which conforms to the spelling used in the exhibition *Peru: a journey in time*.[3]

List of contributors

CÉSAR ASTUHUAMÁN is Lecturer in Archaeology at the Universidad Nacional Mayor de San Marcos, Lima. After his PhD at the Institute of Archaeology, UCL, he returned to Peru to pursue his career in the Ministry of Culture and Universidad Nacional Mayor de San Marcos. He currently runs a number of fieldwork projects across Peru exploring the human use of landscape.

NILDA CALLAÑAUPA ALVAREZ is a native Quechua, Spanish and English speaker from Chinchero, Peru. She has a master's degree in tourism from San Antonio Abad University of Cusco and is the founder, director and board member of the Centro de Textiles Tradicionales de Cusco (CTTC). She leads Andean weaving workshops, sits on panels and attends conferences across the globe.

CAROLINE R. CARTWRIGHT is Senior Scientist at the British Museum. She has led many teams of bioarchaeologists on international projects in the Caribbean, Africa, the Middle East and elsewhere.

RAFAEL VEGA CENTENO SARA-LAFOSSE is Lecturer in Archaeology in the Department of Humanities at the Pontificia Universidad Católica del Peru. His main research projects have focused on the Late Archaic Period in the Fortaleza-Paramonga valley and the Late Epochs of the southern basin of the Yanamayo river (Sierra de Áncash). He is currently conducting research at the Maranga Archaeological Complex, Lima.

MANUEL CHOQQUE runs a family project growing native potatoes at high altitudes in the Andes in his home village of Huatata, near the Inca site of Chinchero in Cusco.

JAGO COOPER is Head of the Americas Section at the British Museum and Director of the Santo Domingo Centre of Excellence for Latin American Research. In addition to his academic publications and museum exhibitions, he has also written and presented a series of BBC documentaries based on his research and international collaborations.

THOMAS A. CUMMINS is Project Curator of *Peru: a journey in time* at the British Museum.

JOANNE DYER is Colour Scientist in the Department of Scientific Research at the British Museum and specialises in the study of colour, colourants and their sources.

PETER FUX is Director at the Museum of St Gallen, Switzerland and was previously curator of the Arts of the Americas and Archaeology collections at the Museum Rietberg, Zürich. He focuses on cooperation with the countries of origin of the collections, both in the exhibitions themselves as well as in conservation

and research. He heads archaeological excavations and cooperative projects in Honduras, Peru and Bhutan.

ANDREW JAMES HAMILTON is Associate Curator of Arts of the Americas at The Art Institute of Chicago and a Lecturer in the Department of Art History at the University of Chicago. His work is invested in analysing objects, how they were made, used and eventually disused, in order to understand why they were created and what cultural meanings they bore. He is the author and illustrator of *Scale & the Incas* (Princeton University Press, 2018), and is working on a forthcoming book examining the royal Inca tunic at Dumbarton Oaks.

ANNA HARRISON is Senior Conservator in the Organic Artefacts Conservation Studio at the British Museum, and Exhibition Conservator for *Peru: a journey in time*.

VICTOR HUAMANCHUMO is a third-generation fisherman from the coastal village of Huanchaco in Trujillo. He builds and uses *totora* reed boats and helps to pass on this knowledge to younger generations.

JULIO IBARROLA is a ceramicist from northern Peru. His practice is inspired by archaeological examples of pottery from excavations.

RICARDO KUSUNOKI is Curator of Colonial and Republican Art at the Museo de Arte de Lima, Peru. Ricardo pursued his art history interests at the Universidad Nacional Mayor de San Marcos and his research focuses on Peruvian art of the eighteenth and nineteenth centuries. His work has led to the creation of numerous high-profile exhibitions at MALI.

GEORGE F. LAU is a Reader in Archaeology at the Sainsbury Research Unit for the Arts of Africa, Oceania & the Americas at the University of East Anglia, who specialises in the archaeology and arts of the Americas, especially of South America and the Central Andes. His research has included excavations at the village of Chinchawas, near Huaraz, and the large fortified centres of Yayno (Pomabamba) and Pashash (Cabana), as well as collections and field studies in different regions of Peru, the United States and Europe.

CECILIA PARDO is Project Curator in the Americas Section at the British Museum and Lead Curator for the exhibition *Peru: a journey in time*. She was formerly Chief Curator and Deputy Director at the Museo de Arte de Lima, Peru. Her recent exhibition catalogues include *Khipus. Nuestra historia en nudos* (2020) and *Nasca* (2017).

AMELIA PEREZ TRUJILLO is an archaeologist at the Instituto Nacional de Cultura, Cusco, Peru. She has extensive experience leading archaeological projects,

including working alongside Bill Sillar in Raqchi and directing excavations at Qotakilli. Most recently, she has worked on arachnological restoration and research projects across Peru.

ELENA PHIPPS is an independent textile scholar and curator currently teaching technical and cultural history of world textiles at the University of California at Los Angeles (UCLA). She has been Senior Museum Conservator in the Textile Conservation Department at the Metropolitan Museum of Art, New York (1977–2010), and co-curator of several major textile exhibitions, including *Tapestries and Silverwork of the Colonial Andes* (2004), and *The Interwoven Globe* (2013). She has numerous publications in the field of Andean textile history, materials and materiality.

GABRIEL PRIETO is an Assistant Professor in the Department of Anthropology at the University of Florida, whose primary research interest is the study of ancient maritime adaptations in the South Pacific coast, with a focus on the north coast of Peru. His research is also devoted to a long-term and multidisciplinary project focused on ritualised human violence in ancient times. At Huanchaco and Huanchaquito, his team has uncovered what is considered the largest ancient child and camelid sacrifice ever found in the world.

MONIQUE PULLAN is Senior Conservator in the Organic Artefacts Conservation Studio at the British Museum.

SOPHIE ROWE-KANCLERIS is Conservator in the Organic Artefacts Conservation Studio at the British Museum.

JULIO RUCABADO is Curator of Pre-Columbian Art at the Museo de Arte de Lima, Peru and was previously Registrar at the Museo de Sitio Pachacamac. His research covers coastal–mountain relations in the context of the formation of the Moche state, and iconographic studies of the Moche and Recuay systems of visual representation.

DIANNE SCULLIN specialises in Musicology at the University of Bristol. She is currently the Network Facilitator on the Leverhulme Network Grant project 'Processional Chants in Early Medieval Iberia', where she investigates the interactions between Old Hispanic liturgical chants and the church architecture of early medieval Iberia.

BILL SILLAR is a Professor at the Institute of Archaeology, University College London. Much of his research has been in the Andean highlands, where he combines ethnographic and archaeological fieldwork with artefact analysis in order to gain a better understanding of Indigenous society before, during and after the Inca Empire.

Notes

Introduction

1. For further information, see Luis Jaime Castillo and Jeffrey Quilter, *New Perspectives on Moche Political Organization*, Washington, DC: Dumbarton Oaks Research Library and Collection, 2010; Katharina Schreiber and Josué Lancho Rojas, *Aguas en el desierto: Los puquios de Nasca*, Lima: Fondo Editorial Pontificia Universidad Católica del Perú, 2006.
2. Gary Urton and Cecilia Pardo (eds), *Khipus*, Lima: Museo de Arte de Lima, unpublished.
3. The republic of Peru declared its independence from Spain in 1821. Since then, political borders have shifted due to conflicts with neighbouring countries.
4. Bernard Lavallé, *En busca del Perú: las dos primeras expediciones (1524–1528)*, Lima: Boletín del Instituto Francés de Estudios Andinos, 2013.
5. Frank Salomon, 'The Khipus of Tupicocha and Rapaz', in Urton and Pardo (eds), *Khipus*, pp. 176–83.
6. For further reading on the history of Peruvian archaeology and museums, see Julio C. Tello and M. Toribio Mejía Xesspe, *Historia de los museos nacionales del Perú, 1822–1944*, vol. X: *Arqueológicas*, Lima: Museo Nacional de Antropología, Arqueología e Historia del Perú, 1967, pp. 1–268.
7. For this statistic, see 'Quechua at Penn' on the University of Pennsylvania website: https://web.sas.upenn.edu/quechua (accessed 1 June 2021).

1 PERU THROUGH TIME

Reflections on the Andean past

1. Reflecting the reality that conversations are at the heart of discussions of how the past should be presented, these excerpts were translated and edited from original conversations in Spanish.

The Peruvian pre-Columbian collections at the British Museum: a brief history

1. 'Questions and Answers', Chairman to Franks, 1860 Select Committee on the British Museum, quoted in David M. Wilson, *The Forgotten Collector: Augustus Wollaston Franks*, London: Thames and Hudson, 1984, p. 12.
2. SD Celar's objectives are to facilitate work by some of the world's leading students and scholars in order to produce and communicate research related to these collections.
3. My thanks go to Thomas A. Cummins, project curator, who collaborated on the research for this article, and to Jim Hamill, who provided helpful data on early acquisitions in the context of the museum's development.

4. David M. Wilson, *The British Museum: A History*, London: The British Museum Press, 2002, p. 15; J. C. H. King, Ethnographic collections, pp. 228–9. See also Arthur MacGregor (ed.), *Sir Hans Sloane: Collector, Scientist, Antiquary, Founding Father of the British Museum*, London: The British Museum Press, 1994.
5. Information from Museum Index +, the British Museum internal database.
6. Baltasar Jaime Martínez de Compañón, *Trujillo del Perú*, c. 1782–5.
7. Cecilia Pardo, 'The Material Construction of the Past: A Brief Account of the Creation of Archaeological Collections', in *Peru: Kingdoms of the Sun and Moon*, ed. Victor Pimentel, Montreal: Montreal Museum of Fine Arts, 2013, pp. 34–7; see also Pascale Riviale, *Un siècle d'archéologie française au Pérou (1821–1914)*, Paris: L'Harmattan, 1996.
8. Julio C. Tello and M. Toribio Mejía Xesspe, *Historia de los museos nacionales del Perú, 1822–1944*, vol. X: *Arqueológicas*, Lima: Museo Nacional de Antropología, Arqueología e Historia del Perú, 1967, pp. 1–268.
9. Wilson, *The Forgotten Collector*, p. 14.
10. Ibid., p. 31.
11. Ibid., p. 32.
12. See the essay by Julio Rucabado in this volume, pp. 114ff.
13. William M. Mathew, *La firma inglesa Gibbs y el monopolio del guano en el Perú*, trans. Marcos Cueto, Lima: Banco Central de Reserva del Perú and IEP Instituto de Estudios Peruanos, 2009, p. 31. Guano, the deposited excrement of seabirds and bats, is a highly effective fertiliser due to its rich mineral components.
14. Catalina Vizcarra, 'Guano, Credible Commitments, and Sovereign Debt Repayment in Nineteenth-Century Peru', *Journal of Economic History*, vol. 69 (2009), pp. 358–87, at p. 368.
15. Correspondence sent to A. W. Franks from J. Moore on 17 July and 5 September 1871. British Museum Archives.
16. Correspondence sent to A. W. Franks by Josiah Harris on 14 September 1871. British Museum Archives.
17. Beatrix Hoffmann, 'Introduction to the History of the Textile Collection at the Ethnological Museum, Berlin', in *Pre-Columbian Textile Conference VII*, ed. Lena Bjerregaard and Ann Peters, Lincoln, NE: Zea Books, 2017, pp. 176–90, at p. 177.
18. Set of correspondence between Adan Digby and George Evelyn Hutchinson in 1946. British Museum Archives.
19. George Kubler, 'Towards Absolute Time: Guano Archaeology', *Memoirs of the Society for American Archaeology*, vol. 4 (1948), pp. 29–50.
20. Ibid., p. 46.
21. Thomas Athol Joyce, *South American Archaeology: An Introduction to the Archaeology of the South American Continent with Special Reference to the Early History of Peru*, New York: G. P. Putnam's Sons, 1912, pp. xv, 292.
22. Note left in one of the three boxes left by Markham, which are currently in the British Museum Archives.
23. Hoffmann, 'Introduction to the History', pp. 186–7.
24. EthnoDocs 1471, Department of AOA, British Museum Archives.

25. Jim Hamill, pers. comm., March 2021. For further information, see also Ben Burt, *Museum of Mankind: Man and Boy in the British Museum Ethnography Department*, New York: Berghahn Books, 2019.
26. Wilson, *The British Museum: A History*, p. 282.
27. Burt, *Museum of Mankind*, p. 104.
28. Ibid., p. 103.

An Andean journey through time

1. Johannes Fabian, *Time and the Other: How Anthropology Makes Its Object*, New York: Columbia University Press, 1983, p. 34. This is quoted by Paul Nadasdy, who uses it to frame his own argument about First Nation state formation in the Yukon and time: *Sovereignty's Entailments: First Nation State Formation in the Yukon*, Toronto, ON: University of Toronto Press, 2017, p. 253.
2. Alfredo López Austin, 'Ecumene Time, Anecumene Time: Proposal of a Paradigm', in *The Measure and Meaning of Time in Mesoamerica and the Andes*, ed. Anthony F. Aveni, Washington, DC: Dumbarton Oaks Research Library and Collection, 2015, p. 29.
3. Francesca Fernandini Parodi, 'The Time of the Past: Exploring the Rhythms of a Pre-Hispanic Urban Settlement in the Coastal Andes (AD 550–850)', *Journal of Social Archaeology*, vol. 20 (2020), pp. 245–67; Silvia Rivera Cusicanqui, *Ch'ixinakax utxiwa: On Decolonising Practices and Discourses*, London: Wiley, 2020.
4. Silvia Rivera Cusicanqui, 'Ch'ixinakax utxiwa: A Reflection on the Practices and Discourses of Decolonization', *South Atlantic Quarterly*, vol. 111 (2012), pp. 95–109.
5. Anthony F. Aveni, 'Understanding Time, Space and Social Organization in the Inca Ceque System of Cuzco', in Aveni (ed.), *The Measure and Meaning of Time*, p. 106.
6. Martina Faller, 'Propositional- and Illocutionary-Level Evidentiality in Cuzco Quechua', *Semantics of Under-Represented Languages in the Americas*, vol. 2 (2020), article 3.
7. Terence N. D'Altroy, *The Incas*, Chichester: Wiley Blackwell, 2015, p. 139.
8. Juan M. Ossio, 'Ages of the World in the Andes', in Aveni (ed.), *The Measure and Meaning of Time*, p. 212.
9. Stella Nair, 'Time and Space in the Architecture of Inca Royal Estates', in ibid., pp. 119–39.
10. Regina Harrison, 'Pérez Bocanegra's Ritual *formulario*: Khipu Knots and Confession', in *Narrative Threads: Accounting and Recounting in Andean Khipu*, ed. Jeffrey Quilter and Gary Urton, Austin, TX: University of Texas Press, 2002, pp. 266–90.
11. Ivan Ghezzi and Clive Ruggles, 'Chankillo: A 2300-Year-Old Solar Observatory in Coastal Peru', *Science*, vol. 315 (2007), pp. 1239–43; Brian S. Bauer, *The Sacred Landscape of the Inca: The Cusco Ceque System*, Austin, TX: University of Texas Press, 2011; David M. Wilson, *The British Museum: A History*, London: British Museum Press, 2002.
12. Bauer, *The Sacred Landscape of the Inca*.
13. Wilson, *The British Museum: A History*.
14. Nadasdy, *Sovereignty's Entailments*, p. 253.
15. Melanie J. Miller, Juan Albarracin-Jordan, Christine Moore and José M. Capriles, 'Chemical Evidence for the Use of Multiple Psychotropic Plants in a

1,000-Year-Old Ritual Bundle from South America', *Proceedings of the National Academy of Sciences*, vol. 116 (2019), pp. 11207–12.

16. Matthew C. Reilly, 'Futurity, Time, and Archaeology', *Journal of Contemporary Archaeology*, vol. 6 (2019), pp. 1–15, at p. 2.

2 LIVING LANDSCAPES

Time, space and living landscapes in the Andes

1. This is a revised version of a text originally published in *Guia MALI*, Lima: Museo de Arte de Lima, 2015.

2. Stephen B. Brush, 'Man's Use of an Andean Ecosystem', *Human Ecology*, vol. 4 (1976), pp. 147–66. See also Instituto de Desarrollo y Medioambiente del Peru, available at www.idmaperu.org (accessed 20 April 2021).

3. John Murra, 'El "Control vertical" de un máximo de pisos ecológicos en la economía de las sociedades andinas', in Iñigo Ortiz de Zúñiga, *Visita de la Provincia de León de Huánuco en 1562*, vol. II, ed. John Murra, Huánuco: Universidad Nacional Hermilio Valdizán, 1972, pp. 427–76.

4. Brush, 'Man's Use of an Andean Ecosystem', pp. 147–66.

5. Dorothy Menzel, John H. Rowe and Lawrence E. Dawson, *The Paracas Pottery of Ica: A Study in Style and Time*, Berkeley: University of California Press, 1964.

6. Luis G. Lumbreras, *De los pueblos, las culturas y las artes del antiguo Perú*, Lima: Moncloa-Campodónico, 1969.

7. Luis Millones and Alfredo López Austin, *Dioses del Norte. Dioses del Sur. Religion y Cosmovisiones en Mesoamerica y los Andes*, Lima: Instituto de Estudios Peruanos, 2008.

8. Nicolas Goepfert, 'The Llama and the Deer: Dietary and Symbolism Dualism in the Central Andes', *Anthropozoologica*, vol. 45 (2010), pp. 25–45.

9. Carlos G. Elera, 'La cultura Cupisnique a partir de los datos arqueológicos de Puémape', in *De Cupisnique a los incas: El arte del valle de Jequetepeque*, ed. Luis Jaime Castillo and Cecilia Pardo, Lima: Museo de Arte de Lima, 2010, pp. 68–111.

10. Thomas B. F. Cummins, *Toasts with the Inca: Andean Abstraction and Colonial Images on Quero Vessels*, Ann Arbor: University of Michigan Press, 2002.

11. Cecilia Pardo (ed.), *Modelando el mundo: Imágenes de la arquitectura precolombina*, Lima: Museo de Arte de Lima, 2011.

12. Juliet Wiersema, 'La relación simbólica entre las representaciones arquitectónicas en las vasijas Mochica y su función ritual', in Pardo (ed.), *Modelando el mundo*, pp. 164–91.

13. David Noble Cook, *Demographic Collapse: Indian Peru, 1520–1620*, Cambridge: Cambridge University Press, 2004.

14. Alexander Koch et al., 'Earth System Impacts of the European Arrival and Great Dying in the Americas after 1492', *Quaternary Science Reviews*, vol. 207 (2019), pp. 13–36.

15. For more information, see Pablo José de Arriaga, *The Extirpation of Idolatry in Peru* [1621], ed. and trans. L. Clark Keating, Lexington: University of Kentucky Press, 1968.

16. See Murra, 'El "Control vertical"'.

Materials and materialities

1. This is a revised version of a text originally published in *Guia MALI*, Lima: Museo de Arte de Lima, 2015. Thank you to MALI for permission to revisit this text.

Qhapaq Ñan: the Andean road system

1. Terence D'Altroy, 'The Imperial Inka Road System: Exploring New Paths', *Asian Archaeology*, vol. 2 (2018), pp. 3–18, at p. 14.

2. John Hyslop, *The Inka Road System*, New York: Academic Press, 1984.

3. Sofia Chacaltana, Elizabeth Arkush and Giancarlo Marcone (eds), *Nuevas tendencias en el estudio de los caminos*, Lima: Ministerio de Cultura/Proyecto Qhapaq Ñan, 2017.

4. D'Altroy, 'The Imperial Inka Road System', pp. 3–18.

5. César Astuhuamán, 'El patrimonio arqueológico en la Región Piura: Investigación, registro y gestión de los sitios y caminos inca', in *Compartiendo el patrimonio: Paisajes culturales y modelos de gestión en Andalucía y Piura*, ed. Javier Hernández-Ramírez and Enrique García Vargas, Seville: Secretariado de Publicaciones de la Universidad de Sevilla, 2013, pp. 183–214.

6. Pedro Cieza de León, *El Señorío de los Incas: 2a. parte de la Crónica del Perú*, Lima: Instituto de Estudios Peruanos, 1967, pp. 213–14.

7. Rob Dover and Nick Fletcher, *Report on Explorations in Northeastern Chachapoyas*, 2011, available at www.academia.edu/11702237/REPORT_ON_EXPLORATIONS_IN_NORTHEASTERN_CHACHAPOYAS (accessed 2 March 2021).

8. Darryl Wilkinson, 'Infrastructure and Inequality: An Archaeology of the Inka Road through the Amaybamba Cloud Forests', *Journal of Social Archaeology*, vol. 19 (2019), pp. 27–46.

9. Sofia Chacaltana, 'Los múltiples significados de la ruta Vilcashuamán-Pisco del Chinchaysuyu: Fuentes rituales y sistema hidráulico', in Chacaltana, Arkush and Marcone (eds), *Nuevas tendencias*.

10. Timothy Ingold, 'The Temporality of the Landscape', *World Archaeology*, vol. 25 (1993), pp. 152–74. See also Edward Swenson and Andrew Roddick, 'Introduction: Rethinking Temporality and Historicity from the Perspective of Andean Archaeology', in *Constructions of Time and History in the Ancient Andes*, ed. Edward Swenson and Andrew Roddick, Boulder, CO: University of Colorado Press, 2018, pp. 3–44.

11. Penny Harvey and Hannah Knox, *Roads: An Anthropology of Infrastructure and Expertise*, Ithaca, NY: Cornell University Press, 2015.

12. Ibid., p. 75.

13. Timothy Ingold, 'Footprints through the Weather-World: Walking, Breathing, Knowing', *Journal of the Royal Anthropological Institute*, vol. 16 (2010), pp. S121–S139.

14. Steve Kosiba and Andrew M. Bauer, 'Mapping the Political Landscape: Toward a GIS Analysis of Environmental and Social Difference', *Journal of Archaeological Method and Theory*, vol. 20 (2013), pp. 61–101.

3 CHAVÍN AND EARLY CULTURES

Early ceremonial centres in the Andes

1. Rafael Vega-Centeno Sara-Lafosse, 'El periodo arcaico tardío en perspectiva regional: Nuevos aportes', in *Repensar el antiguo Perú: Aportes desde la arqueología*, ed. Rafael Vega-Centeno Sara-Lafosse, Lima: IEP and PUCP, 2017, pp. 87–122.

2. Roy A. Rappaport, *Ritual and Religion in the Making of Humanity*, Cambridge: Cambridge University Press, 1999, pp. 170–8.

3. Junius B. Bird, John Hyslop and Milica Dimitrijevic Skinner, 'The Preceramic Excavations at the Huaca Prieta Chicama Valley, Peru', *Anthropological Papers of the AMNH*, vol. 62 (1985), pp. 154–87; Terence Grieder et al., *La Galgada, Peru: A Preceramic Culture in Transition*, Austin, TX: University of Texas Press, 1988, pp. 166–81.

4. For Caral, see Ruth Shady Solis, *America's First City? The Case of Late Archaic Caral*, New York: Springer, 2006. For Ventarrón, see Ignacio Alva Meneses, *Ventarrón y Collud: Origen y auge de la civilización en la costa norte del Perú*, Lima: Ministerio de Cultura del Perù, 2013, pp. 114–33. For El Paraíso, see Frederic Engel, 'El Complejo El Paraíso en el Valle de Chillón, habitado hace 3,500 años', *Anales Científicos de la Universidad Agraria*, vol. 5 (1967), pp. 241–80; Jeffrey Quilter, 'Architecture and Chronology at El Paraíso, Peru', *Journal of Field Archaeology*, vol. 12 (1985), pp. 279–97. For Kotosh, see Seiichi Izumi and Kazuo Terada (eds), *Andes 4. Excavations at Kotosh, Peru, 1963 and 1966*, Tokyo: University of Tokyo Press, 1972.

5. Sheila Pozorski and Thomas Pozorski, *Early Settlement and Subsistence in the Casma Valley, Peru*, Iowa City: University of Iowa Press, 1987; Julio C. Tello and Toribio Mejía Xesspe, *Arqueología del Valle de Casma*, Lima: Universidad Nacional Mayor de San Marcos, 1956.

6. Peter Kaulicke, 'Arte y religión en Cerro Sechín', in *Arqueología de Cerro Sechín*, vol. II: *Escultura*, ed. S. Lerner, M. Cárdenas and P. Kaulicke, Lima: Pontificia Universidad Católica del Perú, 1995, pp. 185–221.

7. For Huaca Lucía, see Izumi Shimada et al., 'Excavaciones efectuadas en el Centro Ceremonial de Huaca Lucía-Cholope, del Horizonte Temprano, Batan Grande, Costa Norte del Perú: 1979–1981', *Arqueológicas*, vol. 9 (1983), pp. 109–208. For Huaca Collud, see Alva, *Ventarrón y Collud*, pp. 187–202. For Huaca de los Reyes, see Thomas Pozorski, 'El complejo Caballo Muerto: Los frisos de barro de la Huaca de los Reyes', *Revista del Museo Nacional*, vol. 41 (1975), pp. 211–51. For Cerro Blanco and Huaca Partida, see Koichiro Shibata, 'El sitio de Cerro Blanco de Nepeña dentro de la dinámica interactiva del Período Formativo', *Boletín de*

Arqueología PUCP, vol. 12 (2010), pp. 287–315; see also Koichiro Shibata, 'Cosmología tripartita en Huaca Partida, valle bajo de Nepeña', *Indiana*, vol. 34 (2017), pp. 13–29. For Garagay, see Roger Ravines and William Isbell, 'Garagay: Sitio temprano en el valle de Lima', *Revista del Museo Nacional*, vol. 41 (1975), pp. 253–72. For Pacopampa, see Y. Seki et al., 'Nuevas evidencias del sitio arqueológico de Pacopampa, en la sierra norte del Perú', *Boletín de Arqueología PUCP*, vol. 12 (2008), pp. 69–95. For Kuntur Wasi, see Yoshio Onuki, *Kuntur Wasi y Cerro Blanco: Dos sitios del Formativo en el Norte del Perú*, Tokyo: Hokusen-Sha, 1995. For Campanayuq Rumi, see Yuichi Matsumoto and Yuri Cavero, 'Una aproximación cronológica del centro ceremonial de Campanayuq Rumi, Ayacucho', *Boletín de Arqueología PUCP*, vol. 13 (2009), pp. 323–46. Finally, for Chavín de Huántar, see Richard L. Burger, *Chavín de Huántar and the Origins of Andean Civilization*, London: Thames & Hudson, 1992; John W. Rick, 'The Evolution of Authority and Power at Chavín de Huántar, Peru', in *Foundations of Power in the Prehispanic Andes*, ed. K. Vaughn, D. Ogburn and C. Conlee, Arlington, VA: American Anthropological Association, 2005, pp. 71–90.

8. Burger, *Chavín de Huántar and the Origins of Andean Civilization*, pp. 149–50.

9. Silvia Rodriguez Kembel, 'The Architecture at the Monumental Center of Chavín de Huántar: Sequence, Transformations, and Chronology', in *Chavín: Art, Architecture, and Culture*, ed. William J. Conklin and Jeffrey Quilter, Los Angeles: Cotsen Institute of Archaeology, 2008, pp. 44–5.

10. Yoshio Onuki, 'Ocho tumbas especiales de Kuntur Wasi', *Boletín de Arqueología PUCP*, vol. 1 (1997), pp. 79–114.

11. Seki et al., 'Nuevas evidencias', pp. 90–1.

12. Luis Guillermo Lumbreras, 'Excavaciones en el templo antiguo de Chavín (Sector R.): Informe de la Sexta Campaña', *Ñawpa Pacha*, vol. 15 (1977), pp. 1–38.

13. Iván Ghezzi and Clive Ruggles, 'Las Trece Torres de Chankillo: arqueoastronomía y organización social en el primer observatorio solar de América', *Boletín de Arqueología PUCP*, vol. 10 (2006), pp. 215–35.

The ceremonial centre of Chavín de Huántar

1. Luis Guillermo Lumbreras, *Los orígenes de la civilización en el Perú*, Lima: Editorial Milla Batres, 1974.

2. These are approximate dates. For a detailed timeline of Chavín, see Peter Fux (ed.), *Chavín*, Lima: Museo de Arte de Lima, 2015, pp. 30–1.

3. Richard L. Burger, *Chavín and the Origins of Andean Civilization*, London: Thames and Hudson, 1995.

4. Luis Guillermo Lumbreras, *Chavín de Huántar: Excavaciones en la Galería de las Ofrendas*, Mainz am Rhein: Verlag Philipp Von Zabern, 1993.

5. John W. Rick, 'Chavín de Huántar: Evidence for an Evolved Shamanism', in *Mesas and Cosmologies in the Central Andes*, ed. Douglas Sharon, San Diego: San Diego Museum of Man, 2006, pp. 101–12.

6. For a broader understanding of the subject, see Fux (ed.), *Chavín*.

7. Burger, *Chavín and the Origins of Andean Civilization*, p. 228.

8. See also John Rick, 'Arquitectura y espacio ritual en Chavín de Huántar', in Fux (ed.), *Chavín*, pp. 161–75.

The history of Andean food and gastronomy

1. John E. Staller (ed.), *Andean Foodways: Pre-Columbian, Colonial, and Contemporary Food and Culture*, Cham, Switzerland: Springer, 2021, p. 2.

2. Martin Morales, *Andina: The Heart of Peruvian Food*, London: Quadrille, 2017.

3. Emiliano Trucchi et al., 'Ancient Genomes Reveal Early Andean Farmers Selected Common Beans while Preserving Diversity', *Nature Plants*, vol. 7 (2021), pp. 123–8.

4. George F. Lau, 'Camelids as Food and Wealth: Emerging Political and Moral Economies of the Recuay Culture', in Staller (ed.), *Andean Foodways*, pp. 61–87, at p. 62.

5. Frances Hayashida, 'Chicha Histories: Pre-Hispanic Brewing in the Andes and the Use of Ethnographic and Historical Analogues', in *Drink, Power, and Society in the Andes*, ed. Justin Jennings and Brenda J. Bowser, Gainesville, FL: University Press of Florida, 2009, pp. 233–56.

6. Crystal A. Dozier and Justin Jennings, 'Identification of Chicha de Maiz in the Pre-Columbian Andes through Starch Analysis', in Staller (ed.), *Andean Foodways*, pp. 187–204, at p. 188.

7. Hayashida, 'Chicha Histories: Pre-Hispanic Brewing in the Andes', p. 233.

8. Gabriel Prieto, 'Chicha Production during the Chimú Period at San José de Moro, Jequetepeque Valley, North Coast of Peru', in *From State to Empire in the Prehistoric Jequetepeque Valley, Peru* (BAR International Series, vol. 2310), ed. Colleen M. Zori and Ilana Johnson, Oxford: Oxford University Press, 2011, pp. 105–28.

9. Carla Hernández Garavito and Carlos Osores Mendives, 'Colonialism and Domestic Life: Identities and Foodways in Huarochirí during the Inka Empire', *International Journal of Historical Archaeology*, vol. 23 (2019), pp. 832–67.

10. William H. McNeill, 'How the Potato Changed the World's History', *Social Research*, vol. 66 (1999), pp. 67–83.

11. Emma McDonell, 'Commercializing the "Lost Crop of the Inca": Quinoa and the Politics of Agrobiodiversity in "Traditional" Crop Commercialization', in Staller (ed.), *Andean Foodways*, pp. 383–406.

4 PARACAS AND NASCA

Paracas and Nasca: life and death in the desert

1. Helaine Silverman and Donald A. Proulx, *The Nasca*, Oxford: Blackwell, 2002.

2. Cecilia Pardo and Peter Fux, *Nasca*, Lima: Museo de Arte de Lima, 2017, pp. 26–7.

3. Markus Reindel and Johny Isla, 'La costa sur en el periodo prehispánico', in Pardo and Fux (ed.), *Nasca*, pp. 40–55, at p. 41.

4. Markus Reindel, Johny Isla and Karsten Lambers, 'Archäologisches Projekt "Paracas en Palpa", Peru', *SLSA Jahresbericht 2004*, 2005, pp. 24–45, available at http://kops.uni-konstanz.de/bitstream/handle/123456789/20863/Reindel_208635.pdf (accessed 5 April 2021).

5. David G. Beresford-Jones et al., 'The Role of Prosopis in Ecological and Landscape Change in the Samaca Basin, Lower Ica Valley, South Coast of Peru, from the Early Horizon to the Late Intermediate Period', *Latin American Antiquity*, vol. 20 (2009), pp. 303–32.

6. Elsie Tomasto-Cagigao, Markus Reindel and Johny Isla, 'Paracas Funerary Practices in Palpa, South Coast of Perú', in *Funerary Practices and Models in the Ancient Andes*, ed. Peter Eeckhout and Lawrence S. Owens, New York: Cambridge University Press, 2015, pp. 69–86.

7. Ann Peters, 'El testimonio de una tumba: La presencia Nasca en Paracas', in Pardo and Fux (eds), *Nasca*, pp. 62–9.

8. Pardo and Fux (eds), *Nasca*, p. 27.

9. Giuseppe Orefici, *Nasca: el desierto de los dioses de Cahuachi*, Lima: Graph Ediciones, 2009.

10. Reindel and Isla, 'La costa sur en el periodo prehispánico', p. 41.

11. Karsten Lambers, 'Los geoglifos: Imágenes y escenarios en el desierto de Nazca y Palpa', in Pardo and Fux (ed.), *Nasca*, pp. 112–23.

12. Anna Gruszczyńska-Ziółkowska, *Detrás del silencio: La música en la cultura Nasca*, Lima: Fondo Editorial PUCP, 2014, pp. 237–9.

13. Pardo and Fux (ed.), *Nasca*, pp. 243–5, fig. 109.

14. Krzysztof Makowski (ed.), *Los Dioses del Antiguo Perú*, vol. I, Lima: Banco de Crédito del Perú, 2000, pp. 292–8, fig. 47; see also Cecilia Pardo and Julio Rucabado, *Fiestas y danzas del Perú*, Lima: Banco de Crédito del Perú, 2019.

15. Pedro Cieza de Leon, 'LXXV: De los más valles que hay hasta llegar a la provincia de Tarapacá', in *Parte primera de la Crónica del Perú* [1553], Madrid: Calpe, 1922, pp. 249–51.

16. Peter Kaulicke, *Max Uhle y el Perú Antiguo*, Lima: Fondo Editorial, Pontificia Universidad Católica del Perú, 1998, p. 48.

17. Julio C. Tello and M. Toribio Mejía Xesspe, *Historia de los museos nacionales del Perú, 1822–1944*, vol. X: *Arqueológicas*, Lima: Museo Nacional de Antropología, Arqueología e Historia del Perú, 1967, p. 156.

18. María Reiche, *Contribuciones a la geometría y astronomía en el antiguo Perú*, Lima: Asociación María Reiche para las Líneas de Nasca/Epígrafe Editores, 1993, p. 29.

19. Ibid.

20. Helaine Silverman, 'Beyond the Pampa: The Geoglyphs in the Valleys of Nazca', *National Geographic Research*, vol. 6 (1990), pp. 435–56; Persis Clarkson, 'The Archaeology of the Nazca Pampa: Environmental and Cultural Parameters', in *The Lines of Nazca*, ed. Anthony Aveni, Philadelphia:

American Philosophical Society, 1990, pp. 115–72; Anthony E. Aveni, *Between the Lines: The Mystery of the Giant Ground Drawings of Ancient Nasca, Peru*, Austin, TX: University of Texas Press, 2000; Johan Reinhard, *The Nazca Lines: A New Perspective on their Origin and Meaning*, Lima: Editorial Los Pinos, 1986.

21. Lambers, 'Los geoglifos: Imágenes y escenarios en el desierto de Nazca y Palpa', in Pardo and Fux (eds), *Nasca*; Masato Sakai, *Centros de líneas y cerámica en las pampas de Nasca, Perú*, Yamagata: Yamagata University Press, 2014.

22. Silverman, 'Beyond the Pampa', pp. 435–56.

23. Reindel and Isla, 'La costa sur en el periodo prehispánico', pp. 40–55; Markus Reindel, 'Life at the Edge of the Desert – Archaeological Reconstruction of the Settlement History in the Valleys of Palpa, Peru', in *New Technologies for Archaeology: Multidisciplinary Investigations in Palpa and Nasca, Peru*, ed. Markus Reindel and Günther A. Wagner, Berlin: Springer, 2009, pp. 439–61.

24. Reindel and Isla, 'La costa sur en el periodo prehispánico', p. 48.

25. Ibid.

26. Directed by Markus Reindel and Johny Isla, the project was created in 1996 as an initiative of the Swiss-Liechtenstein Foundation for Archaeological Research Abroad (SLSA) to explore the historical and cultural meaning of the famous geoglyphs and to study the societies that created them.

27. Johny Isla, pers. comm., December 2020.

28. Luis Jaime Castillo et al., 'The Palpa Figures', *World Archaeology*, vol. 95 (2019), available at www.world-archaeology.com/issues/issue-95/the-palpa-figures (accessed 10 July 2021).

29. Rita Ponce de León and Tania Solomonoff, pers. comm., December 2020.

Walking the lines: exploring the meaning of the Nasca geoglyphs

1. Markus Reindel and Günther A. Wagner, eds, *New Technologies for Archaeology: Multidisciplinary Investigations in Palpa and Nasca, Peru*, Berlin: Springer, 2009.

2. Peter Fux, 'The Petroglyphs of Chichictara, Palpa, Peru: Documentation and Interpretation using Terrestrial Laser Scanning and Image-Based 3D Modeling', *Zeitschrift für Archäologie Außereuropäischer Kulturen*, vol. 4 (2011), pp. 127–205.

3. Karsten Lambers, *The Geoglyphs of Palpa, Peru: Documentation, Analysis and Interpretation*, vol. II: *Forschungen zur Archäologie Außereuropäischer Kulturen*, Aichwald: Linden Soft, 2006; Karsten Lambers, 'Von Bildern zu Bühnen: Die Geoglyphen von Palpa und Nasca (Süd-Peru) in ihrem räumlichen und sozialen Kontext', in *Bild – Raum – Handlung: Perspektiven der Archäologie*, ed. Ortwin Dally, Susanne Moraw and Hauke Ziemssen, Berlin: De Gruyter, 2012, pp. 47–68.

4. See Markus Reindel and Peter Fux, 'Was uns Nasca zu erzählen hat: Perspektiven einer neuen transdisziplinären Diskussion', *Antike Welt: Zeitschrift für Archäologie und Kulturgeschichte*, vol. 1 (2018), pp. 29–32.

Searching for water in the desert

1. Katherina Schreiber, 'Los puquios', in *Nasca*, ed. Cecilia Pardo and Peter Fux, Lima: Museo de Arte de Lima, 2017, pp. 82–8.

Colours of life in the Andes: a scientific perspective

1. This research was made possible by a grant awarded by the Leverhulme Trust to the British Museum (F/00 052/G, 'Andean textiles: organic colourants, biological sources and dyeing technologies'). Dye analysis was carried out by Dr Thibaut Devièse and led by Dr Catherine Higgitt.

2. Elena Phipps, *Cochineal Red: The Art History of a Color*, New York: The Metropolitan Museum of Art, 2010, p. 21, available at www.metmuseum.org/art/metpublications/Cochineal_Red_the_art_history_of_a_color (accessed 17 February 2021).

3. Nathalie Boucherie, Witold Nowik and Dominique Cardon, 'La producción tintórea Nasca: Nuevos datos analíticos obtenidos sobre textiles recientemente descubiertos en excavaciones', *Nuevo Mundo Mundos Nuevos*, 2016, available at http://journals.openedition.org/nuevomundo/69222 (accessed 20 April 2021).

The sound of time passing: Andean music and soundscapes

1. Juan de Betanzos, *Narrative of the Incas* [1551–7], trans. Roland Hamilton and Dana Buchanan, Austin, TX: University of Texas Press, 1996, p. 79.

2. Dianne Scullin, 'What Do Moche Whistles Want?', in *Flower World – Mundo Florido*, vol. IV, ed. Matthias Stöckli and Mark Howell, Berlin: Ekho Verlag, 2015, pp. 13–41.

3. José Pérez de Arce, 'Whistling Bottles: Sound, Mind and Water', in *Music Archaeology in Context*, vol. V, ed. Ellen Hickmann et al., Rahden: M. Leidorf, 2006, pp. 161–82.

4. Miriam A. Kolar, 'Sensing Sonically at Andean Formative Chavín de Huántar, Perú', *Time and Mind*, vol. 10 (2017), pp. 39–59.

5. Henry Stobart, 'The Llama's Flute: Musical Misunderstandings in the Andes', *Early Music*, vol. 24 (1996), pp. 471–82; Dianne Scullin and Brian Boyd, 'Whistles in the Wind: The Noisy Moche City', *World Archaeology*, vol. 46 (2014), pp. 362–79.

6. Anna Gruszczyńska-Ziółkowska, 'Is Sound the First and Last Sign of Life? An Interpretation of the Most Recent Archaeomusicological Discovery of the Nasca Culture (Panpipes)', in *Music Archaeology of Early Metal Ages: Papers from the 1st Symposium of the International Study Group on Music Archaeology at Monastery Michaelstein, 18–24 May, 1998*, ed. Ellen Hickmann et al., Rahden: M. Leidorf, 2000, pp. 191–204.

7. Scullin and Boyd, 'Whistles in the Wind', pp. 362–79.

8. Translation by Jago Cooper. The original reads 'Pero también pienso que los artesanos que confeccionaron estos artefactos estaban orientados a un concepto

de sonido muy propio de los Andes y muy extraño al europeo, cual es moverse en la pura dimensión tímbrica de la flauta, sin melodía o con el mínimo de ella.' José Pérez de Arce, 'Análisis de las cualidades sonoras de las botellas silbadoras prehispánicas de los Andes', *Boletín del Museo Chileno de Arte Precolombino*, vol. 9 (2004), pp. 9–33, at p. 23, available at https://boletinmuseoprecolombino.cl/wp/wp-content/uploads/2015/12/bol9-1.pdf (accessed 20 May 2020).

9. Gruszczyńska-Ziółkowska, 'Is Sound the First and Last Sign of Life?', pp. 191–204.

10. Ibid., p. 195.

11. Max Peter Baumann, 'Andean Music, Symbolic Dualism and Cosmology', in *Cosmología y Música en los Andes*, ed. Max Peter Baumann, Frankfurt: Vervuert, 1996, p. 19.

12. Scullin, 'What Do Moche Whistles Want?', pp. 13–41; Daniela La Chioma, 'La antara en el arte Moche: Performance y simbolismo', in *Música y sonidos en el mundo Andino: Flautas de pan, zampoñas, antaras, sikus y ayarachis*, ed. Carlos Sánchez Huaringa, Lima: Fondo Editorial de la Universidad Nacional Mayor de San Marcos, 2018, pp. 137–74.

13. Pérez de Arce, 'Whistling Bottles', pp. 161–82; Stobart, 'The Llama's Flute', pp. 471–82.

5 UNWRITTEN HISTORIES: MOCHE AND CHIMÚ

Stories from the north

1. Brian R. Billman, 'Reconstructing Prehistoric Political Economies and Cycles of Political Power in the Moche Valley, Peru', in *Settlement Pattern Studies in the Americas: Fifty Years Since Virú*, ed. Brian R. Billman and Gary Feinman, Washington, DC: Smithsonian Institution Press, 1999, pp. 131–59; Krzysztof Makowski, Miłosz Giersz and Patrycja Przadka-Giersz, 'La guerra y la paz en el valle de Culebras: Hacia una arqueología de fronteras', in *Arqueología de la costa de Ancash*, ed. Milosz Giersz and Iván Ghezzi, Lima and Varsovia: Instituto Francés de Estudios Andinos and Centro de Estudios Precolombinos de la Universidad de Varsovia, 2011, pp. 231–70.

2. For little evidence of armed violence, see Susan E. Arkush and Charles Stanish, 'Interpreting Conflict in the Ancient Andes', *Current Anthropology*, vol. 46 (2005), pp. 3–28. For warrior leaders, see Iván Ghezzi, 'Los primeros tambores de la guerra', in *Señores de los reinos de la Luna*, ed. Krzysztof Makowski, Lima: Banco de Crédito del Perú, 2008, pp. 39–53; Krzysztof Makowski, 'Poder e identidad étnica en el mundo moche', in Makowski (ed.), *Señores de los reinos de la Luna*, pp. 55–76.

3. Luis Jaime Castillo and Jeffrey Quilter, 'Many Moche Models. An Overview of Past and Current Theories and Research on Moche Political Organization', in *New Perspectives on Moche Political Organization*, ed. Jeffrey Quilter and Luis Jaime Castillo, Washington, DC: Dumbarton Oaks Research Library and Collection and Harvard University Press, 2010, pp. 1–16.

4. Jürgen Golte, *Moche. Cosmología y sociedad: Una interpretación iconográfica*, Cusco: Centro Bartolomé

de Las Casas and Instituto de Estudios Peruanos, 2009; Krzysztof Makowski, 'El rey y el sacerdote', in Makowski (ed.), *Señores de los reinos de la Luna*, pp. 79–109.

5. See Christopher B. Donnan, 'Moche Ceramic Portraits', in *Moche Art and Archaeology in Ancient Peru*, ed. Joanne Pillsbury, Washington DC: National Gallery of Art and Yale University Press, 2001, pp. 127–39; Christopher B. Donnan, *Moche Portraits from Ancient Peru*, Austin: University of Texas Press, 2004; Janusz Wołoszyn, *Los rostros silenciosos: Los huacos retrato de la cultura Moche*, Lima: Fondo Editorial de la Pontificia Universidad Católica del Perú, 2008.

6. Luis Jaime Castillo et al., 'Ideología y poder en la consolidación, colapso y reconstitución del estado mochica del Jequetepeque: El Proyecto Arqueológico San José de Moro (1991–2006)', *Ñawpa Pacha*, vol. 29 (2008), pp. 1–86.

7. Hélène Bernier, 'La especialización artesanal en el sitio Huacas de Moche: Contextos de producción y función sociopolítica', in *Arqueología Mochica, nuevos enfoques: Actas del Primer Congreso Internacional de Jóvenes Investigadores de la Cultura Mochica. Lima, August 4–5th, 2004*, ed. Luis Jaime Castillo, Lima: Instituto Francés de Estudios Andinos, 2008, pp. 33–51; Elizabeth De Marrais, Luis Jaime Castillo and Timothy Earle, 'Ideology, Materialization and Power Strategies', *Current Anthropology*, vol. 37 (1996), pp. 15–31; Izumi Shimada, 'Late Moche Urban Craft Production: A First Approximation', in Pillsbury (ed.), *Moche Art and Archaeology in Ancient Peru*, pp. 177–206.

8. Paloma Carcedo, *Cobre del antiguo Perú*, Lima: Colección Apu, 1999, p. 61.

9. Walter Alva, 'The Royal Tombs of Sipán: Art and Power in Moche Society', in Pillsbury (ed.), *Moche Art and Archaeology in Ancient Peru*, pp. 223–45; Walter Alva and Christopher B. Donnan, *Royal Tombs of Sipán*, Los Angeles: Fowler Museum of Cultural History, 1993; Christopher B. Donnan, *Moche Tombs at Dos Cabezas*, Los Angeles: Cotsen Institute of Archaeology, 2007; Steve Bourget, *Les rois mochica. Divinité et pouvoir dans le Pérou ancient*, Paris: Somogy Éditions d'Art, 2014.

10. Christopher B. Donnan, 'Moche Masking Tradition', in *The Art and Archaeology of the Moche: An Ancient Andean Society of the Peruvian North Coast*, ed. Steve Bourget and Kimberly L. Jones, Austin: University of Texas Press, 2008, pp. 67–80.

11. Elías Mujica, *El Brujo: Huaca Cao, centro ceremonial Moche en el Valle de Chicama*, Lima: Fundación Wiese, 2007.

12. Luis Jaime Castillo, *La ceremonia del sacrificio: Batallas y muerte en el arte mochica*. Lima: Museo Arqueológico Rafael Larco Herrera and AFP Integra, 2000; Luis Jaime Castillo, 'Taming the Moche', in *Embattled Bodies, Embattled Places: War in Pre-Columbian Mesoamerica and the Andes*, ed. Andrew Scherer and John Verano, Washington, DC: Dumbarton Oaks Research Library and Collection, 2014, pp. 257–82; Jeffrey Quilter, 'Arts and Moche Martial Arts', in Bourget and Jones (eds), *The Art and Archaeology of the Moche*, pp. 215–28; John Verano, 'Communality and Diversity in Moche Human Sacrifice', in Bourget and Jones (eds), *The Art and Archaeology of the Moche*, pp. 195–213.

13. Duccio Bonavia, *Mural Painting in Ancient Peru*, trans. Patricia J. Lyon, Bloomington: Indiana University Press, 1985; Christopher B. Donnan, *Moche Art of Peru: Pre-Columbian Symbolic Communication*, Los Angeles: Museum of Cultural History, 1978, pp. 158–73; Lisa Trever, *The Archaeology of Mural Painting at Pañamarca, Peru*, Washington, DC: Dumbarton Oaks Research Library and Collection, 2017.

14. Donnan, *Moche Art of Peru*, pp. 154–5, fig. 236.

15. Steve Bourget, 'Rituals of Sacrifice: Its Practice at Huaca de la Luna and Its Representation in Moche Iconography', in Pillsbury (ed.), *Moche Art and Archaeology in Ancient Peru*, pp. 89–109; John Verano, 'War and Death in the Moche World: Osteological Evidence and Visual Discourse', in Pillsbury (ed.), *Moche Art and Archaeology in Ancient Peru*, pp. 111–25; Verano, 'Communality and Diversity in Moche Human Sacrifice'; John Verano, 'Warfare and Captives Sacrifice in the Moche Culture: The Battle Continues', in Scherer and Verano (eds), *Embattled Bodies, Embattled Places*, pp. 283–309.

16. Verano, 'Communality and Diversity in Moche Human Sacrifice'.

17. Cecilia Pardo and Julio Rucabado (eds), *Moche y sus vecinos. Reconstruyendo identidades*, Lima: Museo de Arte de Lima, 2016, p. 126.

18. Wołoszyn, *Los rostros silenciosos*, pp. 153–7.

19. George Lau, 'Object of Contention: An Examination of Recuay-Moche Combat Imagery', *Cambridge Archaeological Journal*, vol. 14 (2004), pp. 163–84; Krzysztof Makowski and Julio Rucabado, 'Hombres y deidades en la iconografía Recuay', in *Los dioses del antiguo Perú*, vol. I: *Colección arte y tesoros del Perú*, ed. Krzysztof Makowski, Lima: Banco de Crédito del Perú, 2000, pp. 199–238; Immina Von Schuler-Schömig, 'Die "Fremdkrieger"', *Baessler-Archiv, Neue Folge*, vol. 27 (1979), pp. 135–213.

20. Anne Marie Hocquenghem, 'Sacrifices and Ceremonial Calendars in Societies of the Central Andes: A Reconsideration', in Bourget and Jones (eds), *The Art and Archaeology of the Moche*, pp. 23–42; Krzysztof Makowski, 'Las divinidades en la iconografía mochica', in Makowski (ed.), *Los dioses del antiguo Perú*, vol. I, pp. 137–78.

21. Golte, *Moche. Cosmología y sociedad*, pp. 151–68.

22. Claude Chapdelaine, 'The Growing Power of a Moche Urban Class', in Pillsbury (ed.), *Moche Art and Archaeology in Ancient Peru*, pp. 69–87; Santiago Uceda, 'Los de arriba y los de abajo: Relaciones sociales, políticas y económicas entre el templo y los habitantes del núcleo urbano de las Huacas de Moche', in *Investigaciones en la Huaca de la Luna 2004*, ed. Santiago Uceda, Elías Mujica and Ricardo Morales, Trujillo: Facultad de Ciencias Sociales, Universidad Nacional de Trujillo, 2013, pp. 291–328.

23. Shimada, 'Late Moche Urban Craft Production: A First Approximation'; Santiago Uceda, Ricardo Morales and Elías Mujica, *Huaca de la Luna, Templos y Dioses Moches*, Lima: Fundación Backus and World Monument Fund, 2016, pp. 55–6.

24. Ricardo Tello and Tania Delabarde, 'Las tumbas del conjunto arquitectónico n°35 de las huacas del Sol y de la Luna', in *Informe técnico 2001. Proyecto Arqueológico Huaca de la Luna*, ed. Santiago Uceda and Ricardo Morales, Trujillo: Universidad Nacional Mayor de Trujillo, 2002, pp. 129–75, at p. 155.

25. Pardo and Rucabado (eds), *Moche y sus vecinos*, p. 176.

26. Edward de Bock, 'Appendix B: The Van den Bergh Collection', in *Moche Fineline Painting: Its Evolution and Its Artists*, ed. Christopher B. Donnan and Donna McClelland, Los Angeles: Fowler Museum of Cultural History, University of California, 1999, pp. 301–3.

27. Cristobal Campana, 'El entorno cultural de un dibujo mochica', in *Moche: propuestas y perspectivas*, ed. Santiago Uceda and Elias Mujica, Trujillo: Universidad Nacional de la Libertad, 1994, pp. 449–73; Jean Françoise Millaire, 'Moche Textile Production on the Peruvian North Coast: A Contextual Analysis', in Bourget and Jones (eds), *The Art and Archaeology of the Moche*, pp. 229–45.

28. Millaire, 'Moche Textile Production'.

29. Rafael Larco, *Los Mochicas*, Lima: Museo Arqueológico Rafael Larco Herrera, 2001; José Antonio Salas, *Etimologías Mochicas*, Lima: Academia Peruana de la Lengua, 2012. For a critical analysis of the use of this name, see Henry Gayoso, '¿Por qué AiApaec y Chicopaec no son nombres de dioses?', *Chungara, Revista de Antropología Chilena*, vol. 46 (2014), pp. 345–54.

30. Anne Marie Hocquenghem, *Iconografía mochica*, Lima: Fondo Editorial de la Pontificia Universidad Católica del Perú, 1987; Santiago Uceda, 'The Priests of the Bicephalus Arc: Tombs and Effigies Found in Huaca de la Luna and Their Relation to Moche Rituals', in *The Art and Archaeology of the Moche*, ed. Bourget and Jones, pp. 153–78.

31. Uceda, 'The Priests of the Bicephalus Arc'.

32. Gabriel Prieto, 'Balsas de totora en la costa norte del Perú: Una aproximación etnográfica y arqueológica', *Quingnam*, vol. 2 (2016), pp. 141–88.

33. Ibid., p. 169.

34. Ibid.

35. Verano, 'Communality and Diversity in Moche Human Sacrifice', pp. 202–3, figs 11.18 and 11.19.

The Macabi Island wooden sculptures

1. The microscope was the Hitachi S-3700N SEM, and I used the backscatter electron detector at 20 kV with a chamber pressure of 40Pa.

Chimú: the earthly kingdom of the sea

1. Jerry D. Moore and Carol J. Mackey, 'The Chimú Empire', in *Handbook of South American Archaeology*, ed. Helaine Silverman and William H. Isbell, New York: Springer, 2008, pp. 783–807.

2. Atsushi Yamamoto, 'El reconocimiento del valle de Huancabamba, Jaén, Cajamarca, Perú', *Arqueos, Revista Electronica de Arqueologia PUCP*, vol. 2 (2007), pp. 1–16.

3. Richard W. Keatinge, 'Urban Settlement Systems and Rural Sustaining Communities: An Example from Chan Chan's Hinterland', *Journal of Field Archaeology*, vol. 2 (1975), pp. 215–27; Michael E.

Moseley and Kent C. Day (eds), *Chan Chan: Andean Desert City*, Albuquerque: University of New Mexico Press, 1982.

4. John H. Rowe, 'The Kingdom of Chimor', *Acta Americana*, vol. 6 (1948), pp. 26–59, at p. 45.

5. Jorge Zevallos Quiñones, *Huacas y Huaqueros en Trujillo durante el Virreynato (1535–1835)*, Trujillo: Editora Normas Legales, 1994.

6. Thor Heyerdahl, Daniel H. Sandweiss and Alfredo Narváez, *Pyramids of Tucume: The Quest for Peru's Forgotten City*, London: Thames & Hudson, 1995.

7. John Topic, 'Craft Production in the Kingdom of Chimor', in *Northern Dynasties: Kingship and Statecraft in Chimor*, ed. Michael E. Moseley and Alana Cordy-Collins, Washington, DC: Dumbarton Oaks Research Library and Collection, 1990, pp. 145–76.

8. Barbara J. Mills, 'Performing the Feast: Visual Display and Suprahousehold Commensalism in the Puebloan Southwest', *American Antiquity*, vol. 72 (2007), pp. 210–39.

9. Anthony P. Andrews, 'The U-Shaped Structures at Chan Chan, Peru', *Journal of Field Archaeology*, vol. 1 (1974), pp. 241–64.

10. Santiago Uceda, 'Esculturas en miniatura y una maqueta en madera', in *Investigaciones en la Huaca de la Luna, 1995*, ed. Santiago Uceda, Elias Mujica and Ricardo Morales, Trujillo: Universidad Nacional de Trujillo, 1997, pp. 151–76.

11. Maize beer in the Andes is usually referred to as *chicha*, but this is a Caribbean word borrowed from the Taíno people's language and brought by the Spanish to the Andes during the sixteenth and seventeenth centuries (Denise Arnold et al., 'La chicha: Lubricante por excelencia de la sociedad andina', in *Perú: El legado de la historia*, ed. Luís Millones and José Villa Rodríguez, Seville: PROMPERÚ, 2001, pp. 129–51). The language spoken by the Chimú was Quignam, but there are few references as to how it was spoken. The word *kótzo* means 'maize beer' in the Muchik language, which was possibly the closest language to Quignam and broadly spoken north of the Moche valley along the north coast of Peru.

12. Thomas B. F. Cummins, *Brindis con el Inca*, Lima: Fondo Editorial de la Universidad Nacional Mayor de San Marcos, 2004.

13. Michael E. Moseley, *The Maritime Foundations of Andean Civilization*, Menlo Park, CA: Cummings, 1975; Gabriel Prieto and Daniel H. Sandweiss (eds), *Maritime Communities of the Ancient Andes*, Gainesville, FL: University Press of Florida, 2020.

14. Jorge Zevallos Quiñones, *Los Cacicazgos de Trujillo*, Trujillo: Gráfica Cuatro, 1992.

15. María Rostworowski de Díez Canseco, 'Mercaderes del valle de Chincha en la época prehispánica: Un documento y unos comentarios', in *Etnía y sociedad: Costa peruana prehispánica*, ed. María Rostworowski de Díez Canseco, Lima: Instituto de Estudios Peruanos, 1977, pp. 97–140; Craig Morris and Julián Idilio Santillana, 'The Inka Transformation of the Chincha Capital', in *Variations in the Expression of Inka Power*, ed. Richard L. Burger, Craig Morris and Ramiro Matos Mendieta, Washington, DC: Dumbarton Oaks Research Library and Collection, 2007, pp. 135–63.

16. Robert E. Coker, *Primer diagnóstico de la pesquería peruana: Informes publicados entre 1907 a 1910*, Lima: Tecnológica de Alimentos, 2008; Richard P. Schaedel, *La etnografía Muchik en las fotografías de H. Brüning, 1886–1925*, Lima: Cofide, 1989.

17. Joanne Pillsbury, 'The Thorny Oyster and the Origins of Empire: Implications of Recently Uncovered Spondylus Imagery from Chan Chan, Peru', *Latin American Antiquity*, vol. 7 (1996), pp. 313–40.

Spondylus: the sacred thorny oyster

1. José de Acosta, *Historia natural y moral de las indias* [1590], Mexico: Fondo de Cultura Económica, 1962.

2. Walter Alva and Christopher Donnan, *Royal Tombs of Sipán*, Los Angeles: Fowler Museum of Cultural History, 1993; Yoshio Onuki, *Kuntur Wasi y Cerro Blanco: Dos sitios del Formativo en el norte del Perú*, Tokyo: Hokusen-sha, 1995; Izumi Shimada, *Cultura Sicán: Dios, riqueza y poder en la costa norte del Perú*, Lima: Edubanco, Fundación del Banco Continental para el Fomento de la Educación y la Cultura, 1995.

3. Jorge Marcos, 'Intercambio a larga distancia en América: El caso del Spondylus', *Boletín de Antropología Americana*, vol. 1 (1980), pp. 124–9.

4. Anne Marie Hocquenghem, 'El *Spondylus princeps* y la Edad de Bronce en los Andes centrales: Las rutas de Intercambios', in *Producción de Bienes de Prestigio Ornamentales y Votivos de la América Antigua*, ed. Emiliano Melgar Tisoc, Reyna Solís Ciriaco and Ernesto González Licón, Lima: Instituto Francés de Estudios Andinos, 2010, p. 36.

5. Mary Glowacki, 'Food for the Gods or Mere Mortals? Hallucinogenic *Spondylus* and Its Interpretative Implications for Early Andean society', *Antiquity*, vol. 79 (2005), pp. 257–68.

6. César Lodeiros Seijo et al., 'Short History of *Spondylus* in the South American Pacific: A Symbol that Returns at Present', *Interciencia*, vol. 43 (2018), pp. 872–7.

7. Peter Fux (ed.), *Chavín*, Lima: Museo de Arte de Lima, 2015.

8. Karsten Lambers, 'Los geoglifos: Imágenes y escenarios en el desierto de Nazca y Palpa', in *Nasca*, ed. Cecilia Pardo and Peter Fux, Lima: Museo de Arte de Lima, 2017, p. 120.

9. Alva and Donnan, *Royal Tombs of Sipán*.

10. Alana Cordy Collins, 'El mundo moche al empezar el siglo VIII: Transiciones e influencias', in *Moche hacia el final del milenio*, ed. Santiago Uceda and Elias Mujica, vol. II, Trujillo: Fondo Editorial de la Pontificia Universidad Católica del Perú and Universidad Nacional de Trujillo, 2003, pp. 229–46.

11. Carol Mackey and César Jauregui, *Informe preliminar del Proyecto Arqueológico*, Lima: Instituto Nacional de Cultura, 2002.

12. Carlos Wester, *Chornancap: Palace of the Leader and Priestess of the Lambayeque Culture*, Lima: Ministerio de Cultura, 2016; Alfredo Narváez, *Dioses de Lambayeque: Introducción al estudio de la mitología tardía de la Costa Norte del Perú*, Chiclayo: Ministerio de Cultura del Perú/Proyecto Especial Naylamp Lambayeque, 2014, p. 132, fig. 166.

13. Miguel Cabello de Balboa, *Micelanea Antarctica: Una historia del antiguo Perú* [1586], Lima: Universidad Nacional Mayor de San Marcos, 1951.

14. Johan Reinhard and Maria Constanza Ceruti, *Inca Rituals and Sacred Mountains: A Study of the World's Highest Archaeological Sites*, Los Angeles: University of California Press, 2010.

15. Jerry Moore and Carolina Vilchez, 'Spondylus and the Inka Empire on the Far North Coast of Perú: Recent Excavations at Taller Conchales, Cabeza de Vaca, Tumbes', in *Making Value, Making Meaning: Techné in the Pre-Columbian World*, ed. Cathy Lynne Costin, Washington, DC: Dumbarton Oaks Research Library and Collection, 2016, pp. 221–51; Ministerio de Cultura del Perú, *Proyecto Qhapaq Ñan Rutas Ancestrales del Qhapaq Ñan*, ed. María Helena Tord Velasco, 2020, available at https://qhapaqnan.cultura.pe/sites/default/files/mi/archivo/RutasAncestrales.pdf (accessed 25 May 2021).

16. Maria Rostworowski, 'Mercaderes del valle del Chincha en la epoca prehispánica: Un documento y unos comentarios', *Revista Española de Antropología Americana*, vol. 5 (1970), pp. 135–78.

Death, killing and human sacrifice

1. Gabriel Prieto et al., 'A Mass Sacrifice of Children and Camelids at the Huanchaquito-Las Llamas site, Moche Valley, Peru', *PLoS ONE*, vol. 14 (2019), e0211691.

2. Glenn M. Schwartz, 'The Archaeological Study of Sacrifice', *Annual Review of Anthropology*, vol. 46 (2017), pp. 233–40.

3. Tiffiny A. Tung, 'Trauma and Violence in the Wari Empire of the Peruvian Andes: Warfare, Raids, and Ritual Fights', *American Journal of Physical Anthropology*, vol. 133 (2007), pp. 941–56.

4. John Hemming, *The Conquest of the Incas*, Boston and New York: Mariner Books, 1970.

5. Steve Bourget, *Sacrifice, Violence, and Ideology among the Moche: The Rise of Social Complexity in Ancient Peru*, Austin, TX: University of Texas Press, 2016.

6. Ibid.

7. Elizabeth N. Arkush and Charles Stanish, 'Interpreting Conflict in the Ancient Andes: Implications for the Archaeology of Warfare', *Current Anthropology*, vol. 46 (2005), pp. 3–28.

8. John W. Verano, 'The Physical Evidence of Human Sacrifice in Ancient Peru', in *Ritual Sacrifice in Ancient Peru*, ed. Elizabeth P. Benson and Anita G. Cook, Austin, TX: University of Texas Press, 2001, pp. 165–84.

9. J. Marla Toyne et al., 'Residential Histories of Elites and Sacrificial Victims at Huacas de Moche, Peru, as Reconstructed from Oxygen Isotopes', *Journal of Archaeological Science*, vol. 42 (2014), pp. 15–28.

10. John W. Verano, 'Trophy Head-Taking and Human Sacrifice in Andean South America', in *Handbook of South American Archaeology*, ed. Helaine Silverman and William H. Isbell, New York: Springer, 2008, pp. 1047–60.

11. Dagmara M. Socha, Johan Reinhard and Ruddy Chávez Perea, 'Inca Human Sacrifices on Misti Volcano (Peru)', *Latin American Antiquity*, vol. 32 (2021), pp. 138–53.

12. Richard W. Kaeuper, *Medieval Chivalry*, Cambridge: Cambridge University Press, 2016.

13. Luis Jaime Castillo, *La ceremonia del sacrificio: Batallas y muerte en el arte mochica*, Lima: Museo Arqueológico Rafael Larco Herrera, 2000; John R. Topic and Theresa Lange Topic, 'Hacía una comprensión conceptual de la guerra andina', in *Arqueología, antropología e historia en los Andes: Homenaje a María Rostworowski*, ed. Rafael Gabai Varón and Javier Flores Espinoza, Lima: Instituto de Estudios Peruanos, 1997, pp. 567–96.

14. Daniel H. Sandweiss and Jeffrey Quilter, 'Collation, Correlation, and Causation in the Prehistory of Coastal Peru', in *Surviving Sudden Environmental Change: Answers from Archaeology*, ed. Jago Cooper and Payson Sheets, Boulder, CO: University Press of Colorado, 2012, pp. 117–41.

15. IPCC (Intergovernmental Panel on Climate Change), *Managing the Risks of Extreme Events and Disasters to Advance Climate Change Adaptation*, ed. C. B. Field et al., Cambridge: Cambridge University Press, 2012.

16. Matthew C. Reilly, 'Futurity, Time and Archaeology', *Journal of Contemporary Archaeology*, vol. 6 (2019), pp. 1–15.

17. Johannes Fabian, *Time and the Other: How Anthropology Makes Its Object*, New York: Columbia University Press, 1983, p. 34.

18. Leticia Inés Cortés, 'On Heat and Dryness: Landscapes, Death and Materiality in Early Agricultural Societies of the Southern Calchaquí Valleys (Northwest Argentina, First Millennium AD)', *Time and Mind*, vol. 18 (2020), pp. 165–90.

19. Carolyn Dean, 'The After-Life of Inka Rulers: Andean Death before and after Spanish Colonization', in *Death and Afterlife in the Early Modern Hispanic World*, ed. John Beusterien and Constance Cortez, *Hispanic Issues On Line*, vol. 7 (2010), pp. 27–54.

20. Johan Reinhard and Maria Constanza Ceruti, *Inca Rituals and Sacred Mountains: A Study of the World's Highest Archaeological Sites*, Los Angeles, CA: Cotsen Institute of Archaeology, 2010.

21. Constanza Ceruti, 'Human Bodies as Objects of Dedication at Inca Mountain Shrines (North-Western Argentina)', *World Archaeology*, vol. 36 (2004), pp. 103–22.

22. Andrew S. Wilson, Timothy Taylor, Maria Constanza Ceruti et al., 'Stable Isotope and DNA Evidence for Ritual Sequences in Inca Child Sacrifice', *PNAS*, vol. 104 (2007), pp. 16456–61. See also Hemming, *The Conquest of the Incas*.

23. *Values and Standards of the British Army*, p. 5, available at www.army.mod.uk/media/5219/20180910-values_standards_2018_final.pdf (accessed 15 June 2021).

6 EMPIRES IN THE SKY

The rise of empires: Waris and Incas

1. Admittedly, many people may mistakenly think that Teotihuacan is an Aztec archaeological site due to its proximity to Mexico City and the dearth of intact Aztec architecture.

2. See, for example, Juan de Betanzos [*sic*], *Narrative of the Incas*, trans. Roland Hamilton and Dana Buchanan, Austin, TX: University of Texas Press, 1996, pp. 7–11.

3. See, for example, Jean-Pierre Protzen and Stella Nair, *The Stones of Tiahuanaco: A Study of Architecture and Construction*, Los Angeles: Cotsen Institute of Archaeology, 2013, pp. 203–8.

4. The Field Museum's Proyecto Arqueológico Cerro Baúl has, for many decades, studied the relationship between the Tiwanaku and Wari in the Moquegua valley through excavations at the site of Cerro Baúl. See www.fieldmuseum.org/proyecto-arqueologico-cerro-baul (accessed 18 February 2021).

5. The most important breakthrough in *khipu* decipherment to date occurred in 1923 with the decipherment of the number system. See L. Leland Locke, *The Ancient Quipu*, New York: The American Museum of Natural History, 1923. For a concise study of Wari *khipus*, see Juan Antonio Murro and Jeffrey Splitstoser, *Written in Knots: Undeciphered Accounts of Andean Life*, Washington, DC: Dumbarton Oaks Research Library and Collection, 2019, available at: www.doaks.org/visit/museum/exhibitions/past/written-in-knots (accessed 17 February 2021).

6. Wilhelm Reiss and Alphons Stübel's excavations of a burial site at Ancón were magnificently documented in *The Necropolis of Ancón in Peru*, a set of large illustrated folios serially published between 1880 and 1888. A digitised version from the Harvard University Library is available at https://iiif.lib.harvard.edu/manifests/view/drs:13890340$1i (accessed 18 February 2021).

7. For additional information about the Chancas, see Brian Bauer et al., *The Chanka: Archaeological Research in Andahuaylas (Apurimac), Peru*, Los Angeles: UCLA Cotsen Institute of Archaeology, 2010.

8. Pedro Cieza de León, *The Second Part of the Chronicle of Peru*, trans. Clements R. Markham, London: The Hakluyt Society, 1883, p. 186.

9. For a fuller discussion of reduced-scale Purucaya offerings and their possible origin in Chimú rituals, see Andrew James Hamilton, *Scale & the Incas*, Princeton, NJ: Princeton University Press, 2018, pp. 82–110. In this book, I incorrectly stated that Túpac Inca Yupanqui invented the Purucaya; in fact, Juan Diéz de Betanzos credited Emperor Pachacuti with inventing it. However, Túpac Inca Yupanqui performed the ritual for Pachacuti upon his death.

10. See Ramiro Matos Mendieta and Jose Barriero (eds), *The Great Inka Road: Engineering an Empire*, Washington, DC: National Museum of the American Indian, 2015.

11. See, for example, Thomas B. F. Cummins and Bruce Mannheim, 'The River around Us, The Stream within Us: The Traces of the Sun and Inka Kinetics', *RES: Anthropology and Aesthetics*, vol. 59/60 (2011), pp. 5–21.

12. A digital facsimile of Felipe Guamán Poma de Ayala's manuscript is available at www5.kb.dk/permalink/2006/poma/info/en/frontpage.htm (accessed 18 February 2021).

Machu Picchu

1. Susan Toby Evans and Joanne Pillsbury (eds), *Palaces of the Ancient New World*, Washington, DC: Dumbarton Oaks Research Library and Collection, 2004.

2. Franklin Pease and García Yrigoyen, *The Incas*, Lima: Fondo Editorial de la Pontificia Universidad Católica del Perú, 2011; Henry Mitrani Reaño, *Historia de Machu Picchu: Si las piedras hablaran*, Lima: Telefónica, 2011.

3. Christopher Heaney, *Las Tumbas de Machu Picchu: La historia de Hiram Bingham y la búsqueda de las últimas ciudades de los Incas*, Lima: Fondo Editorial de la Pontificia Universidad Católica del Perú, 2012. See also John Hemming, *The Conquest of the Incas*, Boston and New York: Mariner Books, 1970.

An analysis of coca leaves

1. The microscope was the Hitachi S-3700N SEM, and the team used the backscatter electron detector at 20 kV with a chamber pressure of 40Pa.

2. Tom D. Dillehay et al., 'Early Holocene Coca Chewing in Northern Peru', *Antiquity*, vol. 84 (2010), pp. 939–53, at p. 940.

Capacocha rituals

1. See, for example, Johan Reinhard and Maria Constanza Ceruti, *Inca Rituals and Sacred Mountains: A Study of the World's Highest Archaeological Sites*, Los Angeles: Cotsen Institute of Archaeology, 2010.

Conopas

1. Bill Sillar, 'Miniatures and Animism: The Communicative Role of Inka Carved Stone Conopa', *Journal of Anthropological Research*, vol. 72 (2016), pp. 442–64.

2. Pablo José de Arriaga, *La extirpación de la idolatría en el Pirú* [1621], ed. Henrique Urbano, Cusco: Centro de Estudios Regionales Andinos Bartolomé de las Casas, 1999, p. 36.

3. Ibid., p. 35.

4. Ibid., p. 36.

5. Ibid., p. 50.

6. Ibid., p. 80.

7. Jorge A. Flores-Ochoa, 'Enqa, enqaychu, illay y khuya rumi: Aspectos mágico-religiosos entre pastores', *Journal of Latin American Lore*, vol. 2 (1976), pp. 115–34.

8. Kenneth R. Mills, *Idolatry and Its Enemies: Colonial Andean Religion and Extirpation, 1640–1750*, Princeton, NJ: Princeton University Press, 1997, pp. 96–7.

9. Arriaga, *La extirpación*, p. 23.

Inca architecture and the temple of Viracocha at Raqchi

1. Garcilaso de la Vega, *Royal Commentaries of the Incas and General History of Peru* [1612], trans. Harold V. Livermore, Austin: University of Texas Press, 1989, p. 290.

2. Juan de Betanzos, *Narrative of the Incas* [1557], trans. and ed. Roland Hamilton and Dana Buchanan, Austin: University of Texas Press, 1996, p. 175.
3. Garcilaso de la Vega, *Royal Commentaries*, p. 290.
4. Ibid.

Andean engineering: the power of water and stone

1. Charles R. Ortloff and Michael E. Moseley, 'Climate, Agricultural Strategies, and Sustainability in the Precolumbian Andes', *Andean Past*, vol. 9 (2009), pp. 277–304, at p. 277.
2. Carolyn Dean, *A Culture of Stone: Inka Perspectives on Rock*, Durham, NC: Duke University Press, 2010, p. 75.
3. Henry Tantaleán, 'Andean Ontologies: An Introduction to Substance', in *Andean Ontologies: New Archaeological Perspectives*, ed. María Cecilia Lozada and Henry Tantaleán, Gainesville: University Press of Florida, 2019, p. 2.
4. Luis Jaime Castillo Butters and Santiago Uceda Castillo, 'The Mochicas', in *Handbook of South American Archaeology*, ed. Helaine Silverman and William H. Isbell, New York: Springer, 2008, pp. 707–29.
5. Brian Billman, 'Irrigation and the Origins of the Southern Moche State on the North Coast of Peru', *Latin American Antiquity*, vol. 13 (2002), pp. 371–400.
6. Luis Jaime Castillo Butters and Jeffrey Quilter, 'Many Moche Models', in *New Perspectives on Moche Political Organization*, ed. Luis Jaime Castillo Butters and Jeffrey Quilter, Washington, DC: Dumbarton Oaks Research Library and Collection, 2010, pp. 1–16.
7. Kenneth R. Wright, Ruth M. Wright, Alfredo Valencia Zegarra and Gordon McEwan, *Moray: Inca Engineering Mystery*, Reston, VA: American Society of Civil Engineers Press, 2011.
8. See www.eda.admin.ch/aboutswitzerland/en/home/dossiers/die-schweiz-und-ihre-bergrekorde.html (accessed 10 June 2021).
9. Terence D'Altroy, *The Incas*, Chichester: Wiley Blackwell, 2015, p. 40.
10. Jago Cooper and Lindsay Duncan, 'Applied Archaeology in the Americas: Evaluating Archaeological Solutions to the Impacts of Global Environmental Change', in *Applied Archaeology, Historical Ecology and the Usable Past*, ed. Christian Isendahl and Daryl Stump, Oxford: Oxford University Press, 2016, pp. 432–51.
11. Ann Kendall and David Drew, 'The Rehabilitation of Pre-Hispanic Agricultural Infrastructure to Support Rural Development in the Peruvian Andes: The Work of the Cusichaca Trust', in *The Oxford Handbook of Historical Ecology and Applied Archaeology*, ed. C. Isendahl and D. Stump, Oxford: Oxford University Press, 2019, pp. 422–40.
12. Delphine Renard et al., 'Ecological Engineers Ahead of Their Time: The Functioning of Pre-Columbian Raised-Field Agriculture and Its Potential Contributions to Sustainability Today', *Ecological Engineering*, vol. 45 (2012), pp. 30–44.
13. Clark. L. Erickson, 'Agricultural Landscapes as World Heritage: Raised Field Agriculture in Bolivia and Peru', in *Managing Change: Sustainable Approaches to the Conservation of the Built Environment*, ed. Jeanne-Marie Teutonico and Frank Matero, Los Angeles, CA: Getty Conservation Institute, pp. 181–204.
14. See Kristina Douglass and Jago Cooper, 'Archaeology, Environmental Justice, and Climate Change on Islands of the Caribbean and Southwestern Indian Ocean', in *Proceedings of the National Academy of Sciences of the United States of America (PNAS)*, vol. 117 (2020), pp. 8254–62.
15. Carolyn Dean, *A Culture of Stone*, p. 75.
16. Thanks to George Lau for the thought-provoking discussion and for reading the book in proof form.

7 THE ANDEAN LEGACY

Textiles of the Andes: techniques, traditions and cultures

1. See Thomas F. Lynch (ed.), *Guitarrero Cave: Early Man in the Andes*, New York: Academic Press, 1980; Junius B. Bird, *The Preceramic Excavations at the Huaca Prieta, Chicama Valley, Peru* (Anthropological Papers, vol. 62, pt. 1), New York: American Museum of Natural History, 1985.
2. See Karen E. Price, Catherine Higgitt, Thibaut Devièse, Colin McEwan and Bill Sillar, 'Tools for Eternity: Pre-Columbian Workbaskets as Textile Production Toolkits and Grave Offerings', *British Museum Technical Research Bulletin*, vol. 9 (2015), pp. 65–86; Ana Roquero, *Tintes y tintoreros de América*, Madrid: Ministerio de Educación, Cultura y Deporte. Área de Cultura, 2006.
3. For information about identification of Peruvian dyes, see Jan Wouters and Noemi Rosario-Chirinos, 'Dye Analysis of Pre-Columbian Peruvian Textiles with High-Performance Liquid Chromatography and Diode-Array Detection', *Journal of the American Institute for Conservation*, vol. 31 (1992), pp. 237–55; Dominique Cardon, *Natural Dyes: Sources, Tradition, Technology and Science*, London: Archetype Publications, 2007.
4. See Elena Phipps, *Cochineal Red: The Art History of a Color*, New York: Metropolitan Museum of Art, 2010, available at www.metmuseum.org/art/metpublications/Cochineal_Red_the_art_history_of_a_color (accessed 17 February 2021).
5. Jeffrey C. Splitstoser, Tom D. Dillehay, Jan Wouters and Ana Claro, 'Early Pre-Hispanic Use of Indigo Blue in Peru', *Science Advances*, vol. 2 (2016), available at DOI: 10.1126/sciadv.1501623.
6. See *Ancient Peruvian Textiles: The Fifi White Collection*, Overland Park, KS: Nerman Museum of Contemporary Art, 2007.
7. For spinning, see Grace Goodell, 'A Study of Andean Spinning in the Cuzco Region', *Textile Museum Journal*, vol. 2 (1968), pp. 2–8.
8. See, for example, Verónica Cereceda, 'Semiología de los textiles andinos: Las talegas de Isluga' [1978], *Chungará: Revista de Antropología Chilena*, vol. 42 (2010), pp. 181–98.
9. Ann Rowe, 'Tie-Dyed Tunics', in *Wari: Lords of the Ancient Andes*, ed. Susan E. Bergh, New York/Cleveland: Thames & Hudson and Cleveland Museum of Art, 2012, pp. 192–205.
10. Ann H. Peters, 'Identity, Innovation and Textile Exchange Practices at the Paracas Necropolis, 2000 BP' (2012), *Textile Society of America Symposium Proceedings*, Paper 726, available at http://digitalcommons.unl.edu/tsaconf/726 (accessed 17 May 2021).
11. Johan Reinhard and Maria Constanza Ceruti, *Inca Rituals and Sacred Mountains*, Los Angeles: Cotsen Institute of Archaeology, 2010.
12. See Elena Phipps, 'The Great Cloth Burial at Cahuachi, Nasca Valley, Peru', in *Sacred and Ceremonial Textiles: Proceedings of the Fifth Biennial Symposium of the Textile Society of America*, Minneapolis, MN/Chicago, IL: Textile Society of America, 1997, pp. 111–20, available at https://digitalcommons.unl.edu/tsaconf/871 (accessed 17 February 2021).
13. See Christine Giuntini, 'Techniques and Conservation of Peruvian Feather Mosaics', in *Peruvian Featherworks: Art of the Precolumbian Era*, ed. Heidi King, New York: Metropolitan Museum of Art, 2012. See also Heidi King, 'The Wari Feathered Panels from Corral Redondo, Churunga Valley: A Re-examination of Context', *Ñawpa Pacha*, vol. 33 (2013), pp. 23–42.
14. Felipe Guamán Poma de Ayala, *El primer nueva corónica y buen gobierno* (1615/16) (Copenhagen, Det Kongelige Bibliotek, GKS 2232 4°), available at www5.kb.dk/permalink/2006/poma/info/en/frontpage.htm (accessed 10 February 2021).
15. John Rowe, 'Standardization in Inca Tapestry Tunics', in *The Junius Bird Pre-Columbian Textile Conference*, ed. Ann Rowe and Anne Shaffer, Washington, DC: Textile Museum and Dumbarton Oaks, 1978, pp. 239–64; Ann Rowe, 'Inca Weaving and Costume', *Textile Museum Journal*, vols 34–5 (1995–6), pp. 5–52.
16. Christine Franquemont and Ed Franquemont, 'Learning to Weave in Chinchero', *Textile Museum Journal*, vol. 26 (1987), pp. 54–78; Christine Franquemont and Ed Franquemont, 'Tanka, Chongo, Kutij: Structure of the World through Cloth', in *Symmetry Comes of Age: The Role of Pattern in Culture*, ed. Dorothy K. Washburn and Donald W. Crowe, Seattle: University of Washington Press, 2004, pp. 117–214.
17. See Elena Phipps, Johanna Hecht and Cristina Esteras Martin, *The Colonial Andes: Tapestries and Silverwork, 1530–1830*, New York: Metropolitan Museum of Art, 2004, available at www.metmuseum.org/research/metpublications/The_Colonial_Andes_Tapestries_and_Silverwork_1530_1830# (accessed 17 February 2021).
18. See Sophie Desrosiers, 'An Interpretation of Technical Weaving Data Found in an Early 17th-Century Chronicle', in *The Junius B. Bird Conference on Andean Textiles, April 7th and 8th, 1984*, ed. Ann Pollard Rowe, Washington, DC: Textile Museum, 1986, pp. 219–41; Lynn A. Meisch, 'Messages from the Past: An Unbroken Inca Weaving Tradition in Northern Peru', in *Textile Narratives & Conversions: Proceedings of the 10th Biennial Symposium of the Textile Society of America, October 11–14, Toronto, Ontario* (2006), pp. 380–9, at p. 345, available at https://digitalcommons.unl.edu/tsaconf/345 (accessed 17 May 2021).

Keros, *pacchas*, *tupus* and *unkus*: enduring Andean traditions

1. John H. Elliott, 'El Perú en la Monarquía Hispánica', in *Arte imperial inca: sus orígenes y transformaciones desde la Conquista a la Independencia*, ed. Ramón Mujica, Lima: Banco de Crédito del Perú, 2020, pp. 21–33; Ramón Mujica, 'Arte e identidad: la raíces culturales del barroco peruano', in *El Barroco peruano*, vol. II, ed. Ramón Mujica, Lima: Banco de Crédito del Perú, 2003, pp. 1–57.
2. Juan Carlos Estenssoro, 'Construyendo la memoria: La figura del Inca y el reino del Perú, de la conquista a Túpac Amaru II', in *Los incas, reyes del Perú*, ed. Natalia Majluf, Lima: Banco de Crédito del Perú, 2005, pp. 92–173.
3. John H. Rowe, *Los incas del Cuzco*, Cusco: Instituto Nacional de Cultura, 2003. Abelardo Levaggi, 'República de Indios y República de Españoles en los Reinos de Indias', *Revista de Estudios Histórico-Jurídicos*, vol. 23 (2001), pp. 419–28.
4. Elena Phipps, 'Garments and Identity in the Colonial Andes', in *The Colonial Andes: Tapestries and Silverwork, 1530–1830*, ed. Elena Phipps et al., New York: The Metropolitan Museum of Art, 2004, pp. 16–39.
5. Isabel Iriarte, 'Las túnicas incas en la pintura colonial', in *Mito y simbolismo en los Andes: La figura y la palabra*, ed. Henrique Urbano, Cusco: Centro de Estudios Regionales Andinos 'Bartolomé de las Casas', 1993, pp. 53–86.
6. Joanne Pillsbury, 'El uncu inca: Tradición y transformación', in *Arte imperial inca: Sus orígenes y transformaciones desde la Conquista a la Independencia*, ed. Ramón Mujica Pinilla, Lima: Banco de Crédito del Perú, 2020, pp. 100–31.
7. Gabriela Ramos, 'Los símbolos de poder inca durante el virreinato', in Majluf (ed.), *Los incas, reyes del Perú*, pp. 42–65.
8. Thomas B. F. Cummins, *Toasts with the Inca: Andean Abstraction and Colonial Images on Quero Vessels*, Ann Arbor, MI: University of Michigan Press, 2002.
9. Francisco Stastny Mosberg, 'Pacchas coloniales y jarras de engaño', *Historia y Cultura*, vol. 21 (1991–2), pp. 57–79.

Andean textiles in the Cusco region

1. See the Centro de Textiles Tradicionales del Cusco's website: www.textilescusco.org/about-us (accessed 20 April 2021).
2. Nilda Callañaupa Alvarez, *Weaving in the Peruvian Highlands: Dreaming Patterns, Weaving Memories*, Cusco: CTTC, 2007, p. 101.
3. Denise Y. Arnold and Elvira Espejo, *The Andean Science of Weaving: Structures and Techniques of Warp-Faced Weaves*, London: Thames & Hudson, 2015, p. 223.
4. Ibid., p. 310.
5. José de San Martín (1778–1850) was an Argentinian general who proclaimed Peru's independence from Spain on 28 July 1821.
6. For more information, see www.textilescusco.org/community-detail/pitumarca/10 (accessed 20 April 2021).

Andean values and people power: *ayllu*, *ayni* and *mink'a*

1. María Eugenia Choque and Carlos Mamani, 'Reconstitución del ayllu y derechos de los pueblos indígenas: El movimiento indio en los Andes de Bolivia', *Journal of Latin American Anthropology*, vol. 6 (2001) pp. 202–24, at p. 207. Translation by Jago Cooper.
2. Mario Liverani, *Uruk: The First City*, New York: Equinox Publishing, 2006, pp. 50–2.
3. George F. Lau, 'Camelids as Food and Wealth: Emerging Political and Moral Economies of the Recuay Culture', in *Andean Foodways: Pre-Columbian, Colonial, and Contemporary Food and Culture*, ed. John E. Staller, Cham, Switzerland: Springer, 2021, pp. 61–87.
4. Carolyn Dean, *A Culture of Stone: Inka Perspectives on Rock*, Durham, NC: Duke University Press, 2010, p. 113.
5. John V. Murra, 'Did Tribute and Markets Prevail in the Andes before the European Invasion?', in *Ethnicity, Markets, and Migration in the Andes: At the Crossroads of History and Anthropology*, ed. Brooke Larson, Olivia Harris and Enrique Tandeter, Durham, NC: Duke University Press, 1995, pp. 57–72.
6. Simón Yampara Huarachi, 'The Ayllu and Territoriality in the Andes', *Alternautas*, vol. 4 (2017), pp. 77–87, at p. 82.
7. José Carlos Mariátegui, *7 ensayos de interpretación de la realidad peruana*, Caracas: Fundación Biblioteca Ayacucho, Caracas, 1928; Frank Salomon, 'Andean Ethnology in the 1970s: A Retrospective', *Latin American Research Review*, vol. 17 (1982), pp. 75–128. See also John V. Murra, 'Andean Societies', *Annual Review of Anthropology*, vol. 13 (1984), pp. 119–41; John V. Murra, 'Current Research and Prospects in Andean Ethnohistory', *Latin American Research Review*, vol. 5 (1970), pp. 3–36.
8. Harald Ringbauer, Matthias Steinrücken, Lars Fehren-Schmitz and David Reich, 'Increased Rate of Close-Kin Unions in the Central Andes in the Half Millennium before European Contact', *Current Biology*, vol. 30 (2020), pp. 963–83.
9. Mary Weismantel, 'Ayllu: Real and Imagined Communities in the Andes', in *The Seductions of Community: Emancipations, Oppressions, Quandaries*, ed. Gerald W. Creed, Santa Fe, NM: School of American Research Press, 2006, pp. 77–99, at p. 81.
10. John Murra, '"El Archipiélago Vertical" Revisited', in *Andean Ecology and Civilization*, ed. Shozo Masuda, Izumi Shimada and Craig Morris, Tokyo: University of Tokyo Press, 1985, pp. 3–13. Mary Van Buren, 'Rethinking the Vertical Archipelago: Ethnicity, Exchange, and History in the South Central Andes', *American Anthropologist*, vol. 98 (1996), pp. 338–51.
11. Edward Palmer Thompson, *The Making of the English Working Class*, London: Penguin Books, 2013.
12. Dean, *A Culture of Stone*, p. 113.
13. Irving Finkel and Sébastien Rey, *No Man's Land*, London: British Museum Press, 2018.
14. Sébastien Rey, *For the Gods of Girsu: City-State Formation in Ancient Sumer*, Oxford: Archaeopress, 2016.
15. Weismantel, 'Ayllu: Real and Imagined Communities in the Andes', p. 88.
16. Ibid., pp. 88–9.
17. Carmen G. Escalante and Ricardo Valderrama Fernández, 'Ayllus incas, tierras del sol y agua del Huanacauri en Sucsu Auccaille, San Jerónimo, Cusco', *Anthropologica*, vol. 38 (2020), pp. 161–85; Rory Walshe and Alejandro Argumedo, 'Ayni, Ayllu, Yanantin and Chanincha: The Cultural Values Enabling Adaptation to Climate Change in Communities of the Potato Park, in the Peruvian Andes', *GAIA*, vol. 25 (2016), pp. 166–73; Fernando Untoja Choque, *Retorno al ayllu: Una mirada aymara a la globalización*, Madrid: Fondo Editorial de los Diputados, 2001, p. 194.

Note on dates and orthography

1. Thank you to Andrew James Hamilton for his patient guidance on this matter. For a much more detailed explanation of a complex subject, see the note in his book *Scale & the Incas*, Princeton, NJ: Princeton University Press, 2018, p. viii.
2. Ibid.
3. Other examples of Hispanicised spellings used in this book include 'Viracocha' rather than 'Wiraqocha' or 'Wiraqucha', and 'Conchopata' rather than 'Qonchopata' or 'Qunchupata'.

Select bibliography

Alconini, Sonia, and Alan Covey, *The Oxford Handbook of the Incas*, New York: Oxford University Press, 2018

Arnold, Denise Y., with Penelope Dransart (eds), *Textiles, Technical Practice and Power in the Andes*, London: Archetype Books, 2014

Arriaga, Pablo Joseph de, *La extirpación de la idolatría en el Pirú* [1621], ed. Henrique Urbano, Cusco: Centro de Estudios Regionales Andinos Bartolomé de Las Casas, 1999

Aveni, Anthony F. (ed.), *The Measure and Meaning of Time in Mesoamerica and the Andes*, Washington, DC: Dumbarton Oaks Research Library and Collection, 2015

Bauer, Brian S., *The Sacred Landscape of the Inca: The Cusco Ceque System*, Austin, TX: University of Texas Press

Betanzos, Juan de, *Narrative of the Incas* [1550s], trans. and ed. Roland Hamilton and Dana Buchanan, Austin, TX: University of Texas Press, 1996

Burger, Richard L., *Chavín and the Origins of Andean Civilization*, London: Thames & Hudson, 1992

Cieza de León, Pedro, *The Second Part of the Chronicle of Peru* [1532–50], trans. and ed. Clements R. Markham, London: The Hakluyt Society, 1883

Conklin, William J., and Jeffrey Quilter, *Chavín: Art, Architecture, and Culture*, Los Angeles, CA: Cotsen Institute of Archaeology, 2008

Cook, Noble David, *Demographic Collapse: Indian Peru, 1520–1620*, Cambridge: Cambridge University Press, 2004

Cooper, Jago, and Lindsay Duncan, 'Applied Archaeology in the Americas: Evaluating Archaeological Solutions to the Impacts of Global Environmental Change', in *The Oxford Handbook of Historical Ecology and Applied Archaeology*, ed. Christian Isendahl and Daryl Stump, Oxford: Oxford University Press, 2019, pp. 432–51

Cummins, Thomas B. F., *Toasts with the Inca: Andean Abstraction and Colonial Images on Quero Vessels*, Ann Arbor, MI: University of Michigan Press, 2002

Cusicanqui, Silvia Rivera, *Ch'ixinakax utxiwa: On Decolonising Practices and Discourses*, trans. Molly Geidel, London: Wiley, 2020

D'Altroy, Terence N., *The Incas*, Chichester: Wiley-Blackwell, 2014

Dean, Carolyn, *A Culture of Stone: Inka Perspectives on Rock*, Durham, NC: Duke University Press, 2010

Dransart, Penelope, and Helen Wolfe, *Textiles from the Andes*, London: British Museum Press, 2012

Fux, Peter (ed.), *Chavín*, Lima: Museo de Arte de Lima, 2015

Haas, Jonathan, Shelia Pozorski and Thomas Pozorski (eds), *The Origins and Development of the Andean State*, Cambridge: Cambridge University Press, 1987

Hamilton, Andrew James, *Scale & the Incas*, Princeton, NJ: Princeton University Press, 2018

Hemming, John, *The Conquest of the Incas*, Boston and New York: Mariner Books, 1970

Jennings, Justin, and Brenda J. Bowser (eds), *Drink, Power, and Society in the Andes*, Gainesville, FL: University Press of Florida, 2009

Lau, George F., *An Archaeology of Ancash: Stones, Ruins and Communities in Andean Peru*, Abingdon: Routledge, 2016

Lumbreras, Luis G., *De los pueblos, las culturas y las artes del antiguo Perú*, Lima: Moncloa-Campodónico, 1969

——, *Los orígenes de la civilización en el Perú*, Lima: Editorial Milla Batres, 1974

——, *Chavín de Huántar: Excavaciones en la Galería de las Ofrendas*, Mainz am Rhein: Verlag Philipp von Zabern, 1993

Matos Mendieta, Ramiro, and Jose Barriero (eds), *The Great Inka Road: Engineering an Empire*, Washington, DC: Smithsonian Books, 2015

Mills, Kenneth R., *Idolatry and Its Enemies: Colonial Andean Religion and Extirpation, 1640–1750*, Princeton, NJ: Princeton University Press, 1997

Moseley, Michael Edward, *The Maritime Foundations of Andean Civilization*, Menlo Park, CA: Cummings Pub. Co., 1975

——, and Kent C. Day (eds), *Chan Chan: Andean Desert City*, Albuquerque, NM: University of New Mexico Press, 1982

Pardo, Cecilia (ed.), *Modelando el mundo: Imágenes de la arquitectura precolombina*, Lima: Museo de Arte de Lima, 2011

—— and Peter Fux (eds), *Nasca*, Lima: Museo de Arte de Lima, 2017

—— and Julio Rucabado (eds), *Moche y sus vecinos: Reconstruyendo identidades*, Lima: Museo de Arte de Lima, 2016

Paul, Anne (ed.), *Paracas Art and Architecture: Object and Context in South Coastal Peru*, Iowa City, IA: University of Iowa Press, 1991

Pillsbury, Joanne (ed.), *Moche Art and Archaeology in Ancient Peru*, Washington, DC: National Gallery of Art and Yale University Press, 2001

Prieto, Gabriel, et al., 'A Mass Sacrifice of Children and Camelids at the Huanchaquito-Las Llamas Site, Moche Valley, Peru', *PLoS ONE*, vol. 14 (2019), e0211691

Quilter, Jeffrey, and Luis Jaime Castillo B. (eds), *New Perspectives on Moche Political Organization*, Washington, DC: Dumbarton Oaks Research Library and Collection, 2010

Rappaport, Roy A., *Ritual and Religion in the Making of Humanity*, Cambridge: Cambridge University Press, 1999

Reindel, Markus, and Günther A. Wagner (eds), *New Technologies for Archaeology: Multidisciplinary Investigations in Palpa and Nasca, Peru*, Berlin: Springer, 2009

Reinhard, Johan, *The Nazca Lines: A New Perspective on their Origin and Meaning*, Lima: Editorial Los Pinos, 1986

—— and Maria Constanza Ceruti, *Inca Rituals and Sacred Mountains: A Study of the World's Highest Archaeological Sites*, Los Angeles, CA: Cotsen Institute of Archaeology, 2010

Sillar, Bill, 'Miniatures and Animism: The Communicative Role of Inka Carved Stone Conopa', *Journal of Anthropological Research*, vol. 72 (2016), pp. 442–64

Silverman, Helaine, and William H. Isbell (eds), *Handbook of South American Archaeology*, New York: Springer, 2008

Silverman, Helaine, and Donald A. Proulx, *The Nasca*, Oxford: Wiley-Blackwell, 2002

Staller, John E. (ed.), *Andean Foodways: Pre-Columbian, Colonial, and Contemporary Food and Culture*, New York: Springer, 2021

Stone, Rebecca, *Art of the Andes: From Chavín to Inca*, London: Thames & Hudson, 2012

Tello, Julio C., and M. Toribio Mejía Xesspe, *Historia de los museos nacionales del Perú, 1822–1946*, Lima: Museo Nacional de Arqueología, Antropología e Historia del Perú, 1967

Toby Evans, Susan, and Joanne Pillsbury (eds), *Palaces of the Ancient New World*, Washington, DC: Dumbarton Oaks Research Library and Collection, 2004

Wilson, David M., *The British Museum: A History*, London: British Museum Press, 2002

Acknowledgements

This publication was conceived and written in the midst of a pandemic. Within this worldwide context we are hugely grateful to all the individuals, colleagues, partners and institutions who have collaborated with us and made this extraordinary, albeit logistically challenging, journey possible. Due to national lockdowns, Cecilia Pardo was delayed for seven months in Peru before being able to travel to London to start work carrying out research in the British Museum stores, while the museum itself remained closed to the public.

Our enormous gratitude goes to our supporter, PROMPERÚ, without whom this project would not have been possible. A special thanks to Ricardo Romero, head of the PROMPERÚ office in London, for his trust and commitment to showing the richness and cultural heritage of Peru to international audiences. Likewise, we are indebted to the following people for their tireless and supportive work throughout this process: current Peruvian ambassador Juan Carlos Gamarra and Susana de la Puente, who inspired this project in her role as Peruvian ambassador in London from 2017 to 2018. We are extremely grateful to the Ministry of Foreign Trade and Tourism, and the Ministry of Culture, Peru, who were key to securing the loans for the exhibition. *Peru: a journey in time* has been the result of the generous loans of, and support from, many institutions in Peru and across Europe. We would especially like to recognise the collaboration of our partner in Peru, MALI – Museo de Arte de Lima, for their guidance in the different stages of the exhibition, from conception to production, as well as for their generosity in sharing their magnificent digital assets and collections.

Our Peruvian and international colleagues who agreed to collaborate with their knowledge and written contributions have been instrumental in providing the experience and knowledge materialised in this book. Many thanks to César Astuhuamán, Peter Fux, Andrew James Hamilton, George Lau, Elena Phipps, Gabriel Prieto, Julio Rucabado, Dianne Scullin, Bill Sillar and Rafael Vega Centeno Sara-Lafosse. Likewise, the expertise of our partners in Peru – Nilda Callañaupa Alvarez,

Manuel Choqque, Victor Huamanchumo and Julio Ibarrola – has allowed us to incorporate different Andean practices that have enriched the exhibition and our book in so many ways. Additionally we are indebted to British Museum colleagues from the Conservation and Science departments – Caroline R. Cartwright, Joanne Dyer, Anna Harrison, Monique Pullan and Sophie Rowe-Kancleris – for the analysis carried out and their technical input included in this book.

Many other individuals, from different institutions, guided us in different ways through this process. To all of them, our special gratitude: Rocio Aguilar, Jorge Aldana, Andrés Álvarez Calderón, Karina Aparcana, Nereida Apaza Mamani, Beatriz Barclay, Giannina Bardales, Rubén Buitron, Elizabeth Catunta, Ingrid Claudet, Rosalyn Chávarry Aramburu, Craig Collinson, Claudia Cornejo, John Crock, Thomas B. F. Cummins, Alessandra D'Avanzo, Carlos Del Águila, Rob Dover, Andres Duany, Manuela Fischer, Kerstin Flemming, Edward and Sean Galvin, Manfred Gartner, Maria Luisa Gartner, Ivan Ghezzi, Natalia Haro Carrasco, Maxim Holland, Ulla Holmquist, Baroness Gloria Hooper, Kate Jarvis, Barry Landua, Pedro Germano Leal, Cesar Linares, Luis Angel Lopez Flores, John MacLaverty, Ricardo Malca, Rember Martínez, Sonia Molina, Martin Morales, Ricardo Morales, Gerardo Moreno, Elias Mujica, Amy Oakland, Martín Antonio Olivan Chumbe, Marcela Olivas, Yoshio Onuki, Giuseppe Orefici, Juan Ossio, Maritza Perez, Liz Ramires, John W. Rick, Pilar Rios, Doris Robles, Carla Rodriguez, Alice Samson, Julio Cesar Sandoval, Katharina Schreiber, Ines Seibt, Javier Silva Meinel, María Helena Tord, Gabriela Truly, Moises Tufinio, Rafael Varón Gabai, Celine Wald and Alyson Williams.

This book would not have been made without the individuals and institutions who generously provided contextual images for the publication, whom we would especially like to thank: Cesar Abad, the American Museum of Natural History, Archivo Tello – MNAAHP, Alfonso Casabonne, Bethan Davies, Dumbarton Oaks Research Library and Collection, Ivan Ghezzi, Daniel Giannoni, Billy Hare, Houston Museum of Natural Science,

IWC Media, The John Carter Brown Library, Museo Nacional Chavín, Amy Oakland, PROMPERÚ, Proyecto Qhapaq Ñan, John W. Rick and Mike Rodman.

Thank you to Beata Kibil for her tireless work on the reproduction with Altaimage, and to our designer Rita Peres Pereira, copyeditor Lise Connellan, proofreader Marianne Fisher and indexer Hilary Bird.

We would also like to acknowledge the invaluable efforts of many friends and colleagues at the British Museum, from many different departments and fields of expertise. Special thanks go to Hartwig Fischer, Lissant Bolton and Jill Maggs for their support. We must also thank the exhibition design team, led by Vicci Ward and including Aaron Jones, Helen Eger, David Robertson, Sian Toogood and Clark Henry Brown, for their creativity and patience with trying to cope with our challenging requirements. Thank you to all our other colleagues across the British Museum, especially David Agar, Toni Allum, Claudia Bloch, Maxwell Blowfield, Duygu Camurcuoglu, James Dear, Stephen Dodd, Joanna Fernandes, Stuart Frost, Ana Carreira Galbán, Paul Goodhead, James Hamill, Carl Heron, Tadas Khazanavicius, Eirini Koutsouroupa, Imogen Laing, Joanna Lister, Antony Loveland, Kevin Lovelock, Emma Lyttle, María Mercedes Martínez Milantchi, Rocio Mayol, Cynthia McGowan, Megumi Mizumura, Elizabeth Morrison, Saray Naidorf, David Noden, Saul Peckham, Angela Pountney, Nicole Rode, Michael Row, Hannah Scully, Kim Sloan, Rebecca Stacey, Christopher Stewart, Ian Taylor, Stewart Watson, Keeley Wilson, Helen Wolfe, Bradley Timms, Jonathan Williams and John Williams.

Our sincere thanks in particular to our fantastic project curator Tom Cummins (not to be confused with our dear friend Dr Thomas Cummins from Harvard University), our diligent project manager Jane Bennett, our thoughtful and experienced interpretation manager Claire Edwards, and to Lydia Cooper, who delivered this book in an unbelievably tight schedule with erudite dedication. We wouldn't have been able to make it without you.

Finally, a special thanks to our friends and families, in Peru and the UK, for their patience and support.

Picture credits

Inside cover flaps / endpapers: Design by Rita Peres Pereira, pattern inspired by a textile in the Ethnologisches Museum, Berlin (V A 31526); page 9: Rita Peres Pereira; fig. 0.1: Paul Goodhead; fig. 0.3: Fabrizio Servan, Archivo del Proyecto Qhapaq Ñan – Sede Nacional, Ministerio de Cultura del Perú; fig. 0.4: Courtesy of the John Carter Brown Library; fig. 0.6: Alfonso Casabonne / Casabonne Studio; page 16: Edgardo Solórzano, Archivo del Proyecto Qhapaq Ñan – Sede Nacional, Ministerio de Cultura del Perú; figs 1.1–1.2: Alfonso Casabonne / Casabonne Studio; fig. 1.3: Reproduced by kind permission of Julio Ibarrola; fig. 1.4: Alfonso Casabonne / Casabonne Studio; fig. 1.10: Sueddeutsche Zeitung Photo / Alamy Stock Photo; fig. 1.11: Paul Goodhead; fig. 1.12: PROMPERÚ; fig. 1.13: Centro de Textiles Tradicionales de Cusco; page 36: Daniel Prudek / Alamy Stock Photo; fig. 2.1: Daniel Giannoni; fig. 2.5: Drawing after a rubbing by John Rowe; figs 2.6–2.7: Museo de Arte de Lima / Photographer: Daniel Giannoni; fig. 2.8: Museo de Arte de Lima; fig. 2.9: Museo de Arte de Lima / Photographer: Daniel Giannoni; fig. 2.10: Ministerio de Cultura del Perú, Museo National Chavín; fig. 2.12: Museo Larco, Lima, Peru; fig. 2.17: Museo de Arte de Lima; fig. 2.18: Museo Larco, Lima, Peru; fig. 2.21: PROMPERÚ; fig. 2.22: Museo de Arte de Lima / Photographer: Daniel Giannoni; figs 2.23–2.24: José Luis Matos, Archivo del Proyecto Qhapaq Ñan – Sede Nacional, Ministerio de Cultura del Perú; fig. 2.25: Paul Goodhead; page 62: Daniel Giannoni; fig. 3.1: Museo de Arte de Lima / Photographer: Daniel Giannoni; fig. 3.2: Paul Goodhead; fig. 3.3: Seiîchi Izumi and Kazuo Terada, *Andes 4 Excavations at Kotosh*, Peru, 1963 and 1966, Tokyo: University of Tokyo Press, 1972, p. 175, fig. 102 / With kind permission of Yoshio Onuki; fig. 3.4: Getty Images: Werner Forman / Contributor; fig. 3.5: By kind permission of Cesar Abad, Proyecto Chankillo; fig. 3.6: Museo Larco, Lima, Peru, figs 3.7–3.9: Museo de Arte de Lima / Photographer: Daniel Giannoni; fig. 3.10: Yoshio Onuki / Museo Kuntur Wasi – Ministerio de Cultura del Perú; figs 3.11–3.12: Ministerio de Cultura del Perú, Museo Kuntur Wasi; fig. 3.13: Courtesy of John W. Rick;

fig. 3.14: Rita Peres Pereira; fig. 3.15: Courtesy of John W. Rick; fig. 3.16: Museum Rietberg and ArcTron 3D; fig. 3.17: Daniel Giannoni; fig. 3.18: Janine Costa / PROMPERÚ; fig. 3.19: Ministerio de Cultura del Perú, Museo Nacional de Arqueología, Antropología e Historia del Perú; fig. 3.20: José Luis Matos, Archivo del Proyecto Qhapaq Ñan – Sede Nacional, Ministerio de Cultura del Perú; fig. 3.21: Museo Larco, Lima, Peru; page 82: Getty Images: MARTIN BERNETTI / Staff; fig. 4.1: Paul Goodhead; fig. 4.2: Alfonso Casabonne / Casabonne Studio; fig. 4.3: Billy Hare; figs 4.4–4.6: Ministerio de Cultura del Perú, Museo Nacional de Arqueología, Antropología e Historia del Perú; fig. 4.9: Museo de Arte de Lima / Photographer: Daniel Giannoni; fig. 4.10: Drawn by Rember Martinez / Image with kind permission of the Museo de Arte de Lima; fig. 4.17: Javier Silva Meinel; fig. 4.19: Ministerio de Cultura del Perú, Museo Nacional de Arqueología, Antropología e Historia del Perú; fig. 4.23: Paul Goodhead; fig. 4.24: Heinz Plenge Pardo / PROMPERÚ; fig. 4.25: Museo Larco, Lima, Peru; fig. 4.26: Diagram by Katharina Schreiber / Redrawn by Rita Peres Pereira; fig. 4.27: Zoonar GmbH / Alamy Stock Photo; fig. 4.30: Don Mammoser / Alamy Stock Photo; fig. 4.35: Giuseppe Orefici – Archivo CISRAP; fig. 4.36: Museo de Arte de Lima / Photographer: Daniel Giannoni; fig. 4.37: Redrawn from Daniel Morales Chocano, 1982. Image kindly provided by Museo de Arte de Lima; fig. 4.38: Ministerio de Cultura del Perú, Museo Nacional de Arqueología, Antropología e Historia del Perú; fig. 4.39: Redrawn by Carla Vanesa Rodríguez Rodríguez-Prieto; page 112: Daniel Giannoni; fig. 5.1: Paul Goodhead; fig. 5.6: Moche Archive, Dumbarton Oaks, Trustees for Harvard University, Washington, DC; figs 5.7–5.12: Ministerio de Cultura del Perú, Complejo Arqueológico El Brujo | Fundación Augusto N. Wiese; fig. 5.13: Museo Larco, Lima, Peru; fig. 5.14: Museo de Arte de Lima / Photographer: Daniel Giannoni; fig. 5.15: Moche Archive, Dumbarton Oaks, Trustees for Harvard University, Washington, DC; fig. 5.19: Museo Larco, Lima, Peru; fig. 5.22: Moche Archive, Dumbarton Oaks, Trustees for Harvard University, Washington, DC; fig. 5.23: Museo Larco, Lima, Peru; fig. 5.24: Ministerio de Cultura del Perú, Museo 'Santiago Uceda Castillo' – Proyecto Arqueológico Huacas de Moche; fig. 5.25: Ministerio de Cultura del Perú, Museo Nacional de Arqueología, Antropología e Historia del Perú; fig. 5.26: Moche Archive, Dumbarton Oaks, Trustees for Harvard University, Washington, DC; fig. 5.27: Ministerio de Cultura del Perú, Museo 'Santiago Uceda Castillo' – Proyecto Arqueológico Huacas de Moche; fig. 5.28: Museo Larco, Lima, Peru; fig. 5.29: Moche Archive, Dumbarton Oaks, Trustees for Harvard University, Washington, DC; fig. 5.30: Ethnologisches Museum, Staatliche Museen zu Berlin; fig. 5.38: Image: C. R. Cartwright © 2021 The Trustees of the British Museum;

fig. 5.41: Moche Archive, Dumbarton Oaks, Trustees for Harvard University, Washington, DC; fig. 5.42: Paul Goodhead; fig. 5.43: Gabriel Prieto; fig. 5.44: Antonio Escalante / PROMPERÚ; figs 5.45–5.46: Ministerio de Cultura del Perú, Museo 'Santiago Uceda Castillo' – Proyecto Arqueológico Huacas de Moche; fig. 5.52: The Natural History Museum / Alamy Stock Photo; fig. 5.54: Drawing by Percy Fiestas. Museo Larco, Lima, Peru; fig. 5.55: Museo Larco, Lima, Peru; fig. 5.56: fig. 5.56: Museo de Arte de Lima / Photographer: Daniel Giannoni; fig. 5.57: Gabriel Prieto; page 156: Daniel Giannoni; fig. 6.1: Shutterstock / Oomka; fig. 6.2: Paul Goodhead; fig. 6.3: WikiCommons/AgainErick/CC BY-SA 3.0; fig. 6.4: Paul Goodhead; fig. 6.5: Fundación Temple Radicati – UNMSM / Photo kindly provided by the Museo de Arte de Lima; fig. 6.6: The Royal Library, Copenhagen, GKS 2232 4°: Felipe Guamán Poma de Ayala, *El primer nueva crónica y buen gobierno*, p. 360, no. 143; fig. 6.8: Illustration © Andrew James Hamilton; fig. 6.9: Museo Amano, Lima; fig. 6.12: Ethnologisches Museum, Staatliche Museen zu Berlin / Photograph: Claudia Obrocki; fig. 6.14: Ethnologisches Museum, Staatliche Museen zu Berlin / Photograph: Sandra Steiß; fig. 6.15: The Royal Library, Copenhagen, GKS 2232 4°: Felipe Guamán Poma de Ayala, *El primer nueva crónica y buen gobierno*, p. 258, no. 100; fig. 6.16: Andrew Paul Travel / Alamy Stock Photo; fig. 6.18: © Andrew James Hamilton; fig. 6.21: PROMPERÚ; fig. 6.22: Image: C. R. Cartwright © 2021 The Trustees of the British Museum; fig. 6.31: Bill Sillar; figs 6.34–6.35: Bill Sillar; fig. 6.36: Bethan Davies; fig. 6.37: Tim Whitby / Alamy Stock Photo; fig. 6.39: Miguel Majía / PROMPERÚ; fig. 6.41: Ethnologisches Museum, Staatliche Museen zu Berlin / Photograph: Sandra Steiß; page 190: Alfonso Casabonne / Casabonne Studio; fig. 7.1: Courtesy of the Division of Anthropology, American Museum of Natural History, New York; fig. 7.4: Elena Phipps; fig. 7.5: Houston Museum of Natural Science; fig. 7.7: Mike Rodman. Image kindly provided by Amy Oakland; fig. 7.8: Elena Phipps; fig. 7.9: The Royal Library, Copenhagen, GKS 2232 4°: Felipe Guamán Poma de Ayala, *El primer nueva crónica y buen gobierno*, p. 661, no. 258; fig. 7.13: Private Collection, photograph kindly provided by Juan Ossio Acuña; fig. 7.14: Ethnologisches Museum, Staatliche Museen zu Berlin / Photograph: Claudia Obrocki; fig. 7.18: Museo de Arte de Lima / Photographer: Daniel Giannoni; fig. 7.24: The Royal Library, Copenhagen, GKS 2232 4°: Felipe Guamán Poma de Ayala, *El primer nueva crónica y buen gobierno*, p. 126, no. 42; fig. 7.30: Ethnologisches Museum, Staatliche Museen zu Berlin / Photograph: Dietrich Graf; figs 7.31–7.33: Organic Artefacts Conservation Studio © 2021 The Trustees of the British Museum; figs 7.34–7.36: Centro de Textiles Tradicionales de Cusco; figs 7.37–7.39: Alfonso Casabonne / Casabonne Studio; fig. 7.40: Centro de Textiles Tradicionales de Cusco; fig. 7.41: robertharding / Alamy Stock Photo; fig. 7.42 and pages 222–3: Museo de Arte de Lima / Photographer: Daniel Giannoni.

Index

Page numbers in *italic* refer to
the illustrations